$17

THIRD EDITION

N39
2006

MAKING A LIVING
IN YOUR
LOCAL MUSIC MARKET

REALIZING YOUR
MARKETING POTENTIAL

BY DICK WEISSMAN

HAL•LEONARD®

Cover and book interior design by Hal Leonard Creative Services

Published by Hal Leonard Corporation
7777 Bluemound Road
P.O. Box 13819
Milwaukee, WI 53213

Trade Book Division Editorial Offices
19 West 21st Street
Suite 201
New York, New York 10010

Library of Congress Cataloging-in-Publication Data

Weissman, Dick.
  Making a living in your local music market : how to survive and prosper / Dick Weissman.--
3rd ed.
     p. cm.
  Includes bibliographical references and indexes.
  ISBN 0-634-09924-8 (alk. paper)
  1. Music--Vocational guidance. 2. Music trade--United States. I. Title.
ML3790.W39 2006
780.23'73--dc22
                                        2005031656

Printed in the United States of America
First Edition
Visit Hal Leonard online at **www.halleonard.com**

HAL•LEONARD®
CORPORATION
7777 W. BLUEMOUND RD. P.O. BOX 13819 MILWAUKEE, WI 53213

THIRD EDITION

MAKING A LIVING

IN YOUR

LOCAL MUSIC MARKET

REALIZING YOUR MARKETING POTENTIAL

BY DICK WEISSMAN

HAL•LEONARD®

CONTENTS

PREFACE..xiii

INTRODUCTION BY MARV MATTIS xvii

CHAPTER 1

Can a Musician Make a Living Outside the Major Music Centers? 1

Finding the Right Place 3
Developing and Packaging the Product: You!....................................4
House Concerts 6
Tips for Composers and Songwriters...8
The Multi-Dimensional Musician 8
Financing and Marketing CDs 9
CDs 12
Dealbreakers 13
Other Opportunities in Local Markets..14
Dealing with Rejection..15
Chapter 1 Resources 15

CHAPTER 2

Getting It Together: Developing Your Talent 17

Getting the Group Together...20
Starting a Band..20
Band Agreements..24
Band Names 24
Equipment...25
Chapter 2 Resources 28

CHAPTER 3

Taking It to the Street: Packaging Your Talent for Potential 29

Making Demos—Audio Tapes 29
Making Video Demos..31
Stylists 33
Publicists..34
Sample Press/Promo Kits 34
Chapter 3 Resources..34

CHAPTER 4

Selling Your Act in Places You Never Dreamed Of 37

Booking Yourself 37
Setting a Price 38
The Alan Remington Price Formula 38
Booking Agents 39
Dealing with an Agent 42
Personal Managers 44
The Expansion of Management Roles 45
Sunset 46
Business Managers 46
Other Creative Opportunities 46
Other Sources of Employment 47
Artist-in-Residence Programs 48
Chapter 4 Resources 51

CHAPTER 5

Developing Versatility 53

Teaching 54
College Teaching 56
Private Teaching 56
Chapter 5 Resources 61

CHAPTER 6

Making Use of the Union and Other Organizations 63

Radio and Television Commercials 65
The Musicians' Union as a Source of Work 65
Making Contacts Through the Union 68
Arts Councils and Grants 75
Specialized Casual Work 77
Open Mikes and Jam Session 78
Chapter 6 Resources 78

CHAPTER 7

Expanding Your Recording Opportunities and Developing 79

Jingles 80
Hiring a Sales Representative 85
Writing to Pictures 85
Final Thoughts on Advertising and Film 87
Chapter 7 Resources 87

CHAPTER 8
Working in Multiple Contexts 89
  Working for "The Door" 91
  Contracts 92
  Leaders and Side Musicians 93
  Chapter 8 Resources 94

CHAPTER 9
Producing and Marketing Your Own Record 95
  Today's Record Business 95
  Independent Labels 96
  Other Models 96
  Record Distribution 97
  Singles 99
  Getting a Record Deal 100
  Finding a Producer and an Engineer 100
  Recording Formats: Cassettes, Compact Discs, and Vinyl 102
  Mastering Records 102
  Budgets 103
  Financing Your Project 105
  Choosing a Studio 105
  Time Lines 107
  Promoting and Selling Your Album 107
  Web Sites 111
  Bar Codes 111
  Publishing and Performance Rights 111
  Chapter 9 Resources 114

CHAPTER 10
POLISHING YOUR SKILLS 115
  Studying Music 115
  Sight-reading 116
  Songwriters' Organizations 117
  Improving Your Skills as a Songwriter 119
  Chapter 10 Resources 121

CHAPTER 11

Making Inroads on the National and Regional Scene 123
    Regional Geography 124
    Making National Contacts as a Songwriter..124
    How to Access Artists from Your Home 126
    Making Publishing Contacts by Mail 127
    Small-time Publishers..127
    Contacting Music Publishers in Person..128
    Demos 129
    Tip Sheets 130
    Performing Rights Organizations 130
    Accessing the Major Songwriters' Organizations 132
    Music Print Publishers 132
    Summer Music Festivals 133
    Chapter 11 Resources 134

CHAPTER 12

The Urge for Going: Staying or Leaving...135
    Personal Managers with National Clout...136
    Finding a Manager 138
    Agents 138
    Other Paths to a Record Deal 139
    Music Business Attorneys 139
    Staying or Going Summary 140
    Going but Coming Back 140
    Money Isn't Everything 141
    Living Outside the Mainstream 143
    Developing Local and Regional Music Scenes.......................................144
    Chapter 12 Resources 144

CHAPTER 13

Playing Music Part-Time...145
    Specialized Performing Group 149
    Songwriting 149
    Performing Full-Time, Part of the Time 149
    Dedicated Amateurs and Semi-Professionals..150
    Technology, the Composer, and the Schools...150
    Musical Literacy 151
    Where Do You Fit In? 151
    Chapter 13 Resources...152

CHAPTER 14

The History and Development of Regional Music Markets 153
   Detroit 153
   The Philly Sound...154
   New Orleans 155
   Memphis and Points South 156
   Miami 158
   Atlanta, Macon, and Athens 159
   San Francisco and the Bay Area 159
   Boston 161
   Austin...162
   Minneapolis 165
   Houston 165
   Bloomington, Indiana 167
   Chicago 167
   Portland, Oregon 168
   Other Scenes...169
   Local Markets Ebb and Flow 170
   Chapter 14 Resources..173

CHAPTER 15

Seattle and Denver: A Tale of Two Cities,
with Excursions to Atlanta and Georgia.....................................173
   Seattle...173
   Recording Studios 176
   Personal Managers, Agents, Etc. 177
   Live Music 177
   Other Aspects of Seattle Music..177
   Record Companies..178
   General Ambiance 178
   Can It Continue?...179
   Denver: Some Would Rather Be in Colorado 179
   Atlanta and Georgia Today 183
   Conclusion 184
   Chapter 15 Resources..184

CHAPTER 16
The Music Business in Canada..185
    Staying or Going..186
    Government Aid..187
    FACTOR Awards 188
    The Bad News 189
    The Canadian Record Market...189
    Festivals 191
    Performing Rights 191
    More Aspects of the Music Business in Canada..........................191
    Major Label Interest..192
    Chapter 16 Resources...192

CHAPTER 17
Songwriting Income...193
    Blanket and Per Program Licenses..194
    Legal Controversies 194
    Some Tips to Local Composers 194
    Common Fallacies 195
    New Income Streams 195
    Chapter 17 Resources...196

CHAPTER 18
Music and Technology Futures...197
    Short-Term Technological Hurdles 198
    Copyright Protection 198
    Electronic Commerce/E-Cash 198
    Bandwidth 199
    Music on the Internet 199
    Online Retailing..199
    Web Pages 199
    Internet Cybercasts..200
    Greenhouse Channels 200
    The Evolution of Traditional Music Distribution 200
    Beyond the Internet..201
    The Store Strikes Back: Retail's Revenge 201
    Themed Environments 201
    Desktop Filmmaking...202
    Architectural Entertainment 202
    New Developments 202
    Final Thoughts by Dick Weissman 203
    Blue Sky and Free Music 204
    New Formats...205
    New Revenue Sources 205
    Summary...205
    Chapter 18 Resources 209

CHAPTER 19
Questions and Answers 211

AFTERWORD 215

APPENDICES
State Arts Councils 219
Regional Arts Organizations 223
Canadian Arts Councils 224
State Humanities Councils 225
Young Audiences 229
National Arts and Humanities Councils 232
Arts Organizations Dealing with Special Populations 233
Volunteer Lawyers for the Arts Groups 233
American Federation of Musicians Locals in U.S. and Canada 236
Songwriters' Associations (U.S.) 237
Songwriters Associations (Canada) 239
Performing Rights Organizations (U.S. and Canada) 240
Other Music Business Organizations 241
Information about College Degree Programs in Music Industry,
Music Merchandising, and Audio Engineering 243
Music Trade Papers 244
Songwriters' Tip Sheet 244
Magazines for Songwriters 245
Radio Tip Sheet 245
Magazines: The Best and Most Interesting 245
Bibliographies 245

INDEX 263

PREFACE

Preface to the First Edition

The main purpose of this book is to provide you with an understanding of the options and choices that make up a career in the contemporary world of music. It may not be the easiest life in the world, but a thorough understanding of your career options should provide you with some practical information about whether it is the life that will fulfill your needs.

Special thanks to Marv Mattis, to my editor, Ronny Schiff, Harry Tuft, Dan Fox, and Paul Weissman for computerization. This book is dedicated to all the people who are helping the regional music scenes to grow, especially Ernie Gammage in Austin, TX, Katherine Dines in Denver, CO, and Larry Littman and Richard Ranta in Memphis, TN. I also wish to express my gratitude to all the artists and managers who submitted promotional materials.

For this third edition, add the names of Paul Epstein of Twist & Shout Records in Denver and Terry Currier of Music Millennium and Burnside Distributing in Portland, OR.

Addenda for the Revised Edition

Thanks to John Cerullo at Hal Leonard for getting the revised edition off the ground. Thanks to Paul Weissman for fail-safe computer procedures. Thanks to Arthur Bernstein at the Liverpool Institute of Performing Arts, for shedding light on European perspectives; Alan Remington of Orange Coast Community College, for his nightclub gig formula; and Tim Hayes at Elmhurst College and Bruce Ronkin at Northeastern University, for their ideas and insights about various issues. Finally, thanks to Ron Sobel for his chapter on the shape of the future, and for many stimulating discussions.

Preface for the Third Edition (Second Revision)

Many things have changed in the seven years that have gone by since I last revised this book. During the mid-1990s, I attended a music business seminar in Denver. One of the major speakers was Tommy Noonan, who has a long and distinguished background in the music industry. He was head of National Promotion for Columbia Records under Clive Davis, and held the same position later at Motown Records. He also was instrumental in re-designing the music charts at Billboard. Tommy predicted that by the year 2000 there would only be three or four major record companies. He only missed it by a couple of years. Today we have Sony and BMG in an odd amalgamation where they are run as a single company and Universal has gobbled up such formerly important players as Polygram and MCA. The record and music publishing divisions of Warner Brothers Records are now separate from the rest of the operation, which included the film company, the Time magazine group, and America Online. Only EMI (Capitol in the United States) has retained the same identity that it had when the first edition of this book came out in 1990. There are persistent rumors that Warner Brothers and EMI will also amalgamate in some way, which would leave us with the three-company figure that Tommy projected some twelve years ago.

At the same time as these events occurred, the concert business has boiled down to a small handful of major players, notably Clear Channel, AEG, and House of Blues. Clear Channel also owns 1,200 radio stations, and House of Blues operates a record label and numerous nightclubs.

By consolidating operations, these companies have been able to lower their overhead. For example, in Denver, Clear Channel owns eight radio stations, and they no longer need separate news staff for each station. When BMG and Sony combined, hundreds of people were laid off, because the number of promotion and sales people could be reduced. Clear Channel is currently spinning off its activities into separate companies.

When the second edition of this book came out, the Internet was really just coming into play as a factor in record sales. Since that time, a number of developments have taken place. After some years of growth, American record sales went down during the period of 2001–2003. Although sales went up about 5% in 2004, they headed on the downward trail again in 2005. Various industry observers have attributed the loss of these sales to illegal file sharing through the Internet, the increasing importance of video games, the growth of the DVD format, piracy—the illegal reproduction of recordings—and a general lack of excitement in the musical content of recordings. Piracy is an extremely serious issue in some parts of the world, so serious that major labels have actually ceased doing business in some countries.

On the positive side, the Apple iPod has created a renewed demand for single songs, and there have been millions of legal sales of songs that consumers are placing on these handy devices. Artists Ani DiFranco and Conor Oberst (Bright Eyes) have achieved remarkable success with their artist-owned record labels. DiFranco's company, Righteous Babe, operates out of Buffalo, NY, and Oberst's company, Saddle Creek Records, headquarters in Omaha, Nebraska.

Other artists have been successful selling songs on their Web sites, and house concerts have emerged as an excellent source of gigs for acoustic musicians and singer-songwriters.

As we head toward the second half of the first decade of the twenty-first century, it is important to take a fresh look at the issues that this book originally raised, and to re-appraise opportunities in the regional music markets of the United States. This edition contains discussions of various issues in a new format. These are questions or concerns that I have picked up from teaching classes, seminars, or workshops. In a number of cases, these are discussions rather than solution or answers. The truth is that the music business is complex, and no one has all the answers. Anyone who says that they do is suspect, in my opinion.

Once again, thanks to John Cerullo for believing in this project, and understanding the need for revising the book.

Dick Weissman is available for music business seminars and consulting. You can reach him at r2s@comcast.net.

INTRODUCTION

This is a good book. If you are browsing and haven't bought it yet, buy it. If you own it, congratulations!

The strength of this music do-it-yourself book is that Dick Weissman really knows what he's talking about. He is a savvy music industry professional (a veteran of both the New York and Los Angeles music scenes), who has a finely honed sensitivity to the problems of "out-of-towners" who want to make music their living but who, for one reason or another, have decided to do their living outside of the major music centers—Hollywood, New York, Nashville, and Toronto. He knows the music of out-of-towners well because, as a longtime resident of the Denver area, he is indeed one of them.

Never before in the history of pop music has there been a better time for musicians in regional music centers to seriously pursue music careers with the expectation that their efforts will pay off. The music of the 1950s and 1960s broke the ground for regional centers. It encouraged people from all walks of life and from all areas to create music, and the wide range of musical "bags" or styles that are currently recorded and presented on stage and aired on radio and television reflect the sheer variety of the creative musical opportunities that exist in today's world. It is crystal clear that music is no longer the private property of an elite group of writers and musicians who work out of the four music Mecca cities of North America. Recording equipment has become so inexpensive that basic recording can be done anywhere there is an electrical socket and some talent. Look at the Chart #1–1: *Music Business Centers* on page 3 to get an idea of how decentralized the business has become. In the 1940s, if you wanted to make a record, it was New York, Los Angeles, and, marginally, Nashville. Period!

The scope of this book is remarkable. Weissman crosses all the "t's" and dots all the "i's" in a way that only someone who has lived his subject matter can do. That kind of attention to detail puts this book in a very special category of self-help music books.

If that's all it did, this book would earn a place on many a book shelf. Happily, however, the book offers even more. It is not simply a manual on how to get things done, but it also offers considerable scope and insight into the business of music.

The only negative I feel about *Making a Living in Your Local Music Market* is that I'm green with envy that I did not write it.

—Marv Mattis
Hollywood, September, 1989

Author's note: I guess Marv did take this book seriously. After a sojourn in Santa Fe, NM, he now lives in Crestone, CO.

CHAPTER 1

Can a Musician Make a Living Outside the Major Music Centers?

Thirty-five years ago I wrote a book about the music industry entitled, *The Music Business: Career Opportunities and Self-Defense*. My goal in writing that book was to provide a general outline for musicians about the way the music industry works, how artists get contracts with major record companies, what these contracts commit the artist and the record company to, the function of agents, managers and music publishers, etc.

The more I used that book in my own teaching, and the more I read about the music industry in the numerous books that have appeared since then, I began to realize that there was a whole other area of the business that I had neglected. The music industry in North America is centered in the cities of Los Angeles, Nashville, New York, and Toronto. Outside these cities you will not find any major record company headquarters. Chicago is an important center for the production and recording of commercials, but has much less activity in the areas of records and television. Few network radio or television commercials are conceived or produced outside of the major music markets, and only a handful of major talent agencies or personal management firms can be found in regional markets. Yet there is a lively music business, with many musicians and singers working in such markets, and there are many others trying to break into the business.

This book is intended to help you explore the options for musicians and singers who want to pursue music-business careers, and who are not necessarily concerned about the "big time," but are worried about whether they can make enough money to put bread on the table and gas in their cars. Each chapter of this book covers various aspects of local music markets.I have done almost all of the things I am writing about, and I continue to do them today. I've sung and played in a touring group that recorded three albums for Capitol, recorded solo albums for major and minor labels, worked as a contract song-writer for two different publishers in New York and Los Angeles, written two feature film scores for low-budget films produced in Colorado, and have done extensive studio work. I have also written songs and instrumental music for several theatrical works and produced records as a staff producer for various large and small record companies on a local, regional, and national basis, published over fifty music instructional folios and eleven books about music and the music business.

Thirty-four years ago, I moved to the Denver-Boulder area, where out of necessity I gained a new perspective on the nature of the music industry. Why did I move to Denver in the first place? After working on and off for more than ten years in the New York market, I realized that as long as I stayed in New York, I would earn the bulk of my income from playing on commercials. Although I don't have anything against doing commercials and was always happy to get the healthy re-use checks for commercials that ran as long as ten years, I did not make the mistake of confusing this income with the reasons that caused me to choose music as a profession. My original motivation was to play and write music as a means to express my feelings and ideas. The point that I'm making is that after building up a network of contacts in New York, I had to start over again in order to learn what life was like in the music world outside the "big city." This book is designed to help you to avoid my somewhat haphazard trial-and-error process, to steer clear of my mistakes, and to be able to scope out local opportunities while developing an overall understanding of the music industry. There are four major music markets in North America. (See the chart below.) These markets are in Nashville, New York, Los Angeles, and Toronto. Although all these cities provide work in all aspects of music, Los Angeles and Toronto are centers for a tremendous amount of film and television work, Nashville specializes in records and New York remains the center for recording radio and television commercials.

Edmonton Vancouver	Boston Cleveland Indianapolis Philadelphia Cincinnati Pittsburgh Omaha
TORONTO	**NEW YORK** Kansas City, MO
Seattle **LOS ANGELES**	**NASHVILLE** Athens
Portland	Chapel Hill
Denver	Memphis
San Francisco	Dallas Atlanta
Albuquerque	Austin Muscle Shoals
Las Vegas	Houston Miami
San Diego Phoenix	New Orleans

Although most of the major business of music takes place in the four music centers, there is a great deal of regional and some national recording work in what are called the secondary music markets: Atlanta, Austin, Boston, Chicago, Dallas, Memphis, Miami, Minneapolis, Montreal, New Orleans, Omaha, Philadelphia, Portland, San Francisco, Seattle, and Vancouver. They are active in different ways, as you'll see later. For example, Austin is an important center for songwriters and records, while the Dallas-Fort Worth area is a very active jingle center. Another group of cities have an even smaller, but still tasty piece of the pie. These include Albuquerque, Athens (Georgia), Chapel Hill, Cleveland, Calgary, Denver, Houston, Phoenix, and San Antonio. Some cities are noted for a specific role in the music industry. Athens, Georgia for example, is recognized as a hotbed of live music, with hundreds of performance venues. Try to think of the music business as a large circle, with the four major areas in the center, the secondary markets constituting the satellites somewhat removed from the center of the circle and the less-active areas surrounding the far edges of the circle. The basic assumption governing this book is that for one reason or another you do not wish to, or cannot move to one of the major music business centers. This may be because you are not comfortable in a high-pressure, heavy-hype sort of environment. The major music centers, with the possible exception of Nashville, are congested, overpopulated and share a high cost of living. It may be that you simply like the place where you live, or that you have developed a variety of music contacts in your town that you are reluctant to abandon. It is also possible that family commitments or other business opportunities require you to stay where you are.

Finding the Right Place

Even if you do not wish to relocate to one of the major music business centers, you may wish to live in a city where there is a bit more action than your current location offers. I have a friend named Jerome Gilmer who moved from Macon, Georgia to Denver, Colorado, where he has established a thriving, although not gigantic, business doing music for commercials and film and video projects. He consciously chose to move to a larger market, but not to one of the four major cities where he felt that he might be lost in the music-business shuffle. How can you tell whether there is more happening in another town than where you are currently living or working? There are a number of sources that you can turn to for assistance. You can write to one of the many locals of the Musicians' Union (American Federation of Musicians), get in touch with local songwriters' organizations or check out weekly entertainment papers from various towns. The Appendix of this book will tell you how to access these sources. You can also check with music schools in the area, consult the Yellow Pages, look for lists of recording studios in the annual *Mix* magazine directory or look for the annual *Musician's Atlas*. It is an excellent idea to visit your prospective hometown. Check out how it feels to you, find out what housing and food costs are like, and try to determine whether the skills that you have to offer seem to be in short supply, or if the market is flooded with possible competitors. Remember, there are many types of work available for musicians. You should also be conscious of the changes that develop over time. Today's regional hotspot may become tomorrow's ghost town, or vice versa. The Seattle music market went from being invisible to being the center of "grunge" music, and subsequently has eased back to a position as an important regional music marketplace.

Developing and Packaging the Product: You!

Can you make a living in music? The first rule of survival is to have a product to sell. Whatever your musical skill, package it in a form that is accessible to people who are not musicians, and who may lack interest or knowledge about complex aspects of musical style. When a club owner asks what kind of music you play, don't simply tell him "everything." Hand him a CD, a video, or a promo kit that explains who you are and what you do.

Once you have a product to sell, whether it's a Dixieland band, a rhythm-and-blues combo, or whatever, *package the product*. A promo kit should contain such items as pictures, a group bio, reviews, set lists, lists of places you have played, a recording (if you have one), and a list of significant appearances at clubs or schools that your client will recognize.

Packaging the product includes coming up with a name for your group—one that is attention-getting, but not too bizarre (unless, of course, you plan to build your reputation by emphasizing the bizarre).

For example, "The Monday Night Band" is not a good name for an alternative rock group. On the other hand, "Twisted Methuselah" is not a good name for a cocktail lounge group. Know who you are, and design your promo kit to stress the particular style of music you are selling. Then direct it in a way that will be comfortable for the type of client who is apt to buy your sound. The style in which you write your bio and the sort of pictures that you include should reflect the spirit of your musical focus.

Once you have packaged your presentation, it's time to get that package to local buyers, local agents, and anyone else you can think of who might offer you work. If you don't plan to pursue a career outside of the area where you live, it is probably unnecessary for you to have a personal manager.

Local agents may have access to employment opportunities "behind the scenes." I call these jobs "invisible work." Invisible work involves performances that are not open to the general public. Certain cities are popular convention centers for regional meetings or national conventions. Sometimes a one-hour job for such a group pays better than a whole week of working in a club for four or five hours a night. (Chart #1–2 on the next page breaks down the differences between visible and invisible work.)

Visible and Invisible Work

Visible Work	
Type of Work	**Primary Sources of Work**
Night clubs, concerts, resorts, restaurants	Booking agents; occasionally personnel managers; auditions
Recording artist career	
Songwriting	Personal manager; sometimes music business attorney; rarely audition tape or word of mouth
School performances through Young Audiences or other arts organizations	Music publishers
Symphony jobs	Auditions
	Solo performances through personal managers; regular orchestral jobs by audition

Invisible Work	
Type of Work	**Primary Sources of Work**
Conventions	Booking agents; caterers; event planners
Writing Commercials	Personal contacts; a demo
Writing special material (e.g. songs for specific events)	Agents; personal contacts
Freelance musical work (touring shows, pops symphony gigs)	Personal contact with contractors; word of mouth; referral
Grants	Contact state, community or federal arts councils or foundations; research books about grant programs
Weddings parties, funerals, celebrations, proms, fraternity parties, church work	Agents; union; direct contact
Studio work	Recording studios; contractors; word of mouth
Overseas tours, cruises	Direct contact (see resources)

Other Sources of Work
Ads in Yellow Pages; demo tape or video; union referral books; cards at wedding party supply or music stores; cold calls to prospective clients; auditions for band leaders; referrals from your teacher; sharing leads with others

One of the reasons that agents have access to conventions is that often there is more talent being booked than simply music. The agent may book typists, models, comedians, and together with a caterer, may even be partly responsible for the physical arrangement of the meeting. Caterers, by the way, are another source of invisible work, and so are wedding planners. These people may even recommend you to a client without you knowing about it.

Grants provide another source of invisible work. There are state, federal, and city grants for musicians and composers, and there are also grant monies available through private, family run, or corporate foundations. Each state has an artist-in-residence program, which sends artists (including musicians) into schools, nursing homes, prisons, and communities in any part of the state. Additional grants are available through state or federal humanities programs. Humanities grants usually involve critical studies about various forms of music. There are also state and federal grant programs in the folk arts.

House Concerts

A relatively new source of gigs that work for soloists and duos is the house concert. These events are run by people who love to have live music in their homes. They contact friends and sometimes have their own e-mail lists. The audiences are small, generally twenty to fifty people, but they are very attentive. On the plus side, the artists often sell a high percentage of CD's to those in attendance, because they are generally listening intently. The artist receives the door fees, usually about $10 per person. Occasionally the host deducts a small amount for refreshments. Since these events are held in living rooms, they don't generally require a PA system. In a populous area, like New York City, you can do a half dozen or more house concerts in the various boroughs and suburbs.

The hostess often offers the artist food and lodging. House concerts are a great way to establish a following in an area where you are not well known. However, you should anticipate some loss of privacy. The "promoter" will probably make some demands on your time, and the audience wants a high degree of interaction. This isn't a good platform for aspiring divas or superstars.

As far as I know, there is no national list of house concert presenters. Since you really can't expect to do more than an annual concert, you can find out about opportunities by sharing contacts with other musicians. Relatives and fans are often willing to promote house concerts. Beware of people who have never done a concert in their home before, because they may not have the willingness to do enough phoning or e-mailing to get you an audience. At the end of this chapter, I list a book that details the house concert experience from a performer's viewpoint.

A key factor in pursuing a lifetime career in music is *developing versatility*. The more instruments that you can play, and the more musical styles that you master, the better are your chances of getting freelance work. This work may be in local recording studios, dinner theaters, playing for touring Broadway shows, the circus, or for touring ice shows. Besides having the ability to play more than one musical instrument, it is desirable to develop your skills both in reading music at sight and being able to improvise. Usually, there is one relatively short rehearsal before you are expected to go out and do a professional performance, where you sound good and play in tune. If you play rhythm-section instruments such as guitar, keyboard, electric bass, or drums, you also need to have instruments and accessories that are used in current musical styles.

There are also some psychological aspects involved in pick-up jobs such as the ability to get along with conductors, contractors, and other musicians. You must be able to perform well under what can be intense pressure. It is also important to have a broad grasp of musical styles, so that you can understand the nuances of, say, swing versus Dixieland jazz or bebop.

Full-time music teachers have a steady source of income, and hopefully enough job security to enable them to survive. Teaching part-time can provide you with a useful source of extra income, and may even prove helpful in improving your own skills. Teaching opportunities can be found at local colleges, community colleges, music studios, private schools, in your own home or music studio, and through grant-funded artist-in-residence programs. Other possibilities are after school programs or local schools, YWCA/YMCA classes, churches, private schools, or community centers.

At this writing, many private teachers are charging handsome fees for lessons. Thirty-five to forty dollars an hour is not considered unusual. The key to developing a good teaching practice is to be businesslike. It's a good idea to charge by the month, and to collect in advance.

On your side, a committed teacher should not regularly cancel lessons because a gig comes up that is more fun. Teaching is a business and includes obligations on both sides.

Another key to your ability to getting work is to *use organizations as a source of referrals*. There are some two hundred and fifty locals of the American Federation of Musicians in North America. They all receive calls asking for harpists to play at weddings; bluegrass or Dixieland bands to play outdoor concerts; organists to perform at churches, etc. There are pros and cons of union membership, but the union can provide a considerable amount of work for local musicians. Together with record companies, they co-sponsor the Music Performance Trust Fund, which provides matching funds to subsidize concerts in malls, hospitals, and schools all over North America. Some local unions have actually begun to act as booking agencies for their members.

Unions are only one of many possible sources for job referrals. Local recording studios, music stores, and state or community arts councils can also provide you with job leads. One friend of mine got a six-month residency in Saipan through a referral from the Colorado Arts Council.

Tips for Composers and Songwriters

If you feel you have skills as a composer, local work that you can access includes writing words and music for jingles, doing musical arrangements for jingles or theater works, scores for short of feature films, music for slide shows, and writing special material for such venues as planetariums. Celebrations of special events can offer additional opportunities. Cable television or public TV may offer other possibilities for work. Some churches commission music for special events or holiday celebrations.

If you are a songwriter, the publisher of your music has the legal right to control the first recording of a song. Under copyright law, once that recording is issued, anyone can record a song, provided they pay royalties to the publisher. Songwriting can also provide the writer with entry into the world of the recording studio. It is quite possible that the songwriter may be used to singing or playing background parts on a record. This is a double opportunity, because you can contribute musically to the realization of your song, and you can also earn good money for performing on the recording session. You should certainly pursue such opportunities, but never push your talents so aggressively that an artist or producer not only refuses to hire you on the session, but also turns against your song. Because the modern world of recording includes the use of synthesizers, drum machines, sequencers, and samplers, it may be possible for a composer to "realize" most of the musical score without the aid of other musicians. Another possibility is to use a few other players or singers to provide a specific sound that a machine can't successfully emulate, but to do most of the work with synthesizers.

The opportunity of hearing your own work on tape or CD will undoubtedly lead to further progress in your own musical career. You may find that some of the instruments that you play don't sound good enough for a recording, or that your skills on, say oboe, are considerably less than what you had hoped or fantasized. Recording generally serves to deepen a musician's understanding of what he can do, and perhaps also what's best to avoid. Sometimes an understanding of your own limitations will lead to collaborations which themselves may bring you more work through the network of contacts that your collaborators have developed.

The Multi-Dimensional Musician

As a musician or singer, you may find that you are perfectly able to function in more than one musical group. In one group you may be the leader, hiring the other musicians, taking responsibility for the sound system and musical arrangements, and receiving as much as double the wages of the other musicians. In another group, you may simply be a side musician, taking a call from another leader to play a particular date for a given fee. As a side musician, you should not be responsible for anything other than playing the date. The headaches are the leader's problem.

Some musicians function better as leaders, and some prefer less responsibility and willingly (or unwillingly) accept less money. An alternative is to form a cooperative group, where everyone splits the money evenly, and tasks are also shared. One person may be responsible for the sound system, one may actually book the job, another may own the van, and so forth.

Sometimes a group starts out as a cooperative, but various people drop out. The remaining leader actually owns the name and hires new musicians for set (usually lower) wages. This is what happened when Kenny Rogers took over the First Edition, which subsequently became known as Kenny Rogers and the First Edition. Many of the touring 1960s and 1970s rock bands like the Mamas & the Papas and Kiss have evolved in a similar way.

There are innovative ways of participating in more than one musical group. In Aspen, Colorado (a small town that is renowned for its skiing and its summer music festival), during the busy ski season, some local musicians work as many as three musical jobs a day, playing such events as breakfast meetings, after-ski jobs in clubs or ski lodges, and evening nightclub gigs. Some of the rock groups turn into country groups by adding or subtracting a key player or two.

A bluegrass group based in the Denver-Boulder area came up with an entertaining solution to the problem of wanting to play more than one style of music, and yet having a specific musical identity to sell to the public. As Hot Rize, this four-piece vocal and instrumental group played bluegrass and newgrass music, using the traditional instrumentation of banjo, fiddle, or mandolin, guitar and bass. After the first set of their shows, they came back on stage in different outfits, with electric and lap steel guitars. The "second band" was called Red Knuckles and the Trailblazers. The two bands dressed differently, and the performers even referred to one another by different names in the second band.

They carried this device to such extremes that they even recorded a number of albums under each bands' name. Hot Rize stuck to bluegrass and Red Knuckles performed Texas swing and some rock and roll oldies. The band no longer exists on a regular basis, but during occasional re-union tours they retain both identities.

Besides greatly expanding their audience-appeal, these musicians found an amusing and innovative way of gaining acceptance for more than one musical genre. This kept their music fresh and vital, while expanding their opportunities to work.

Financing and Marketing CDs

Many musicians dream of making their own recordings, setting down on tape their own musical concepts, and selling them in the marketplace. For the vast majority of musicians, the dream of finding a national recording contract with a major label is just that, a "dream." More and more musicians are producing their own recordings, usually in relatively modest quantities for their own local markets. These recordings can be financed and marketed in a number of ways. One option is for musicians to finance the recordings themselves. Good studios are now available in almost all local markets with engineers who are conscientious and capable. They may not have the latest multi-track digital machines or automated mixing consoles, but every major city has a number of twenty-four track studios, not to mention the proliferation of everything from one-inch sixteen-track equipment, pro tools digital set-ups, and semi-pro four- and eight-track basement studio operations.

There have also been major changes in the picture since the first edition of this book was published in 1990. Currently, used eight-track A-DAT machines are available for under $1,000. The machines can be ganged together, so that three machines gives you the capability of twenty-four tracks, for an investment of under $10,000. This does not include the purchase of microphones and a mixing console. The bottom line is that with an investment of $10,000 to $15,000, your band can have a sixteen- to twenty-four-track studio at your rehearsal space. Another piece of good news is that the cost of A-DAT tapes is about $15 for a forty-minute tape, or $42 if you use twenty-four tracks. Compare this with tape costs of $600 and up to make an album in the old analog format.

Many musicians are recording on computer-driven hard-disc systems, using Pro Tools. These systems don't require the use of tape, and editing can be done with a minimum of trouble. Some artists use combinations of analog and digital recording, recording on analog tape but mixing to digital. Some musicians record on a hard-disk system at home, but mix their albums at a studio in order to use better gear. In any case, the process of recording has become cheaper and more efficient and whether an order as small as 1,000 CDs, your manufacturing cost per album will be about $1.50. Some duplicators can also provide graphic services at a relatively low price. (To find manufacturers, check with your local studio, or check out the ads in *The Music Connection* or *Billboard*.)

Studio rentals for Pro Tools recording are as low as $30 to $50 an hour in many cities. Large studios are hurting because of the proliferation of home recording, and if you need to use one, you can probably make a better deal than would have been possible ten years ago.

Let's get back to the subject of financing your project. It is possible to raise money from a specific investor, or a group of investors. These may be people who are friends of the artist(s) and have a real and sincere interest in helping the artist(s) find an outlet for their music. One friend of mine in Denver actually sold shares for his recording project to a group of investors. He was able to raise a considerable amount of money for what was basically a local project. Other artists have sold subscriptions to their records in advance, raising the money to record before even going into the studio. A Canadian artist named Bob Bossin did this, titling his album, *Thanks to the Following*, and listing all the subscribers in the album notes.

If you raise money from a group of investors it is important for you to explain that there is a good chance that they will either lose most of their investment or that they will end up making little or no income from the project. Many investors have some sort of fantasy of financing a massive supergroup operating out of a city like Terre Haute, Indiana. Of course, anything is possible in the music business, but it important that you explain the risks inherent in music projects to your investors. Since the investors are often family members, if you don't give them an accurate picture of what is involved, relationships may be irreparably damaged.

Even some artists of national stature like John Prine or Arlo Guthrie have begun to release of their own recordings. As the record companies become larger and become increasingly corporate, the break-even point on a record is so high that even sales of a hundred thousand records are considered unsatisfactory. Through the complicated arithmetic of the record business, with its many deductions from royalties for packaging, promotion copies, and "breakage" fees, a locally produced record may actually generate more revenue for an artist than one that is produced by a major label.

Some artists, like Ani DiFranco and Fugazi, prefer to establish their own record labels because they simply don't want to be marketed or controlled by multi-national conglomerates whose primary interest is often not in the artist's music but in the sales of a "product." DiFranco has even established her own label in Buffalo, New York. Instead of receiving a royalty of 10% to 12% of the retail selling price of her recordings, she owns the record company. A few aspects of control that disturb artists are the way an album is advertised, the cover art, the use of outside record producers who do not always share an artist's musical vision, and, in general, the world of the corporate "suits."

If the artist owns the record label, she must undertake all of the financial risks, but she also gets all of the profits. Since DiFranco has begun to earn gold records (over 500,000 copies sold), the profits have become considerable. If a major label had sold 500,000 of her records, she would probably be in a situation where she would have started receiving, let's say $1.50 an album when sales reached 250,000 to 300,000 albums. The first half of her sales would have gone back to the record company to pay back the cost of making her album.

Another interesting situation is the rise of Saddle Creek Records in Omaha, Nebraska. It is a sort of collective of musicians, with Bright Eyes (Connor Oberst) being the one that the jackpot. He owns part of the label, and many of the artists play on each other's records. Since Bright Eyes has hit the pop charts, most people in the business have become aware of the label.

Remember that the ability to sell a locally produced recording involves such matters as getting airplay, newspaper publicity, store displays, collecting money from record stores or distributors, and most of all, selling recordings before, during, and after performances.

CDs

With the exception of dance music and some alternative or punk rock projects, vinyl is a dead item. Regardless of whether you personally like the medium of vinyl, the fact is that turntables are a dying breed except for disc jockeys performing at dance clubs. These days, cassettes are essentially a dead item. Issuing product on a cassette in the twenty-first century marks the artist as an amateur.

CDs must be duplicated in quantities of a thousand to be cost-effective. There are duplicators that will sell you five hundred copies, but usually the price of a thousand albums is only half again as much as a five hundred CD run. In other words, five hundred CDs might cost you a thousand dollars, and a thousand albums might come in at $1,200 to $1,500. The final price will depend on such issues as whether you are providing cover art, who is printing the CD booklets, and whether or not you want the company to design the package, etc. Low budget CDs feature two-color generic album covers, but they also have little individuality or appeal. Another new development since the first edition of this book is the use of CDRs for mastering. A CDR is a CD reference disk that can be made in many recording studios today. The cost of making this disk is now down to $10 or less. It is no longer necessary to send records out to a separate mastering facility to be processed. This saves about $500, depending on what studio is used, and how much time is spent on the mastering. Some people prefer to use mastering studios to provide a final shot at equalizing the sound of different album cuts, and to smooth out imperfections in the mixing process. Mastering studios often charge as much as $150/an hour, and represent an additional expense. I know people who swear by them, and others who do their mastering on smaller systems that many studios now own.

One of the keys to selling recordings locally is to develop an extensive mailing list. These people constitute a ready audience for your product. They are interested in an artist on a personal and musical level, and provide a ready market for any recordings that you may make. Below is a chart that illustrates the advantages of recording for a record company as opposed to producing your own album.

Before we leave the subject of independent recording, Eugene Chadbourne presents a dissenting opinion about cassettes in his entertaining book: *I Hate the Man Who Runs This Bar*. Chadbourne has achieved an "underground" reputation as a creative guitarist who spans many musical styles. He prefers to make cassettes, re-recording over old cassettes and actually hand-making creative covers for each unit. This may strike you as being extremely impractical, but consider whether you have the equipment to duplicate cassettes at home. Since Chadbourne has a reputation as an innovative musician in the first place, it could well be that his way of doing things is indeed quite appealing to his fans.

Record Companies vs. Producing Your Own Album

Advantages	
Self-production	**Record Company Production**
Total creative control of music	Better budget
More money per unit	Better distribution
Control of advertising and imaging	Possible overseas release
Retain all publishing rights	Access to radio and record stores
Control cover art, notes, production	Possible access to major producer
Disadvantages	
Self-production	**Record Company Production**
Bookkeeping, bill collection if albums are consigned	Could be lost in the shuffle of a company's other products
Must pay for pressing, recording, graphics, etc.	Company will probably control cover art, imaging of group
Necessity of raising funds	Most records never earn any royalties at all
Paperwork, promotion, constant follow-up calls	Reduced publishing royalties or loss of publishing rights

Dealbreakers

Over the years, I have produced many projects for artists who released their own recordings. I also have many other friends who have produced similar projects, and know many artists who have released their own recordings. Far too many of these projects went astray because the artist had devoted considerable thought and preparation to the artistic and technical aspects of recording but very little consideration to the marketing of the recordings. In my opinion, there are two fundamental questions that an artist must answer before pursuing this avenue. They are:

1) How will the record be sold and/or distributed? Will the record be in stores, will it be available outside of your hometown? Will there be any effort made to get radio play?

2) Who will follow up to get paid for records that are consigned, keep appropriate receipts for tax records, obtain a bar code for the record (if it is sold in stores), and work with the graphic artist, etc? If no one in your

band is willing or able to do this boring but important work, do you have a manager or is there a family member who can do it for you?

If you are unable to answer either of the above questions that it would be wise to delay making a record until you figure out the business side of your particular story.

Other Opportunities in Local Markets

Even an artist who has no particular desire to tour nationally can maintain and utilize national contacts to advance his/her career in such areas as songwriting, developing instructional materials for other musicians, and obtaining some regional college bookings. Regional college booking conferences provide the opportunity to expand the geographic area that an artist covers. Other opportunities are available for high school concerts, performances in public schools, and for specialized audiences, such as senior centers and nursing homes. In the appendix of this book are resources for contacting the people who can provide this type of work.

One of the ways to keep a musical career alive and vital is to keep studying new or old forms of music. This can be done at local colleges or through private teachers. Developing new skills is a good way to maintain your interest in music, and, in turn, it may open up new employment opportunities. Classes and seminars are offered in many areas of the country that will enable you to meet successful professionals who are working in fields such as songwriting and arranging.

There is more involved here, however, than jobs. A musician should strive to keep his level of enthusiasm high. This is a necessity for successful performing, but it is also important in terms of maintaining a long-term career in music. The longer one has been playing music, the more exciting it is to find new musical areas to explore. If you are able to continually expand your musical horizons, you will be able to renew your enthusiasm about music as a profession.

It is also possible to work and tour nationally, but to live in an area outside the major music centers. By utilizing business help in the form of a personal manager, booking agency, or attorney who is knowledgeable about music-business procedures, a performer can live anywhere she chooses, as long as his business is being run by skilled professionals. These days John Cougar Mellencamp lives on an Indiana farm, Gloria Estefan in Miami, Pearl Jam and a number of other artists in Seattle, and other artists are spread out all over North America. Some artists maintain more than one residence, sharing their time between idyllic spots like Aspen, Colorado and Los Angeles, California. All of the artists mentioned are active in the business and tour on a regular basis.

Dealing with Rejection

No one enjoys being turned down for anything, whether it's a job, a date, or gig. The best approach to this problem is to understand that often the turn-down has nothing to do with you personally. A club owner may have already booked a band, your music might not be right for a particular venue, or your CD or audition may indicate that you aren't quite ready for prime time. There is a fine point between being persistent and being a nuisance. Try to find out what you can do to improve your music. Listen to what critics, club owners, or record people say, and decide whether their advice is valid, or if you should ignore it. Remember that the Beatles were turned down *twice* by every record company in England. At the same time, remember that you probably aren't as good as the Beatles were!

Chapter 1 Resources

In addition to the more detailed information available in the Appendix, each chapter lists some useful basic resources that provide the reader with information that is relevant to the chapter itself.

Marty Buttwinick, *How to Make a Living as a Musician So You Never Have to Work a Day Job Again!* Glendale: Sonata Publications, 1993. This guide is detailed to the point of being irritating, but it is has many useful tips for freelance musicians. It is particularly valuable if you are contemplating leading any sort of band.

Eugene Chadbourne, *I Hate the Man Who Runs This Bar: The Survival Guide for Real Musicians.* Emoryville, CA: Mix Publications, 1997. Chadbourne definitely has an off-beat approach, but if you are interested in musical styles that are off the beaten track, this book is for you. Useful for freelancers and members of musical groups.

David Heflick, *How to Make Money Performing in Schools.* Orient, WA: Silcox Productions, 1996. An extremely detailed guide for performers and teachers.

Mike Levine, *How to Be a Working Musician.* New York: Billboard Books,1997. Probably the best guide currently available for those whose goal is to be freelance musicians. The book presupposes that you are living, or want to live in a large city, and offers information about writing and playing on jingles, working in one dance band group that plays for weddings or social functions, theater work, etc. A number of brief but helpful interviews with other musicians are included.

Douglas McLeod and Kimberly, *Random House Concerts: A Guide for Musicians and Hosts.* Austin, TX: Woodworks Publishing, 1999. The book provides information on what house concerts are like.

Billy Mitchell, *The Gigging Musician: How to Get, Play, and Keep the Gig.* San Francisco, CA: Backbeat Books, 2001. A practical guide to gig work.

Note: A number of other books on this subject have appeared in the last few years. Many of them are listed in the Appendix, but these are, in my opinion, the best currently available.

Making and Selling Your Own Records

Veronica Kalmar, *Label Launch: A Guide to Independent Record Recording, Promotion, and Distribution*. New York, NY: St. Martins Griffin, 2002. This book contains some good launching strategies, including helpful Internet info.

Diane Sward Rapaport, *How to Make and Sell Your Own Recording: A Guide for the Nineties*. Englewood Cliffs: Prentice Hall, 1999, Revised Fifth Edition. The best source of information on album design, graphics, consignments, building a mailing list, etc.

Jana Stanfield, *Making and Selling Your Own CDs and Cassettes*. Cincinnati, OH: Writer's Digest, 1997. Somewhat similar to Rapaport, but the author is herself a writer and performer, and has a somewhat different perspective.

Tim Sweeney and Mark Geller, *Tim Sweeney's Guide to Releasing Independent Records*. Torrance, CA: TSA Books, 1997. Sweeney has a very realistic perspective on contemporary radio.

Note: The Rapaport and Stanfield books tend to focus on folk, new age, and singer-songwriter sorts of records, and Sweeney's book is almost entirely oriented to rock records. None of these books are very useful in regard to what it takes to make records, as opposed to selling them. Kalmar's book is the most up-to-date of the group.

CD Pressing

Two publications feature many advertisements for pressing and album production facilities: *Billboard* and *The Music Connection*. These ads also appear to a lesser degree in other music business periodicals. See the Appendix for addresses.

CHAPTER 2

Getting It Together: Developing Your Talent

How do people learn to sing and play an instrument, and what enables them to parlay that early talent into a career in music? There is no single, simple answer to this question. To a great extent, it's primarily a matter of desire. Watch any three- or four-year-old child. Invariably, kids of that age hum and sing to themselves, and make up their own tunes. Sometimes the words don't make a lot of sense, but are simply a single phrase that the child repeats over and over again. When my son was that age, he became fixated on the phrase, "Colorado railroad train," and he would sit in the back of the car singing and humming that phrase repeatedly.

The point is that for most people, talent is not necessarily as significant as most people think it is. It's a question of how talent is developed, and in what direction it is taken. Most people probably have some musical talent; they simply don't bother to use or direct it.

Over the years I have watched some students who I thought had very little natural musical ability mature into excellent musicians. They did it by practicing longer and harder than their more gifted peers. Some of these musical "ugly ducklings" went on to achieve successful careers as professional musicians.

Even today, the young child who likes rock or country music is not apt to get much musical help in school. School music programs are oriented toward band instruments and the performance of existing materials. Vocal music programs tend to stress choral singing, except for occasional forays into musical theater productions. There are some exceptions, and some schools do have guitar programs, but the orientation of school music continues to be toward band and choral music.

Studying various kinds of music in school can be a very useful and even exciting experience, but most schools don't allow much flexibility in what the student is allowed to study. Because of this fact, we have the phenomenon of a well-trained teacher who has never heard of the musical artists that his students listen to, appreciate, and whose records they actually "study."

Schools have not adjusted to the notion that pop music, whether country, rock or rap, is essentially a rhythm-section-oriented form. The principal instruments are electric bass, drums, keyboards, and guitars. Other instruments perform auxiliary roles. This is not true in middle-of-the-road (MOR) styles of pop music performed by such singers as Barbra Streisand or Céline Dion, nor is it necessarily true in jazz, where horns or saxes often dominate.

Many rock and country stars are self-taught or have taken lessons outside the school music setting. Schools often take the position that everything starts with the study of classical music or swing-style big band jazz. It follows from these assumptions that each student must learn to play band or orchestral instruments and learn these styles of music before attempting any other musical genres.

If you want to play or sing rock or country music, don't expect a lot of help from the academic world. This is not to say that you're left on your own out in the cold. There are good rhythm section players all over North America. The ones you want to seek out for lessons are the ones who not only play the music that you like but also have the ability to teach what they know. A good teacher is not always a "monster" player, but is someone who has the ability to analyze musical styles, and to translate that analysis into a form that a student can grasp.

Look for people who have some teaching experience and who enjoy sharing their knowledge of playing or singing. Avoid those with too many outside commitments who don't seem to remember your name or what assignment they gave you last week. Try to avoid teachers who have such a heavy teaching load that they seem to be unable to concentrate on the lesson.

One of the difficulties in learning pop and rock music is that written music is not necessarily the best vehicle for transmitting this information.

Some of the best pop or country performers read music, but many don't. Artists who do know how to read music often bypass that skill in their everyday work. It's easier to make a rough tape of a song than to bother writing out the melody in music notation. An interview with Stevie Winwood mentioned that he had played music in church at an early age and had even taken college music classes for a year. He then disclosed that he seldom wrote down any music anymore because he could use the medium of tape or could store information on computer-based synthesizers.

Reading music should be viewed as a useful tool rather than a substitute for developing your ear or learning how to "fake" and improvise. You can acquire many musical skills by listening to records and singing or playing along with them. There are series of CDs that are designed for that purpose, with the rhythm section on one channel of the stereo, and the lead part of the opposite speaker. You can play along, or you can shut off the lead singer or player and do the solos yourself. There are also CD players that allow you to slow down recordings without changing their pitch, so that you can easily play along with the artist.

More and more music instruction videos are coming out. The advantage of video instruction is that it shows you how a player holds an instrument, breathes into it, or fingers it. A student with a good ear can benefit from audio or DVD instruction tapes even if he is unable to follow the written music. However, the easiest way for a composer to communicate his music is still to write it down and have singers and instrumentalists read it. Being able to read music also makes it easier to move from band to band or to play in more than one band at the same time.

There are a variety of ways to find teachers. Ask for referrals from better-quality music stores. Some of these stores also employ teachers, so they are apt to recommend their own people. Since the store wants to continue doing business with you, they will probably refer you to someone who is at least competent. You should also check with your local musician's union. Most of the good, working professional players will be members of the union, although some good teachers may no longer play professionally. You can also call upon the resources of the music departments of local colleges. Many colleges offer music classes or lessons through their continuing education departments. Be sure that your lessons will cover things that you want to know, rather than a prescribed course of study that has no relevance to your needs. Check out some of the teacher's credits. With whom have they played, what is their musical education, what kind of music do they like, do they write any music or have any recording experience? A top-quality teacher can prove to be an excellent source of job referrals, sending you on gigs that he can't make, or chooses not to play. A teacher will seldom refer you for a job that could prove too difficult for your skill level. After all, any recommendation refers back to the person who makes it, and the teacher's reputation will be adversely affected if he gets a call complaining about the poor job her/his student did.

Studying voice presents its own set of challenges. There are many different styles of vocal production. Aretha Franklin, for example, doesn't (usually) sing like an opera singer. Singers who have had a great deal of operatic training almost invariably sound stiff when they try to sing contemporary popular music. Broadway vocalizing is sort of halfway between current pop styles and "legitimate" singing.

The difficulty here is that if you are at the early stages of a musical career, you may not even know what sort of musical style you are striving to achieve. Try consulting the music department of a local college, or check with a singer who performs locally and whose vocal technique you admire. Where did he study, and is he happy with his teacher? Perhaps he gives lessons.

A good voice teacher is a rare gem. He can save your life by teaching you how to sing through a cold or when you're tired, and he can show you vocal exercises that will extend both the top and the bottom of your vocal range. This is particularly valuable if you are basically an instrumentalist whose vocal goals are to sing passable harmony back-up parts. If you are able to sing, you will become that much of an asset to your band.

Beware of the voice teachers who are too psychologically oriented. It is true that your voice will show the effects of tension or illness, but if what you really need is psychological help, you shouldn't be getting it from a voice teacher. Be sure that your teacher has a good idea of what kind of musical help you are seeking. Don't let her/him transform your musical style into something grotesque or inappropriate.

Getting the Group Together

Let's assume that you have your singing and playing together and you have now decided to put a band together, or join an existing group. How do your find people with whom to sing or play, and what are some of the problems that are apt to come up?

You need to identify exactly what kind of music you want to play, and how serious you are about it. Most daily newspapers have ads after their "musical instruments for sale" classifieds that are placed by bands looking for new or additional members, or individuals starting to put a band together. If there is a local entertainment weekly or monthly in your town, you will find similar advertisements in it. Other sources of information are the bulletin boards at music stores and the music departments of local college or community college music departments, community centers, record stores, or even supermarkets. Your local Musicians' Union may have a newsletter as well as a bulletin board, and if there is a songwriters' organization in your town, attend some of their meetings and try to hook up with someone who shares your musical interests. Recording studios and instrument repair people are another possible vehicle for your search.

Starting a Band

When you start a band, there are several things you'll need to figure out. First of all, there is the question of leadership. Is one person going to lead the band? If that is the case, that person will usually call the rehearsals, work out some way of getting promotional materials together, book the band him/herself or talk to booking agents about getting work, set up auditions with club owners, and be the contact person for your band. The leader also may provide and transport the group's sound system. In return for accepting all of these responsibilities, the leader may want to take an extra share of whatever money the group earns. In the big band era of the 1930s and 1940s, the bandleader always made at least twice as much money as the rest of the band. In fact, even today most union contracts specify that the leader of the group must earn double scale, or twice the minimum wages that the other musicians receive. Some groups split this money, but others do not.

In some groups, one person naturally seems to gravitate toward a leadership role. Often the other people in the band don't mind; in fact, they may feel a sense of relief that someone is willing to take most of the responsibility. Trouble can start when it comes time to decide how the music you are going to perform will be chosen. Although a musician may be indifferent to what brand of microphone is on the stand, who is booking the group, rehearsal hours, or even what the group wears, most people will show a great deal of concern about whether their own songs or their choice of cover tunes will be performed, and who is going to sing and play the solo parts.

Sometimes a group will have one person who acts as the music director, another one who handles the sound equipment, a third who owns the van and a fourth who does the booking. In these groups, the band usually splits the money as well as the responsibilities.

It is also possible, although clumsy, to apportion income to different group members on an uneven basis. One or two people may actually own the group's name, and they may simply hire other people to fill in empty slots. This is typically the case with revival rock groups, where it is the original member or two who owns the name. A new band can't readily afford such a course of action, because the group rarely has a guaranteed income.

Sooner or later, your band will have to make an important choice. Are you going to be a cover band, doing tunes that are already on the charts? Or are you going to use your band as a vehicle for developing the writing skills of those in the group? Sad to say but a cover band will have quicker access to work in most local markets, but if you don't write songs there is nothing that will set you apart from the hundreds of other bands performing in your region.

Most groups come up with some sort of compromise. They agree to learn a certain number of contemporary hits in order to get work, but they insert their own tunes into the show, especially very early or late in the evening.

One of the first things you will need to do is to find a name for your musical organization (this will be covered in the next chapter). You will also need to figure out a rehearsal schedule and find a place to practice. You will need to decide the frequency and length of your rehearsals as well as who is going to be at them.

The answers relate to what your goals are. Partly it's a question of how old you are, and whether you are going to be able to work in bars. Like it or not, the bulk of work in most music markets is in the bar scene. In most states this means that you will have to be twenty- one years old in order to work. The chances are that some of the people in your group have other commitments, whether they include school, jobs, sports, or boyfriends or girlfriends. Sometimes the best way to judge the seriousness of a musician's intentions is by measuring their other commitments.

There are several rules that should work for most rehearsals:
- Start at a set time, and work for approximately the same amount of time whenever you practice.
- No visitors should be allowed, unless they are there for a specific reason. For example, you might want to ask another musician to come to a rehearsal to see if the vocal balance is correct.
- Don't allow friends, people that you are dating, fathers, mothers, or other relatives or friends to visit.
- Never have anyone who is visiting a rehearsal (who, remember, you are not supposed to have invited) take sides in a group dispute. Its not fair to your fellow band members, and it puts the visitor in an embarrassing spot.

Where are you going to rehearse? The answer may depend on the instrumentation and size of your musical group. If you are an acoustic guitar duo, you can probably rehearse in a basement or garage without bothering your family or neighbors. If you're a hard-rock band, though, you need to look for some "industrial" space where you can scream your lungs out without annoying anyone else. A garage that is soundproofed or set away from the house might do the trick. You may need to consider a space that is not in use at night or on weekends. This could be a school, a warehouse, loft, or something similar.

In larger cities, rehearsal space is available in buildings that are set up for that purpose. Sometimes they have keyboards or drum sets available with the room. This is a great convenience, but chances are the rental fees will wreck your budget. Some locals of the Musicians' Union allow members to rehearse in their buildings. This is a good solution, but it may obligate you to join the union at an earlier time in your career than you might otherwise choose. Depending on your situation, this may be a worthwhile move.

Develop some practice routines that will help move your rehearsals along smoothly. Try running over a few old favorites to warm up. Time should be set aside for working out new songs, experimenting with new arrangements, and perhaps learning some of the latest hits. There is a certain psychology to knowing when to keep rehearsing a song, when to put it aside for another rehearsal, and knowing when to "abandon ship." Not every group can do every song.

Common musical goals are an important part of the glue that can bind a group together in tough times. Without these goals, the group can be destroyed by senseless bickering. One of the most divisive aspects of group decisions is the question of whose material is going to be performed, and how that choice will be made. It seems that 90% of the time when a person in the band writes a song, she is going to sing the lead part. There is no rational reason for this—it's simply a question of ownership. Most groups would be much better off if they dealt with the question of who sounds best on a particular song, rather than assuming that since Jane wrote it, she ought to sing it. The writer needs to accept that he may not be the one with the best vocal quality for a particular song.

Group members need to be able to criticize each other honestly, without any feelings of bitterness or holding back opinions. This doesn't mean that a person needs to be insulting or hostile, simply that ultimately there is no way to disguise bad news.

Try to look at this from a positive point of view: if you have a band member who is not really a singer, but has a true writing talent, the idea that he won't have to sing the song in order to get it performed can be a very liberating feeling. The writer may then open up, and start to compose songs with more demanding vocal parts that he could never personally perform. A spirit of cooperation can develop, where band members make suggestions on minor revisions of a lyric, or a new chord change that brings the tune to a whole new musical or emotional level.

The process of auditioning, whether you are the one on the griddle or the one making the decision, is never much fun. If you are looking for people to form a band, think out clearly what you want them to do. If you want someone who can read music, then obviously you are going to need to have some charts ready to test their reading skills. Can they read fluently, slowly, or not at all? Remember that auditions usually make people nervous. Don't expect a faultless performance from the outset.

What about musical styles? Do you want a guitar player who is fluent in rock and roll, but who can also play an occasional fingerpicking guitar part on ballads? Be sure that you go through the entire range of music that you expect the person to be able to play. Don't just set up a group jam session where everyone plays every blues lick they know as fast and as loud as possible. Try to get to know the person who you are auditioning, both musically and from the standpoint of what it would be like working with him on a daily basis. Does he play other musical styles, like reggae or bluegrass that your band hasn't ever attempted? Get as much information as you can. Does he play any other instruments that could add spice to your sound? Many musicians have been through a high school band program where they learned how to play a horn or a string instrument. Maybe that's just the sound you need to add to a song that has never sounded exactly right.

Be sure to check out the type of equipment your future band member owns. Does she have effects pedals? Is her amp loud enough for the sort of rooms you are going to be playing? Does she have a van that could be used to haul equipment? Does she own any extra microphones or sound equipment? What kind of attitude do you surmise she will project onstage? Can you imagine rehearsing with her, day after day, for months at a time? Does she have a serious interest in music, or is this something to pass away a little time before she goes away to college?

If you are the one who is auditioning for a band, try to see things from the band's side. Be frank about your strengths and weaknesses. Don't try to pretend that you are a hot jazz player if you don't know what a C6 chord is. Don't dwell on the negative, but try to figure out what you could add to a band that would convince them to hire you. Have you written any songs? Can you write arrangements? Do you own recording equipment? Do you have up-to-date equipment? Could the band rehearse in your garage? Finally, is this a band you want to be in?

Just because you're offered a job, that doesn't mean that you have to take it. Don't waste time doing something that you don't want to do. On the other hand, if this is your first band, it may be worth your time to get some experience, even though you know the group isn't really going anywhere, or you don't like the bass player's attitude.

Joining a band is a matter of chemistry and goals. Sometimes you'll run into a wonderful musician who is just not the right fit for your group. Perhaps when he learns something new his attention wanders, or he plays too loud over the vocals. Possibly, he's too egotistical. You won't want to work with someone on a regular basis who only seems to think about how great he is, without relating to the other people in the group. Music needs to be give-and-take, and cooperation will help to produce good music and, ultimately, financially rewarding results. It's a different matter if you have a musical group where one person is featured and well known, as are Garth Brooks or Bruce Springsteen. In these cases, the leader has most of the responsibility, and the jobs that come in are largely a result of how managers and/or record companies have built up the name of that performer. The people in the band, out of necessity, are going to play subsidiary roles. In these situations, the featured artist usually writes all or most of the material, and the only hope a band member has of getting something recorded is by co-writing a song with the artist. It is also not unusual for the "road band" to be replaced by studio musicians for the recordings.

There is nothing wrong with joining this kind of a band, as long as you have a realistic view of what is going to happen. You can then use this situation to help your own career move to another level.

Band Agreements

It is a good idea to get some sort of band agreement in writing that defines what will happen if a member of the group decides to leave, or is fired. The agreement should specify whether the group as a whole owns equipment, or whether it belongs to a specific individual. Does the group have a co-op publishing company, owned by all? If so, you may have quite a bit of conflict when the drummer gets fired, you go on to make a hit record, and he collects his share of the publishing royalties forever. Some bands even give everyone equal credit for songwriting, and if one member leaves the band, the same problem could occur.

Bands usually start with musical respect and personal friendships, but endless rehearsals and tours can easily erode that reservoir of good will. If you're in doubt about a band agreement, you might want to consult a lawyer. (See the Appendix for information on reduced-price legal services, which is probably what you will need if you are at the start of your professional life.)

Band Names

It's a good idea to check with everyone you can think of—the American Federation of Musicians, AFTRA, the singers' union—and to do a Google search, to see if your band's name is being used by some other group in Rapid City, South Dakota. You can register the name with the secretary of state in the state that you live in for a nominal fee, and this will at least establish that your name is in use, and dates from a particular time period. Hiring a lawyer to legally register your name will be more expensive, but if you start to tour regularly, it's a step you will want to take. Some bands have gotten into serious legal difficulties for performing under names that were already in use before they began their careers.

Equipment

Whether you're an acoustic soloist or in a jazz combo or a heavy metal band, you're going to need some sort of sound system in order to work. If you are a solo acoustic act, or even a duo, you may be able to survive temporarily without any sound reinforcement. Even then, you will be dependent on the not-so-tender-mercies of second-class microphones that constitute the sound system of most nightclubs or school gymnasiums. Most dances and quite a few concerts are held in high school and college gyms.

The first thing to do is to figure out what you need, and what the equipment is going to cost. How many microphones do you need to properly reproduce your vocals and instruments? What kind of mixing board will be necessary, with how many microphone inputs to send sound out to the audience? Do you require any special effects? Do you need to update your keyboard sounds by buying a new synthesizer? What about a computer and a sequencer? Does the drummer have a quality drum machine, octapads, and electronic drums? Does your guitar player have an effects rack that's set up so that all of her effects are ready to go? Is the rack activated by foot pedals that are easy to reach?

If you want your band to develop a contemporary sound, you are going to have to invest in equipment. How are you going to come up with the necessary cash, or obtain credit to buy what you need?

If the group is going to be run as a cooperative, with each band member assuming areas of responsibility and with income equally distributed, then each player should try to save some money that can be set aside for equipment (such as sound equipment, microphones, a mixing board, speakers, and, possibly, a van). Sometimes this money is set aside by the band placing a portion of the receipts from each gig in a special bank account.

Each player should own his own equipment and amps, and if the band breaks up, or if one or two people leave, they can either be bought out of their share of the sound equipment, or they can buy it from the remaining group members. Remember that equipment loses its value as it ages and is constantly used, so that a $3,000 sound system will certainly not be worth $3,000 in four years.

Back to the issue of raising money to buy the equipment. You may be able to buy some equipment on a credit basis, if your parents, an older brother or a sister, or a manager is willing to co-sign a loan at a music store. Another option is to buy the equipment on time, if a store owner is willing to trust you or if you have a good credit rating. Make sure that the interest rate, if there is one, is not excessive.

Where can you buy a good sound system or musical instruments at a fair price? A lot depends on how many music stores there are in the area where you live. Major cities have giant discount stores that offer large discounts off retail prices. However, discount stores may not always be reliable about servicing the equipment that they sell, and often they're too busy to offer much advice or consultation. This is even more apt to be true of mail-order discounters. If the store or mail-order company that sells you equipment doesn't service it, you may find yourself in the annoying position of having to ship it back to the manufacturer, instead of having the store deal quickly with the problem. A good local store hopes to start a long-term relationship with you, while a big city discounter or mail-order company is much more impersonal and understands this may well be your only purchase from them.

Now that you are getting outfitted with better, larger, and more expensive equipment, you may need a larger vehicle to carry all of it, and the group, too. You may even need a roadie to help you carry and load or unload the equipment, and to operate the mixing board while the band plays. Your roadie or road manager can also take care of any questions that a club owner or manager may have, in the absence of an agent or manager being there at the club to represent you.

Some people pay the road manager a percentage if their own gross income, or a weekly salary, while others make her/him an equal member of the band. Initially, you may find a friend or brother or sister who is willing to help you out, but if the band starts to work regularly, you will need help on a regular basis.

How do you find a road manager? You can advertise in the newspaper or weekly entertainment guide, or you can put up a sign at local music stores or in schools. Your road manager is as important a member of your team as anyone in the band, so you want to choose her/him with great care. You want someone who is dependable and even-tempered, but who won't put up with any outrageous nonsense from a patron or a club owner. Frankly, it helps if your road manager is big and strong, and looks it.

One last word about equipment: now that you are starting to play paid jobs, you need to keep good records of any equipment that is purchased—musical instruments, sound equipment, a van, musical accessories, and any music lessons or classes that you are taking to advance your skills. Keep a record of all miles driven to and from jobs, auditions, and rehearsals. You can deduct mileage that is driven to and from professional engagements or any promotional or business expenses from your taxes. You can also work out a depreciation schedule for your instruments and sound system, and possibly for your van, that can save you quite a bit of money on taxes. The Internal Revenue Service demands precise records. If you are audited and are unable to produce such records, you may not be able to deduct your expenses, even though they are legitimate business expenses. You will also have to pay interest penalties, if the IRS disallows your deductions. Keep a log of all car repairs and of all instrument and PA repair expenses.

Another deductible item that you may be able to take advantage of is the cost of buying and maintaining costumes, provided that they are not worn off-stage. You will need to keep a record of what your costumes cost, and a steady log of dry-cleaning costs. Most bands have one person in the group who is more organized and careful than the rest. Make that person keep a record of expenses. Buy a car mileage log from your local stationery store, and record the miles driven on a daily basis.

Sample Instrument Record Card

Equipment & Brand	Guitar Amp., Global
Source	Joe's Music
Price	$800
Length of Warranty	90 days, ending June 1, 2006
Service, Availability of Parts	No repair, factory warehouse in Los Angeles

If you keep careful records, you will have a good idea of what you are spending on equipment, and what it will take to service each piece of your gear. It will refresh your memory when a problem arises whether servicing will be convenient or awkward.

Expense Chart

The following chart is a sample of an expense log that includes a month's worth of income and expenses.

Income and Expense Sheets for Bitter Roots Band, June, 1999

Income & Source / Mileage / Musical Expenses / Other Expenses				
Date	Income	Expenses	Description	Miles
6/1/99	$400.00		OK Club	82
6/7/99	$650.00		Jackson PTA	39
6/9/99		$12.50	Dry Cleaning, Al's	
6/10/99	$500.00	$100.00	City Golf Club Commission to Fast Ed's Agency	61
6/12/99		$28.50	Ralph's Printing (Business Cards, fliers)	6
6/14/99		$15.40	Guitar Strings, Maine Music	12
6/15/99		$60.00	Local 14 quarterly union dues	
6/19/99			Audition, Mix & Max Bar	112
6/20/99		$80.00	Irene's voice lessons	20
6/22/99		$68.00	P.A. Repair, Maine Music	12
6/26/99		$100.00	Photo Session, Al Brunson Pictures	
6/28/99		$200.00	Rent, rehearsal studio	
6/30/99	$1,000.00		Bill's Bar	150
TOTAL	**$2,555,00**	**$664.40**		**494**

Total Income:	$2,555.00
Music Expenses:	$323.40
Business Expenses:	$341.00
Net Income:	*$1,890.60*
	Mileage 494

Chapter 2 Resources

There are an ever-increasing number of books that discuss how musicians can get a band together. They tend to be at their best when examining the protocol for rehearsals, and the way that musicians can develop into better players through study and the acquisition of new skills and better instruments. Most of these books are less successful in their attempts to provide insights into the music business. Four of the better books that I have run into are:

Marty Jourard, *Start Your Own Band: Everything You Need to Know to Take Your Band to the Top!* New York, NY: Hyperion, 1997. Contains useful guides to equipment and some basic information about music.

Kathryn Lineberger, *The Rock Band Handbook: Everything You Need to Know to Get a Band Together and Take It on the Road*. New York, NY: Berkeley Music Co., 1996. If you've never been in a band before, and don't really understand what each instrument is supposed to do, this book is a good beginning guide.

Norton York, (Ed.), *The Rock File: Making It in the Music Business*. Oxford: Oxford University Press, 1991. This is a collection of articles by various British writers. The first half of the book, which discusses the role of rhythm instruments, vocals, and horns is equally applicable to American musicians.

Patricia Shih, *Gigging: A Practical Guide for Musicians*. New York, NY: Allworth Press, 2003. This book contains some excellent practical situation on real-life situations.

Sound Reinforcement

There are tons of books about recording and sound reinforcement. The one below is a good place to start:

Sokol, Mike, *Acoustic Musician's Guide to Sound Reinforcement and Live Recording*. Upper Saddle River, N.J.: Prentice Hall, 1998. A practical guide.

CHAPTER 3

Taking It to the Street: Packaging Your Talent for Potential Buyers

You now have the opportunity to test your performing repertoire, see which members of your group like to talk on stage, and which ones need to concentrate simply on playing their instruments. You'll find out which of your songs seem to get the most reaction from audiences. Try experimenting by performing the same song in different keys at different tempos. You may be surprised to find out that a song you thought was a fine musical arrangement works far better in a different tempo or key.

Once you have honed your performance chops to a fine point, perhaps after six months or more of free performances for various audiences, you'd like to get paid for what you do! How do you get this to happen?

There are booking agents in all local markets whose professional expertise is in matching performing artists with buyers of talent. These buyers exist in all sorts of venues, as you will see in the next chapter. How can you package your product to get the attention of buyers, whether you are booking yourself or working through one or more booking agents?

You will need to put together some sort of promotional or press kit that you can show to prospective clients. The kit should include:

- Pictures of the group, preferably both in color and black and white
- A group biography, with some information about each member of the band
- A list of styles of music that your band performs
- A set list (if the song titles are recognizable to a club or bar owner)
- An audio demo of your group on cassette tape or CD
- Videos (discussed later in this chapter)
- Any positive reviews of your music in the press

Making Demos—Audio

First, analyze your intended audience. Where do you want to work? If you want a gig in a Top 40 bar where bands perform current hits, then you need to do Top 40 material on your demo. You may want to put together medleys of these tunes, performing excerpts from a number of songs, rather than trying to record the complete tunes. For example, you might have a 1950s medley or a group of songs by a current artist. Medleys demonstrate the depth of your repertoire to a club owner.

How should you go about recording a demo? A good place to start is by having your own four-track cassette studio, an eight-track A-DAT, or a hard-disk recorder. You can keep your mini-studio in your rehearsal space. It helps if someone in the group has some knowledge about the recording process, and the sound mixing. There are several current books that deal with home studios listed in the Appendix. As your talents develop and you become more critical, you may want to upgrade your equipment, mix your tape at a local recording studio, or do the whole project at a high-tech professional studio.

If this is your first recording venture, prepare yourself for a shock. You may be about to discover that you don't always sing in tune, that your vocal enunciation is unclear, and that that wonderful $200 guitar you love sounds awful on tape. Don't despair. Part of the problem may lie with the microphones that you are using. A cheap microphone can make you sound terrible. The spot where you place the microphone also radically influences the sound quality of your recording. For example, if you are recording a guitar with one microphone and you place the mike very close to the bass strings of the guitar, the guitar will lack brightness. The microphone should be placed wherever it reproduces the sound in a way that reflects the vision of the player. If the player is striving for special effects, this may call for unusual procedures of microphone placement, or the effects may be obtained through equalizing the sound on the recording console.

After you have logged some time in your home studio "woodshed," it's time to evaluate what you have done. Are you getting a good enough sound to make a demo for your press kit? Have you captured the essence of your group's sound on the tape? If you are working with a four- or eight-track machine, unless you are dealing exclusively with a drum machine, it's going to prove very difficult to capture a real contemporary drum sound.

Now you have more decisions to face. Should you try to buy a better tape recorder, a second A-DAT machine, a computerized recording set-up, or better-quality microphones? Should you try to enlist a friend who is a technical wizard to help produce your demo? Will she charge you for her help? Or, should you go with a professional studio recording with an experienced engineer at the controls?

If you decide to go to a studio, be sure to talk with the engineer who is going to work on your project and get a feel for whether he will be comfortable be recording your style of music. Above all, listen to other projects that he's recorded in the same studio.

If you aren't sure whether you need a studio-quality demo to achieve your objective of getting work, take your home tape and play it for prospective employers and booking agents. How do they react to the tape? It's best not to rely on family or friends for this sort of information. They may not have the basis for making an informed judgment, or they may be afraid to be critical. They may also bring some unwelcome personal biases to the situations with comments like, "I told you that bass player was no good. Look at the way he dresses." This is not the sort of information you need.

Today there is a wide range of recording equipment available. Before you buy anything, it's a good idea to listen to what it can do. Listen to some tapes that other people have made using that equipment. If possible, try to arrange a rough demo session for your band, however brief, where you can check out what your band will actually sound like using that tape recorder and microphones. Find a music store owner who has the patience to work with you, and then give him your loyalty by buying exclusively from him.

Another possibility for making a cheap demo is to do it at a local college's recording studio. You may be able to find a student who is majoring in audio engineering and will be able to do your demo as a college project. She'll get some experience and fulfill a course requirement, and you'll get a demo for the cost of the tape. Some of these college studios are well equipped with sixteen-, twenty-four-track, or hard-disk facilities.

If the college ploy fails, look for a non-professional audio fanatic who spends much of her free time recording bands as a hobby. Many non-professionals love experimenting in a studio and buying high-quality professional gear financed through some other career. It may be work for you, but it's fun for them. For example, a few years ago, an airplane pilot in Denver had a well-equipped eight-track studio, which he rented out for next to nothing. He didn't use the studio to make money, but because he enjoyed recording music.There may be someone like that in your hometown or nearby. Some successful recording artists have home studios that they allow their friends to use, just for the practice of recording music in that particular room, or as a favor.

At times, a new recording studio needs somebody to try out their equipment, and they will allow you to use studio time free, or at minimal expense. A professional audio shop may also let you use their studio, and they will use your demo as an example of what can be done with their equipment.

If you are paying for the recording studio, be sure that your band is well rehearsed before you set foot in the door. A studio is not a cost-effective place to re-work musical arrangements or argue about repertoire. You should work out the kinks of your repertoire in your home studio before renting elsewhere.

How many songs should be on a demo? No more than three, or at most, four. If you are recording cover tunes, you may want to do portions of a dozen songs or three or four medleys. If you want to work in a bar that features cover bands, limit or omit original music on your demo. If you won't perform it at the club, don't put it on your demo. Make sure your strongest song or medley is the first thing on your demo, because if the owner of a venue doesn't like the first song, he may never bother listening to any more material.

Making Video Demos

Making a video is an expensive proposition, but there are some ways of saving money. The American Federation of Musicians (the Musicians' Union) has a number of locals that allow members to make videos cost free, using equipment owned by the union local. Of course, you must be a member in good standing of the local to obtain such services. The union probably will not allow you to take possession of the video. They will show it to prospective buyers at union headquarters. This enables them to be sure that your group will file a union contract on any jobs you receive, but it also means you can't shop the tape yourself. There are many film, television, and mass communications students at local colleges who may be able to use your video as a class project.

The community access division of your local cable television supplier may provide similar services. Many of the cable companies have agreements with the communities that they serve that require them to teach people in the community to run video equipment and to produce local shows.

A possible drawback that many of these free services share is a lack of editing facilities. Sometimes a college or union local may have some editing equipment, but it is not usually state-of-the-art quality. Any sort of student project starts with the assumption that most students lack experience. This is definitely going to limit the scope of your video. Another problem with free or low-cost video services is the number of cameras involved in the shoot. A camera video shoot may portray your group accurately, but it offers little chance of capturing unusual artistic or humorous effects that top artists use in their MTV videos. High-quality, professional videos require the use of three or more cameras, access to a sophisticated editing facility, a quality director, and unfortunately, the expenditure of considerable sums of money.

If none of these strategies have enabled you to get a free or low-cost video, I recommend that you wait until the group has achieved a solid financial base before you make a video. It is too expensive to attempt such a high-risk proposition early in your career. It is safer and far less expensive to combine an audio recording with some quality photos that can demonstrate your abilities and charisma.

Why bother with a video at all? Remember your goals: to communicate whatever visual strengths your group possesses, along with a good audio track. For one thing, you can sometimes use a video as a substitute for live auditions at clubs. If the video is reasonably good at capturing what your group does, you won't have to lug equipment across town for an audition. The alternative to getting video services free is to be prepared to spend $25,000 and up to capture your group in a thoroughly professional vein.

If your video comes out well, you may be able to promote it to be shown on cable television as part of the cable company's neighborhood access program commitment. Some public or private channels have programs that devote time to local videos. If your group has a particularly magnetic lead singer or player, a good video can help you to get a record deal.

Now you have a video and/or audio insert that you can place in your promo kit. What else do you need? You'll certainly want some good photos of the group, together with some biographies and some favorable critical reviews.

If you want the photos to be useable in newspapers and magazines, be sure to use glossy photos. How do you assemble these materials? Once again, you need to resort to whatever talent and ingenuity your group possesses. If you have done a video, or any sort of local television performance or interviews, you may be able to use some stills for your promo kit. Be sure to get permission from the broadcaster, or you may get a nasty letter from a lawyer threatening a lawsuit if you don't pay up. Do you know anyone with a good camera who is looking for experience as a photographer? Remember, all you really need are one or two decent photos. The more copies of a photo that you can get duplicated, the cheaper the cost per photo.

You can always hire a photographer. Try to find someone who has some experience working with musicians. Look at some of the work she has done before making any commitments. Check with the Musicians' Union or with local agents or other bands. The Denver local of the Musicians' Union provides free photos for members. They can be done with a photographer that the union recommends or one that the group chooses.

Student photographers at colleges and even high schools are another source of getting free or low-cost photos. It's most important that a photo captures the spirit of the group. It's a good idea to have the photographer listen to some of your music before she does the shoot. This will help the photographer to match the image of your music with the "look" of the band.

Stylists

Costuming and appearance can be an important part of developing a group's image. Getting the attention of the public is an important step in building a performing career. Some of today's pop stars (not to mention athletes and politicians) expend considerable effort on creating a visual image that coordinates with their musical or personal style. To accomplish this, some groups hire stylists or costume designers who create a particular "look" that the public will identify with a musical act.

Although this may strike you as an extravagance, remember that getting the attention of the public (or, for that matter, of record companies) is one of the first major hurdles to your music career. Working with a stylist or costume designer can be one of the ways to overcome public indifference to accepting a new musical group. The visual aspect of the package that you present to the public can be as important to your career as its musical contents.

To save a bit of money, try writing your own biographies, and/or group history. Tell what the members in the group have done that might be of interest to the general public, not only in the areas of music, but in terms of hobbies or unusual skills or interests. Maybe one of you collects snakes, plays professional table tennis, or set a state record for the women's javelin. As your career develops, you should include a list of satisfied clients. If no one in your group has the ability to write well, you can always hire a professional writer or a journalism student to compile your biographies.

Be sure to include a list of any musical credits. Has anyone in the group studied with a famous musician? Does anyone have music degrees? Did someone play in an honor band or win a local or state music contest? Have any members of your band played with other well-known bands?

Publicists

Once a group has started an active touring career, it is often desirable to hire a publicist. The role of a publicist is to make sure that anything positive about an artist gets attention in the media. Even hobbies or skills that are totally unrelated to music may enable you to get publicity in magazines or on television shows that may not feature music. For example, athletic skills, cooking specialties, or unusual hobbies can earn a story in an appropriate newspaper or magazine. The publicist attempts to control any media coverage of the artist to fit the image of the group that the group itself or their manager is attempting to formulate.

Media attention leads to record sales and to public interest in a group. This, in turn, stimulates concert appearances and further record sales. Hiring a publicist isn't cheap, but in the long run it can be quite cost-effective. (See Resources at the end of this chapter for books about publicity.)

Sample Press/Promo Kits

Now that you have taken a look at the various forms of publicity that you will need, the following are some sample press/promo kits and photos. Note that different musical groups try to relate the style of their publicity to the style of their music.

Chapter 3 Resources

See the Chadbourne and Levine book in the resource section of Chapter 2.

Two reasonable books about music publicity are:

James Gibson, *Getting Noticed: A Musician's Guide to Publicity and Self-Promotion.* Cincinnati, OH: Writer's Digest Books, 1987. Readable and intelligent.

Jim Pettigrew, Jr., *The Billboard Guide to Music Publicity.* New York, NY: Billboard Books, second edition, 1997. Including sample press releases, and information about technology and media guides.

CHAPTER 4

Selling Your Act in Places You Never Dreamed Of

At this point, you have developed a promo kit that includes group photos, bios, and a demo tape, and you have a sound system and a vehicle in which to transport it. What you need now are more jobs.

There are two ways to go about finding work. One way is to do it yourself or have one person in the group represent the band. The other way is to be represented by a booking agent.

Booking Yourself

Getting a musical organization together is a full-time job in itself. You need to work out musical arrangements, choose the tunes you want to perform, buy equipment, select clothing to be used in your performances, and set aside many hours (and a place) for rehearsals. If you are doing original material, then you will need to set aside time for writing and re-writing songs.

If you plan to book yourself, you will need to:

- Do a good deal of legwork, such as making numerous phone calls to check out all sorts of leads from friends or other bands.
- Figure out ways to advertise your talent. This may include ads in the Yellow Pages, printing posters and flyers, designing T-shirts with your logo, and contacting schools, clubs, religious groups, social and business organizations, caterers, etc.
- Be prepared to negotiate prices. You want to make as much money as possible, and the client wants to get great entertainment at a low price.

Of the hundreds of musicians I've known, I can only think of three or four individuals who actually enjoyed booking themselves or their groups, and were good at it. The most successful salesperson of the bunch books himself and does a brilliant job of it. This is mostly because he has an office with maps on the wall, huge card files, and six full-time assistants who return phone calls immediately. They run their operation like a business. The owner-bandleader only involves himself during the final stages of the negotiation.

Another person who was good at booking his group quit doing it after a couple of years. He found that it took up too much of his time. It was easier to hire someone else who didn't need to spend his time practicing, rehearsing, performing, and recording. Booking can be a full-time job, if it's done well.

Setting a Price

The most obvious factor in setting a price is to know as much as possible about where you're going to perform. Is there a cover charge or a minimum number of drinks that the customer must buy? What kind of money do they charge for drinks? Does the cover charge apply for the whole evening, or just for one show? Do you know other bands or soloists who have played this particular room?

If you're working for an organization at a party or a charity event held in a room they've rented out, what sort of people are hiring you? Are they well-heeled doctors and lawyers, truck drivers at a Christmas party, or a group of environmental activists? Obviously you don't charge a regional convention of IBM the same price as you would a benefit for a safe house.

This brings up the subject of benefit concerts. Many of the local chapters of the Musicians' Union follow the rule that a group can only do a benefit if all of the people at the facility—the ticket-takers, stagehands, ushers, etc.—are contributing their services free of charge. This is a great out for you, if you feel that you are being taken advantage of. One final ploy that I have used when the client is being particularly aggressive about getting me to donate my services is to tell the client that I will be happy to do a benefit for them if they can get my dentist and my auto-mechanic to donate free services for me. Many clients have a terribly inflated idea of how much money an average musician earns. They may figure that if you are charging them $100 for an hour, since the ordinary work week has forty hours that you are earning $4,000 a week. If only this were true! I regret to say that, with a few exceptions, whenever I have done benefits, I have generally been treated worse than when I was doing a paid job. For whatever reasons, people seem to value your talents based upon how well they are paying you.

I suggest that you find a particular cause or charity that appeals to you, and simply tell others that you contribute your services to Organization X. By the way, if you do play benefits, be sure to get a tax receipt that will enable you to deduct the value of your services from your income tax. To make this work, the organization must have non-profit status.

The Alan Remington Pricing Formula

Alan Remington is a friend of mine who has taught music and music business at Orange Coast Community College in Costa Mesa, California. Alan has had a long and successful career as a conductor, composer arranger, and head of his own band. His own band was so successful in playing one night casual gigs that he sent out as many as a dozen bands to different events in the Los

Angeles area in the same night. This is the formula he devised after playing at many clubs and talking with other bands and club owners:

1) Figure out the number of patrons during the peak hour. By Alan's estimation, they will usually consume two drinks per hour. Typically, the two drinks will average out to a cost of $4 to $5.

2) Double this figure, because the average customer will stay for two hours. Let's say the room holds two hundred people. During the two hours they will spend $8 a head, bringing in $1,600 to the club.

3) Since there are two shows, the total receipts will be $3,200. Alan's formula is that the band should get about a third of the bar receipts. In this case, this would be just under $1,100.

This assumes that there is no cover charge. If there is a cover charge the band should either get the amount of the cover charge, or 75% of it, plus an additional percentage of the receipts from the bar. If the room doesn't serve alcohol, the numbers must be adjusted to reflect the prices of coffee and dessert, or whatever constitutes the bill of fare.

One way to convince the owner that your band is earning its keep, is to try to establish how many people are coming to the club because the band is there. Of course the club owner will say that they would come to drink and party anyway, but he is usually quite aware that this is not necessarily true. Another argument that can be used is that the club has to have entertainment because it is available at competing venues.

Booking Agents

What do booking agents do and how do they do it? A booking agent is someone who sells acts to a variety of clients on a short-term or a long-term basis. Agents service wedding receptions, parties, conventions, and special events such as political rallies. They also work with caterers and halls, schools, county or state fairs, and anyone or anyplace that might require the use of live entertainment.

Some booking agents specialize in clubs, some in conventions. An agent may book one type of entertainment, or provide anyone under the sun on request. That could range from a Hawaiian hula group to a pair of trained bears and a juggler. Agents generally have offices, although a few may work out of their homes (depending on state laws). They charge the musician a commission of 15% to 20% of the musician's gross wages. The higher fee is what is paid for a one-night engagement, and the lower one is what the agent takes for a long-term booking in a club.

Agents build up a certain clientele who will give them repeat business. For example, an agent might book the local IBM Christmas party every year, unless his contact at the company leaves or they're dissatisfied. Agents may book a particular club on an exclusive basis or compete for the account with other agents.

How do you find an agent to represent your group? Some agents may be willing to give your group a live audition in their office, rehearsal studio, or club. Others may prefer to see you working in front of a live audience. This means that you may have to go out and get some work yourself before you can get an agent. You will find agents listed in the Yellow Pages, and you can get a list of those who have union franchises from the nearest local of your union.

One way to find out who the viable agents in your town are is to ask some of the local groups who work regularly for recommendations. You'll probably hear the names of two or three agents repeatedly (unless you live in a very large metropolitan area where there are dozens of them).

If you have friends in working groups, ask them to recommend you to an agent, or if you can use their name when calling the agent. There's a much greater chance than an agent will come out to see you if someone they know and trust suggested doing so.

Provided that an agent has some interest in your band, she will need some selling tools in order to represent you to the best of her ability. If you have a good promo kit with attractive photos, a few reviews, a set list, some letters from satisfied clients, and a good audio or video demo, an agent is more likely to take you seriously than she would with an act who simply wanders in the off the street and says, "Book me."

It is crucial for you and your agent to reach a clear agreement on a number of issues. What kind of music do you like to play, what sort of music can you play in a pinch, and what styles of music are you unwilling or unable to perform? Do you want to work in bars, or is this impossible because of some of the band members' day jobs? Are you willing to do some travelling, at least on the weekends? There may be more work available in neighboring ski resorts or beach clubs than exists in the town where you live. Some agents simply don't deal with out-of-town accounts. Others may send you on a six-month Holiday Inn tour, if that is what you want.

You also need to reach some agreement on the price of the band. Initially, the agent may have a better notion of what your band can make than you do. After all, she's been booking bands in the area for a while. She also knows the clients ands the size of their budgets. That is her business.

This brings up another subject. It doesn't much matter who books you for your first few gigs, but don't let a buddy or a relative book your band on a long-term basis. It's very unprofessional. Although they may be enthusiastic, they probably have little business knowledge or skill. Agents know when to lower the price, and when to hold out for top dollar. They recognize when a client is bluffing and could easily afford to pay the band double the initial offer.

In many sections of the country, conventions are a daily event. They may be gatherings of local business people, regional meetings of medical or sales groups, or even national meetings. Convention gigs often pay more for one hour of work than you could earn working in a club for three days of four one-hour sets.

If some of the people in your band work day jobs and some don't, you may be able to form a smaller group within your regular band. You might also be able to do a solo lunch hour show, or a duo during "happy hour," usually from around 4:00 P.M. to 6:00 P.M. Happy hour gigs are common in many downtown areas, or near the airports of cities where business people may be quartered. After a hard day of meetings and selling, they like to go to the motel bar and unwind. You can provide the (usually happy) background music. Many "singles' bars" also offer happy hours. Not all happy hours include entertainment, however. Some just feature special deals on food or drinks. If that is the case, try to convince the manager of the venue to feature music at least one day a week, or ask your agent to check it out. Friday is usually a good bet, because it marks the end of the workweek and the start of the weekend.

Never try to steal jobs from an agent. If your agent has booked you on a gig and someone comes up and asks what the band charges, it is best to hand them your agent's card. She was the source of the job and is probably more adept than you are at negotiating deals. If the people for whom you are performing say that they would like to book you again and ask if they can contact you directly, do the honorable thing and say, "No." If the agent finds out that you are booking jobs directly, she will probably never call you again. She may even bad-mouth you to other agents in your locale, who will then be reluctant to book you.

What can an agent offer you? Sometimes agents book certain clubs exclusively, so that they may be able to get you booked in a club on a long-term basis. If you are seeking consistent gigs, either for financial reasons or to make the group musically tight, this can be a great opportunity. If you sign an exclusive agreement with an agent she may be willing to share in the costs of your promo kits or photos, or even to invest in helping you to make a better demo.

Some agents have ready access to work outside your hometown or the region where you live. Most agents will insist on an exclusive agreement if you expect them to perform this kind of service. They will also want to place their name and phone number on your photos and promo materials.

If an agent has been booking you on a non-exclusive basis and everything is going well, it may be worthwhile for you to sign an exclusive deal. An exclusive deal means that the agent is the only one with the right to book you or your band, and she will collect commissions on any job you work, even if you book it yourself. You need to understand that if you *have* signed an exclusive deal, you cannot work for other agents.

It would be foolish to sign an exclusive agreement with an agent who has seldom if ever booked you unless the contract contains some guarantees of work or income. For instance, if your band has been together six months and you have been able to make $500 a week for the four of you, an agent will have to get you work that pays over $620 in wages to compensate for her 20% commission. You can and should work out an agreement that gives the agent a certain amount of time to get your income over, say, $750 a week, or the contract can be dissolved. If you are a union member operating under a union agreement, the agent has to get you a certain amount of work or the agreement can be dissolved. Check with your local to find out about this requirement.

In the "dirty tricks" department, watch out for this maneuver. Rather than talk about commissions, an agent may ask you what your group charges to play at a particular event. You will quote a price and they will accept it. What you don't know is that you are getting the $600 fee that you requested, but the agent has sold the group for $1,200, pocketing 50% of the fee. This sort of trick is difficult to prove. The client is rarely interested in getting in the middle of a dispute between an agent and a band. All they know is that they were billed for $1,200, and the band showed up and did a good job. I've had friends who played convention gigs where an out-of-town client gave the band a check and asked them to give it to the agent. Much to the band's surprise, they found out that the agent was making as much money as the band received for playing the gig. Do your best to find out what the job pays, rather than quoting a price up front to the agent.

Another issue that you should discuss with your agent is the question of doing repeat jobs at a higher fee. If you've played the Cheyenne Elks Club twice, and each time the band drew bodies like flies, then it's time to ask for a higher fee on the next go around. The trouble is that sometimes the agent's loyalty to the client is stronger than her attachment to the band. If she books a club one hundred nights a year, and you only play six or seven of these nights, the chances are that she will be more concerned with the club manager than with your band. Under these circumstances, you may have to get tough with the agent and turn down the gig. If the agent is representing your interests, she should fight to get you more money. If she doesn't, perhaps you should look for new representation.

Dealing with an Agent

The question of meals is one that is a persistent problem in the relationship between agents and talents. It should be clearly specified whether the act gets a meal break, and whether the client will feed the band. Many agents leave this matter to be resolved on the gig, which put the musician(s) in the embarrassing position of being a beggar, waiting for the client to make an offer. This is a particularly acute problem if the gig is out of town, and at a location where there is no other place for the band to eat. On the other hand, musicians should be careful not to wolf down huge quantities of the client's food, as some musician like to do.

Generally speaking, musicians should not drink on the job. It isn't professional, and can lead to problems. Another recurring problem between musicians and agents is that clearly if you have to drive a hundred miles to get to the gig, you should be paid more than if it's a five-minute drive. Be sure to find out exactly how far away the gig is. Some clients want the band to set up before the event begins. This may require you to hang out on the job for as long as two or three hours. Under those circumstances the band should be paid more money, and it is essential that some provision be made for the band to eat. A client certainly doesn't want a surly, hungry band with a bad attitude to entertain them.

A contract for a gig, with or without an agent, should specify the hours of employment, specify breaks during the course of the evening, offer discounted or free food or drink, provide lodging or a lodging allowance if the gig is not near your home base, and should specify how and when the band will be paid. It is a good idea to get a 50% deposit on any contracted job. If something goes wrong, at least you will get to keep that money. What sort of things can go wrong? Occasionally a club owner spaces out that he booked a band, or books two bands for the same gig at the same time.

Sometimes the person who hired you quit his job, or was fired. The new manager or owner may not even be aware that you have a signed contract. The American Federation of Musicians (AFM) will provide legal help and even pay you the union minimum if you get caught in such a situation. However, this requires that your band all be members of the union, and use a signed union contract filed in the jurisdiction of the local where the gig is taking place. The AFM also franchises certain booking agents, limiting the percentages of their commissions. If you decide to use a union agent, it is best to join the union. Even though some union agents will book non-union talent, they are not supposed to do so.

The truth is that many local rock bands don't bother to join the union, and think of it merely as a bunch of old swing and symphonic musicians. In some locals that's probably true. It's also true that if younger musicians would join the union and take a more active role in it, they might transform the shape of their locals. A number of locals are making more of an effort to deal with young rock and country musicians. Almost all the big-time rock and country musicians belong to the union, because their recording contracts and TV appearances require that affiliation.

In cooperation with the record companies, the union co-sponsors local concerts through a fund called the Music Performance Trust Fund (MPTF). These concerts are free and open to the public. They take place all over North America in shopping malls, hospitals, schools, parks, nursing homes, prisons, and other locations. They pay whatever the union minimum for that local determines is appropriate. Each local sets its own wage scales, and as you would expect, wages in New York or Los Angeles are higher than they are in Dubuque or Tupelo. Working a couple of MPTF jobs a year will often pay enough to cover your union dues. Of course, you may get other jobs as a result of playing these gigs.

MPTF can be a great "cop-out" for all the requests you get to do benefits. These clients can be referred to the union with a recommendation to apply for MPTF funds. You will still be paid minimum scale, and the client only pays part of the tab. If an organization is truly poverty-stricken, it may even be able to get MPTF to pay most or all of the costs of the gig. Note that MPTF jobs must be requested forty-five days in advance, recommended by the local unions, and approved by the trustees of the fund in New York.

There is an organization called NACA (see Resources) that books colleges. They hold regional and national conventions, which showcase acts for college buyers. A similar group exists in Canada. The attendees at these conferences are buyers for college entertainment, so a successful audition can result in weeks of work at colleges.

It is possible to do NACA auditions without an agent. Once again, you need to face the question of whether you are the best person to do the necessary bargaining. If they like an act, a group of several colleges will try to "block book" it. This means that several colleges will get together and offer you a series of concerts at a reduced fee. You get more work, and they'll get a bit of a bargain. Whether this will prove to be worthwhile depends upon the distances you traveled to get the job, the distance between the various jobs, and the amount of work that they are offering.

There are also regional arts organizations, such as Arts Northwest, that put on annual conferences. Bookers, presenters, and talent are the attendees, and juried acts are showcased. To obtain a showcase, you must submit promotional materials and a CD or video. It is a good idea to attend one of these conferences first before trying to get on the program. You can go to educational workshops, scope out the scene, and even make contacts with agents and presenters. In the Appendix is a list of these regional arts organizations, with information on how to contact them.

It is not necessary to have a booking agent to appear at a showcase. If you don't have an agent, you may want to rent a booth to further promote your group.

Personal Managers

Agents get jobs for acts. They function as an employment agency for the act, and as bargaining agents who needs to satisfy both the buyers and sellers of talent. Generally speaking, agents don't offer acts long-term career plans. Their work is to get jobs and keep the buyer happy by providing good entertainment.

A personal manager, on the other hand, does attempt to build long-term careers for her acts. She is usually the one who gets a record company contract for the artist, and negotiates that contract with the help of a music business attorney. A manager is also a sort of buffer between an act and the booking agent, monitoring the agent's work to make sure that everything benefits the act. Managers do not usually function as booking agents, except in the classical field, where it is customary to do so. State laws vary on the exact limitations of a booking agent and personal manager, but some are very stringent. It's to your advantage to check them.

Since the premise of this book is that you want to stay in your local music market, either by choice or necessity, you probably won't require the services of a personal manager, unless you expect to record and tour on a national level. Also, to put it bluntly, you usually cannot afford the additional commissions that a manager will require. A good personal manager charges anything from 10% to 50% of your gross wages, with 15% to 20% being the most common amounts required. If you put this on top of the 15% to 20% fees you are paying to your booking agent, there isn't much left for the band to split.

Why do people hire managers? When an act is on the road, they rarely have time to take care of their business. Someone has to make decisions as to which jobs to take and which ones to turn down. Negotiations with a major record company can take months of hard work, negotiating offers and counteroffers. In short, for a full-time touring act that is after national exposure and big-time record deals, a manager is virtually a necessity. Record companies may judge the viability of an act by the reputation of the group's manager and/or attorney. The best and most influential managers have immediate access to major record company personnel.

For an act aiming to work only in a secondary market, a personal manager may be an unaffordable luxury. Most local managers have other full-time employment commitments and may not have the time to commit to developing an act. Examine your goals. What can a manager do for you that you aren't already doing? (Long-term goals are discussed in depth in Chapters 11 and 12.)

At this point you may be wondering how in the world you can afford to pay a manager, an agent, and travel expenses, too. If you have already established something of a career, and are working regularly, you may want to have a provision in your managerial contract that has certain performance guarantees. Let's say your three-piece band grossed $75,000 last year. If you make $100,000 this year, and pay a manager 20%, you won't be doing much better than you did last year. You might require the manager to take a lower commission on amounts under $75,000, with the commission escalating when and if the band makes more money. You may also include a provision that states that if the band *doesn't* make $100,000 this year, then the contract is dissolved.

Another important part of a management contract, one that also can be placed in a record company contract, is known as a "key man clause." Some of the large management firms might include half a dozen managers or even more than that. If your manager leaves the company, you may find yourself represented by someone who doesn't know your music, or doesn't believe in it. With a key man clause, if the person that signed you leaves the company, then you are out of the contract.

The Expansion of Management Roles

Because record companies have been laying off many of their employees, some of the more aggressive management firms have become increasingly active in record promotion. They are assuming duties usually undertaken record companies, like making contacts with radio stations. If your group has ambitions on a national level, this can be a very important matter.

Sunset

One of the most controversial aspects of management contracts is what will occur when a management contract ends. A contract can end with bitterness, when a band fires a manager, or a manager resigns, or the contract may simply run out after three to five years, and one side or the other chooses not to renew the contract. The sort of issues that come up are:

- Should a manager continue to get a percentage of record royalties after she is no longer working with a group?
- Does the manager own part or all of a music publishing company that contains songs written by the act?
- Should a manager be paid commission on gigs that were booked while she was still working for the band, even though the gigs took place after the relationship has ended?

If you are signing with a new manager, be careful that you are not paying double commissions. Some agreement should be reached where the old manager and the new one take reduced commissions during a transition period.

Business Managers

Superstar acts usually hire a business manager to deal with their investments and tax problems. This usually represents another 5% off the gross income of the act. Since the lion's share of the people reading this book are not competing in the superstar area, it is not really something that you should worry about at this time. If a high degree of success comes your way, believe me you will get many people soliciting you to provide these services. Business managers and personal managers often want power of attorney, which enables them to sign contracts in your absence. Be very careful in granting *anyone* power of attorney, because it offers opportunities for unscrupulous people to embezzle from you. In these days of e-mail and faxes, you ought to be able to deal with most contractual signatures no matter where you are.

Other Creative Opportunities

In the category of special projects, a number of cities have commissioned songs to celebrate their history, attract tourists, or to build local pride. Local Chambers of Commerce and tourist bureaus are possible sources of such work. If you get any nibbles, send a demo of any songs that could be considered appropriate, or write a fragment of a potential song. Do some research to check out historical events in your town, and what musical style is popular in your community, and appropriate for the subject. It is always good to throw in a few references to local tourist attractions or prominent landmarks. Churches also sometimes commission new music to celebrate particular holidays or events.

Other similar projects can include state songs, celebrations of historical events or songs built around tourist attractions, and political campaign songs. These songs can be lucrative, and are fun to write. If you excel in writing melodies or in crafting lyrics, but not in both, you may find it helpful to find a collaborator to complete the project.

Two other sources of local recording work are industrial films and slide shows. Industrial films usually require only instrumental music. They are usually short films, running from five to fifteen minutes. Occasionally, a song may be appropriate at the beginning or end of the film, much as in a feature film.

Slide shows usually also focus on a product or event, but they are done with smaller budgets and less elaborate productions. With either slide shows or industrial films, you should include creative fees as part of your budget, as well as the union scales for yourself and any other musicians. These wage minimums vary in each medium, so you should get the necessary information from your local union. Many of the clients for these projects will not be signatory to union agreements, so you may have to do the necessary paperwork. If the client uses the film in another medium, for example, as in a commercial, there will be additional payments that need to be made to the musicians. Be sure that your agreement with the client specifies that he will be responsible for any payments if the work is used in a new medium.

Local news programs and cable television will sometimes buy snippets of music for use during five- to fifteen-second segues that run between shows or behind credits. Check your local cable supplier or news station to see if they need such music, and what kind of musical style they prefer. In Chapter 7, there is an extended discussion of work available doing local or regional commercials.

One final source of jobs is film editors. They put the final touches on film and video products, and often they have input on who will provide the music. In some instances, they may even do the hiring and payment. You can find who the film editors are in your community by consulting the better photo and film processing labs, or by checking with college film departments or any recording studios that are capable of recording sound with picture. Occasionally, recording studios hire composers to work on projects that the studio is recording.

Other Sources of Employment

There are some organizations that do not work through booking agencies. One of them is called Young Audiences. This group hires groups or soloists to do school concerts. (See the Appendix for their various offices.) It is often necessary to audition in order to work for them. They want a combination of a lecture and a performance, oriented to children of various ages. You may be asked to spend a portion of your program demonstrating vocal or instrumental techniques or answering questions. It is a good idea to do a brief history of the musical styles that you perform or to talk about the history of the music you are playing.

The great advantage of Young Audience performances is that almost all of them take place in the very early hours of the morning (try 8:00 A.M. on a snowy day in a distant suburb)! The performances are usually the length of a school period, forty to fifty minutes, and you usually do two consecutive performances at the same school.

Income from Young Audiences won't make you rich, but it's a nice way to supplement your income. Many of the Young Audience jobs are limited to union members, because they are partially funded through MPTF.

There are organizations in some cities that deal with disadvantaged people or special populations. Some of these shows are for people in correction facilities, or physically or mentally disadvantaged people. Typically, these performances also take place during the day. They provide a wonderful opportunity to get paid for what is really community service. They are a reminder of the tangible evidence that music is something that almost anyone can relate to, no matter what their age, intellectual or social level, physical or mental handicap. Denver also has an organization called ArtReach that brings the arts to special populations, varying from halfway houses for juveniles to senior centers. Check with the Department of Social Services in your local city government to see if there are similar organizations in your community. Sometimes these organizations require the artist to volunteer their services. Bread and Roses in San Francisco, and Outside/In in Santa Fe are groups that sponsor performances and workshops for special populations, such as seniors, people in prisons, and at-risk youth.

Another source of work is communities that only allow people over the age of fifty-five to live there. Often these housing developments have a community center. A recent article about performing in these venues claimed that many of them will pay a performer $300 to $500 for a performance.

Artist-in-Residence Programs

Another significant area of possible employment is available through government or foundation-supported grant programs. Every state in the United States has an arts council and a humanities council. Similar programs are available in Canada. Arts councils exist to promote an appreciation of the arts and to help local artists and arts organizations to achieve recognition. Each state arts council has a program called Artists-in-Residence (AIR) or Artists in the Schools. These programs hire artists to work in schools for periods ranging from half a day to an entire school year.

A "residence" means that you work in a school or community setting. To be eligible you must live in or near that locale. If you live in a large state, the residency may require you to temporarily relocate. The arts council may provide you with free or low-cost housing, but you may lose the ability to work at your normal evening musical gigs in your hometown.

Each state administers this program in its own way using broad federal guidelines. There are many employment opportunities available through these programs. The state gives a local school district some "matching funds" to pay for an artist to work in a school. The extent of the match varies from state to state. In some areas of the country, Young Audiences administers these programs.

Usually these jobs are for soloists, or small groups. The reason that more work is available for solo acts is that the Arts Council and the local school district must come up with more money for each member of the group. In these days of budget cutting for school programs, this is unlikely to happen.

The AIR aims to offer new experiences to children in a particular school. Music is only one of a number of disciplines represented. Dance, drama, creative writing, video and visual arts specialists may also apply for the programs. (The usual procedure for an AIR position is to submit a form together with a resume and a tape of your work.) The Arts Council staff then screens the application. If you get past the preliminary screening, the council calls you to do a short audition. The judges are selected from people with previous working experience in the program, some of whom will undoubtedly be musicians. Others on the panel will include council staff members, and some educators who have had artists in their schools and are familiar with the program.

The judging of your work is based on an evaluation of your talent together with some consideration of whether your work will fit into a public school program. You need to be able to communicate with children as well as demonstrating that you have artistic ability.

The forms will ask whether you can work in different areas of the state, and what lengths of time you are willing to commit to the work. The less restrictions you place on where and when you are willing to work, the better your chances of being employed in the program. However, take into account the size of the state in which you live, and whether travel will be a hardship.

One of the things that you can do to try and improve your chances of getting AIR work is to contact a school and work with them on proposing a program. The school goes through roughly the same process that you do with the council. Their grant proposal is scored by a panel on the basis of the validity of the program and how much it can contribute to the artistic learning of the children, together with some judgments as to whether the program has been well planned, and is workable as described in the grant form.

There are some pitfalls of getting a school to do a grant proposal. They may be funded, and you may not have passed the artist audition. Or you might be chosen, but the school's grant is rejected as being poorly planned or not sufficiently interesting. It is still wise to get schools to write grants, however, because it increases the odds in your favor.

Is all of this worth the trouble of doing the paperwork and an audition? Most of the AIR programs pay the artist approximately $500 a week, plus mileage. They may or may not provide a housing allowance, if you need to travel many miles away from your home. Usually the local hosts will, at the very least, attempt to assist you in finding low-cost housing.

The beauty of the AIR program is that almost all events take place during the day, leaving your nighttime hours free for practicing, writing, or even performing. There are also generally no weekend obligations, so that if you are not far from home, you can continue to work weekends, at the very least. Some states allow applicants from other states. You are less likely to actually get work unless you have a fairly unique skill, or have developed a reputation that has spread to that state. You will have to do more hustling and try to contact schools in the other state to be sure that there are some requests for your services. Unfortunately, it is possible to be listed on the AIR roster, but not to actually get any work from it. Each state has its own specific procedures. Some states encourage community arts residencies, where your residency is in a city, rather than in a school. The same general rules apply, except that you will be working with adults, as well as with children.

Once you are accepted into an AIR program, you have entered another network that can supply you with additional opportunities for employment. The state arts councils often get requests from local arts councils or from various areas of the state to recommend musicians to play at festivals or special events. Once the people working at the arts council get to know you they may well recommend you for other work. Many of them are artists themselves, and they have a pretty good idea of how artists work. Best of all, since they are state agencies and not-for-profit companies, you do not pay any commission on this work. Other arts council grant programs are discussed in Chapter 6.

Other sources of grant money include city arts programs and private foundations. Consult your local librarian, particularly at a college library, for a list of private foundations in your state. Often the money offered by private foundations is related to education or disadvantaged populations. For example, they might be willing to fund a songwriting program for juvenile delinquents, but they are not apt to fund a demo of your band. Many uses of music are appropriate in the area of mental health programs, such as improvising music with disturbed children. Use your imagination, and consult with the foundation office for help.

There is also a fair amount of work available performing music for "special populations," such as people in penal institutions, seniors, disturbed children, and numerous other groups. Performing for special populations involves more than setting up a sound system and getting everyone to "boogie." Seniors are apt to be interested in hearing songs that were popular when they were teenagers or young adults. Research your audience, much as you would do in a normal performance. You wouldn't play bossa nova in a country bar, would you? Check with local seniors' organizations and with your city or state Department of Social Services.

Through working with special populations, you may develop skills and an interest in learning about music therapy. Some friends of mine have been able to get steady work performing for and with patients in mental hospitals. They find the work is very satisfying. There are a number of full- and part-time jobs available in the field of music therapy. Should you become more interested in this area, you may want to take some college courses, or even get a degree in this field.

Chapter 4 Resources

The Buttwinick, Chadbourne, and Levine books recommended in Chapter 2 are also relevant to this chapter.

The annual book, *Songwriter's Market*, published by Writer's Digest in Cincinnati, lists producers of audiovisual materials and short films who are looking for music. It is an invaluable resource.

Most state arts councils are located in the capital city of your state. Check for their addresses in the telephone book under "State Government."

The address for NACA is: National Association for Campus Activities, P.O. Box 6828, Columbia, SC, 29260.

There are a several books available on personal management, and most books about the music business have a chapter on it. A good current resource is Dr. Stephen Marcone's *Managing Your Band, Artist Management: The Ultimate Responsibility* from High Marks Publishing, Wayne, NJ, 2003. Distributed by Hal Leonard.

The best book about booking is Jeri Goldstein's *How to Be Your Own Booking Agent*. Be sure to get the second revised edition, published by the New Music Times in Charlottesville, VA in 2004. Whether or not you want to book yourself, Goldstein's volume offers an excellent explanation of how the booking process works.

CHAPTER 5
Developing Versatility

Developing versatility is the key to expanding your opportunities to work in the music business. Whatever you know how to do, or are doing, there are ways to expand your employment opportunities by using the skills that you already possess.

Start with the most basic and obvious skills. What instrument do you currently play? How many other related instruments could you add to your arsenal? If you are a guitarist, do you also play banjo, mandolin, or ukulele? If you play electric guitar, do you have both jazz and rock-type guitars, a rack of effects pedals, a MIDI adaptor, or a guitar synthesizer? Do you own both acoustic and electric guitars? What about a twelve-string? If you play acoustic guitar, do you own both nylon- and steel-string models? Can you play both pick and finger style? Can you use fingerpicks or play slide guitar?

Even if you only play a single instrument, there are options open to you that can increase your musical scope and ability to tackle new musical projects. The fact that Jimmy Page could play excellent acoustic guitar, as well as his wild electric rock leads, enabled Led Zeppelin to use a wider sound palette that was not in the repertoire of most of their rock competitors. Expanding your musical sphere will help vary the musical arrangements of your band and will make you a greater asset for any future musical endeavors.

Other rhythm instrument players have similar opportunities. If you are an electric bass player, do you own both fretted and fretless bass instruments? Can you play an upright acoustic bass? Do you know how to use a bow? Do you have effects pedals that will expand the range of the music that you play? Do you play the newer five and six string electric basses? If you play drums, do you own a drum machine or synthesized drums? Can you follow a chart? Do you play Latin percussion, or own any exotic percussion instruments such as Irish bodhran or African or Greek percussion instruments?

Keyboard players, do you own one or more synthesizers? Do you have your various keyboards hooked together via MIDI? Do you play organ, harpsichord, and acoustic piano? Can you read and improvise with equal skill? On the previous page is a chart of various instrument families, designed to indicate ways of improving your employment prospects and musical skills. Adding

Family of Instruments

Instrument Family	Instrument	Related Instrument or Skills
Rhythm	Guitar	Acoutic; various electric; 12-string; 5-string banjo; tenor banjo; dobro; mandolin; ukulele; effects pedals; MIDI; synthesizer; pedal steel guitar
	Bass	Fretted; fretless; acoustic; use of the bow; 5-string; 6-string; tuba
	Keyboards	Acoustic; synthesizers; piano; organ; harpsichord; celeste; clavinet; sequencers; samplers; accordion
	Drums	Congas; bongos; woodblocks; tympani; tambourine; drum synthesizers; drum machines; Latin & African percussion
Woodwinds	Saxophones	Clarinet; flue; oboe; english horn; bass clarinet; alto flute; recorder family; piccolo; tenor, alto, baritone, soprano, and bass saxophones; EWI
Brass	Turmpet	Flugelhorn; piccolo; trumpet; mutes; EWI
	Trombone	Bass and tenor trombones; sackbut; mutes
Strings	Violin	Viola; mandolin; electric violin; cello
	Bass	See rhythm bass above
All		MIDI adaptors are now available for virtually all instruments, enabling players to achieve effects that were previously impossible. Sampling devices allow players to achieve the sounds of any instrument.

variety will help keep you excited about playing music, and will also lead to more and better paying jobs.

Some of the work in smaller music markets may actually demand more versatility than what is required in a major music market. For example, in New York, it is possible to make a living (though admittedly, usually a modest one) simply by playing jazz. If you live in, say Idaho Falls, you will need to explore additional options. Teaching is one of the more obvious choices.

Teaching

If you have a college degree with a major in music education, or you are getting one, you may want to consider teaching in the public school system. In order to get certification, you must have completed courses in music education and completed practice teaching in a school. The course work includes the basics of study in different families of instruments, so that you can work with school ensembles. No one can play many instruments with equal facility, but taking method courses in the various families of instruments will enable you to develop a basic understanding of the orchestra. Other parts of the music education curriculum include the study of conducting and music transposition. These subjects are essential in dealing with a school band. The same general sort of study leads to jobs conducting school choral groups. In small schools a teacher may have to conduct both a chorus and an orchestra. Because of cuts in school music budgets, some band teachers have found themselves having to conduct a chorus, and vice versa.

Public school music generally includes music programs to celebrate the holidays, a spring and/or graduation program, and music during sporting events.

Work is also available as a substitute music teacher. The advantage of subbing is that you can work when you choose, providing work is available.

The disadvantage is that although the pay is reasonably good, you probably will not qualify for dental or medical benefits, nor will you be paid during summer vacations. Part-time or substitute teachers are unlikely to accumulate pension benefits.

Teaching in private schools is another possibility. Private or religious schools may not demand state certification, and their programs may have a bit more flexibility than the standard public school offerings.

Many teachers continue an active playing career, working weekend gigs and even touring in the summer. Summer music camps offer teachers additional opportunities to earn extra income. Many musicians thrive on teaching music, and it actually fuels their enthusiasm to play. Others find that teaching music all day is not conducive to inspiring one to practice or perform music on a regular basis. You need to decide for yourself which sort of reaction you are apt to have to a full-time teaching position. It is also important to keep in mind that opportunities in public school teaching seem to be diminishing. Despite research that validates the importance of music in a school program, state legislatures and school boards seem to always cut music and art budgets as their first steps toward balancing the budget. On the other hand, if you are able to find full-time employment as a music teacher, you will receive pension, medical and dental benefits, and a fair amount of vacation time. For the average musician, these benefits are unheard of, outside teaching or employment in a major symphony orchestra.

If you do decide to pursue a career in teaching music in the schools, it is a good idea to try to study ways of integrating music into the overall school curriculum. This includes the use of music in teaching American history, and the mathematical and acoustical foundations of music.

College Teaching

Full-time college teaching usually requires that you have a graduate degree in music. Some subjects, such as music history, generally require that the teacher have a PhD. Other areas, like sound recording or music business, usually demand that professors have a master's degree. Occasionally, colleges will substitute real-world experience for these requirements.

Most colleges have tenure track jobs. After six years the teacher applies for tenure. The teacher undergoes a comprehensive review, examining teaching, creative work, and service to the college and the community. If tenure is granted, the professor usually goes from being an assistant professor to an associate, and a considerable wage increase is also given. Ultimately the professor can apply for a position as a full professor, and a similar process occurs.

Colleges also hire instructors, who teach more classes, and are required to do less creative work or publications. Part-time work is also available at many colleges, community colleges (two-year programs), and universities. Depending upon the school, a bachelor's or a master's degree is usually sufficient for instrumental or vocal instructors.

Private Teaching

Many musicians set up a private teaching practice in their own homes. Some teachers even go to the student's home, which may represent a considerable investment of your time, not to mention the price of gas and car maintenance. However, you may be able to charge more and get a more upscale group of students. Many music stores employ teachers to give private lessons, but they usually charge the teacher from 10% to 20% for recruiting students and setting up lessons. Some stores leave all the arrangements to the teacher, simply rent space to the teacher by the hour.

Working for a music store can provide you with a regular income, but it also can be a deadening experience. Many store studios are small cubicles, and spending hour after hour in such an environment is not particularly conducive to your physical or mental health. This condition is aggravated in warm weather, if the studio is not air-conditioned.

One way to avoid teaching burnout is to schedule forty-five minute lessons, and leave fifteen minutes at the end of the hour for relaxing, getting outside for a breath of air, making notes on the last lesson, making phone calls, or talking to the student. Although this will cut into your income, it will make you a better teacher and a saner person.

For children under the age of fourteen, a half hour is a good amount of lesson time. Many children don't practice enough to justify a longer lesson or don't have a sufficiently long attention span to get through a longer lesson. Naturally, there are exceptions, such as children who are unusually mature or motivated. In such circumstances, you can always experiment with a longer lesson time.

If you play keyboard or guitar, or write songs, you may also be able to teach group classes. Teaching groups of people is sometimes less musically satisfying than teaching individuals, because people who take group lessons are usually less serious about the work involved. Groups can be fun, though, because of the interaction between the various personalities in the class. They also pay better than private lessons, even though the fee per person will be smaller.

My favorite group lesson experience took place with one adult male student. He seemed to grasp everything quite well during the lessons, but each week he would come back and seem to be at exactly the same level of skill. After three weeks of this I tried to diagnose the problem. It turned out that he never practiced at home, because he thought that since he was learning the material in class, there was no need to spend time at home repeating the same things he had learned in the class.

In order to teach classes, you will need a location that is suitable for approximately five to ten students. Community centers, religious institutions, community colleges, or music stores are possibilities. You can advertise the class through sponsoring organizations, or you can rent the place yourself and advertise the classes by printing up fliers or making posters. The advantage of having a sponsoring organization is that they will publicize the class on bulletin boards or in their own catalog or newsletter. Usually they will have a large mailing list, which gives you a good chance of filling your classes.

You should set a limit on the size of your classes, so that people are comfortable in the space and can get to know one another. Several friends of mine have run successful guitar classes lasting two hours. The second hour is a sort of sing-along social hour, combining beginners with students who have a bit of playing experience. Since many people who take group lessons are adults and have no illusions about becoming guitar heroes, the second hour is sometimes more fun than the actual lesson. The Old Town School of Folk Music in Chicago offers large group classes, combining stringed instruments and several teachers. They have had success with this format for over forty years.

What should you charge for lessons? You will need to check the going price in your area. It may be anywhere from $10 to $25 for a half hour lesson. It is possible to teach two students in one lesson, especially if they are friends or siblings. A fair arrangement is to charge less than you would for two private lessons, but more than you would for a regular group lesson. Group lessons usually cost $5 to $10 per person, and the fee is usually paid ahead of time. Most group lessons run in series of six to eight weeks. The biggest problem with group lessons is making sure that you have enough enrollment to offer the classes. One way to accomplish this is to offer a pre-payment discount for classes, in the same way that many shows charge more at the door than if tickets are bought in advance.

Many teachers collect by the month, on the first lesson of the month. Some teachers give a slight discount for pre-payment, such as offering all "lesson months" as though they had four lesson days per month. This gives the student a free lesson every third month when there are actually five lesson days during the month.

Make-up lessons are a ticklish issue. A teacher should not allow make-ups unless the cancellation takes place twenty-four hours in advance. If you do not adopt this policy, you will get last-minute cancellations from parents who forgot about beauty parlor appointments or golf dates. Some teachers simply don't offer make-ups, but that's probably pushing things a bit too far. Make-ups can be scheduled on a day when you normally don't teach. If you have a large teaching practice, trying to schedule make-up lessons on a hit-and-miss basis can be disastrous. Don't allow students to cancel because they haven't practiced. Use that situation for a lesson in improvisation or sight-reading or for analyzing records.

Another consideration in teaching is your own attendance. If you are going to teach on a regular basis, then you can't leave to take a last-minute luncheon gig. Deal with your students in the same way that you expect them to deal with you. If you need to make a last-minute cancellation, you can offer a free lesson to the student who you have inconvenienced. If these changes in your work schedule keep happening, you should consider cutting down on your teaching load.

Summer is a time when many students drop out of lessons. They may leave because of vacations, work, social commitments, or athletic interests. You need to anticipate this drop off in your income. Very few students will want to take lessons during holiday breaks. If you charge by the month, you should charge for these "vacation times."

If you are consistent about following most of the policies outlined, you can count on teaching as a good supplementary source of income. It can even provide your major bread and butter, if you want it to, and if you can develop a regular clientele. Music stores that don't themselves offer lessons are a good source of referrals. Another source of potential students is to advertise in the local entertainment weekly, or even in the daily newspaper.

You will need to find a source of rental instrument, especially if you are teaching group lessons. If you rent any instrument yourself, be sure to get a deposit to cover damage or loss. Renting provides a reasonable alternative to the jaded parent who has watched her child go through many fads and temporary hobbies or interests.

If you are teaching for a music store or studio, the store will encourage you to have the student buy instruments and supplies there. There is nothing wrong with this, provided that the store does not tack on unreasonable mark-ups. Be sure to advise the store as to the supplies and sheet music you'll be recommending for your students. You should resist the tendency of some store owners to get you to pressure the parent to spend money for a higher quality instrument, even if the store owner offers you a commission on the sale. A good teaching relationship that can continue for several years is worth a lot more to you than $10 or $20 in commission from the sale of an instrument that is not needed. It is the teacher who should be the judge of when the student is ready to up-grade their instrument.

Record at least a portion of your music lessons on a cassette tape or a CD. The student can then refresh her memory by playing the tape/CD at home. This will also prevent unnecessary phone calls between lessons. Be sure to have some blank tapes available, because students invariably forget to bring theirs. It is also a wise idea to have the student write down all lesson assignments in a notebook. You should also have a notebook in which you keep track of each student's progress. Sometimes when a teacher gets busy, he too can forget what pieces he has assigned, or what sections of a piece the student needs to work on.

Sample Pieces at Medium Skill Levels

On the following pages are examples of rhythm parts, lead parts, lead sheets, some difficult instrumental parts, etc. I have tried to give you a feel for what you are apt to meet on a normal club date or on a record date. Here's an original bebop line in D♭ for a lead player.

Here is a sample of a regular piano part for a standard tune.

Here is a typical example of a rhythm lead sheet for guitar, bass, or keyboard.

Chapter 5 Resources

There are dozens of books about teaching music in schools. The best resource I have found about private teaching is David Heflick's book *How to Make Money Performing in Schools*. It was published by Silcox Productions, Orient, WA, in 1996.

CHAPTER 6

Making Use of the Union and Other Organizations

Many musicians see themselves as purveyors of some sort of glamorous lifestyle, rather than blue-collar workers. When the question comes up of uniting with their colleagues in a labor organization, they invariably ask, "What can the union do for me?"

Union leaders often resort to blue-collar answers to what is really a white-collar question. The union sets wage scales, offers pensions and benefits for those participating in national contracts, and provides a measure of job protection. A number of AFM locals also offer pensions based on contributions for work done locally.

Many younger musicians see the union regulations as restrictions on their work life: a member is not supposed to work with non-union musicians, contracts are supposed to be filed on all jobs played, members must pay work taxes on these jobs, and many of the younger musicians feel the cold shoulder coming from older union officials, whose idea of a contemporary rock tune is "Kansas City."

However, the union is what its members make it. The truth is that many musicians are out in the cold if they're working without the protection of a signed contract. Unfortunately, there are a fair number of sleazy agents out there booking jobs at low wages, and a considerable group of club owners who tend to treat musicians like mildly educated cattle. The real question is not whether a serious professional should join the union, but how she can make it work to her best advantage.

Some professional engagements absolutely require union membership. Professional symphony orchestras work under collective bargaining agreements. These contractual agreements not only cover wages, but every aspect of working conditions. They are hammered out in complex negotiations between lawyers representing both sides. Players in such orchestras require union membership within thirty days of employment. When you consider that symphony orchestras employ from 60 to 105 musicians, it would be a disaster if each musician had to negotiate such matters as length of rehearsals, instrument insurance, dental and medical plans, disability, and a procedure for arbitrating disputes. Fortunately for the symphony musician, the union negotiates such agreements on a daily basis around North America.

What about musicians in pop or country music? Anyone recording for major record companies must be a union member because the major record companies have all signed union agreements that require it. Musicians who want to appear on national or syndicated television and are performing on-camera are required to join AFTRA (the American Federation of Radio and Television Artists) as well as the AFM.

Should those who wish to make their own records bother with the union? Meet the Special Payments Fund—one of the least understood benefits of union member-ship, and one that can actually assist you in financing your own recordings.

The Special Payments Fund pays a yearly bonus to all union musicians who participate on recording sessions with filed union contracts. The bonus is based on the amount of each musician's gross wages earned in recording sessions. It has nothing to do with the sales of the recordings that you played on, but is a small percentage of the sales of *all* recordings. The payments continue on a reduced scale for an additional four-year period after the first year.

How can this help a four-piece country band in Boise? If this group files union contracts, pays work dues, and makes the 10% pension contribution to the AFM Pension Fund, they will then receive bonuses based on their gross wages during the recording sessions. The pension money is put into the AFM Pension Fund and comes back to the musicians involved, at ages fifty-five and sixty-five. To qualify for a pension, a musician needs to have earned $1,500 in pension-covered wages for a period of five years. One-quarter, one-half, and three-quarters of a year's credits are given for those who earned $375, $750, and $1,125 in covered wages. A number of locals have pension plans for work done in their jurisdiction, so that the amount of your pension will escalate if you are a member of one of these locals.

Self-contained groups (those who do all of their own playing) generally file six sessions for each album recorded. One album a year will cover you for a full pension credit. Any commercials, film scores, television shows, slide shows, or industrial film scores that you perform on that utilize union contracts will also add to your pension credits.

How important is the Special Payments Fund? A few musicians make over $30,000 from their bonuses; many others earn anything from $50 to $1,000 and up. The size of your check depends on how many union sessions you played and the overall sales of records. Digital sales are also now part of the picture.

A similar bonus plan exists for musicians who play on feature film scores that utilize union contracts. In the bonus fund for film, you are paid the bonuses based on the gross of the particular film that you performed on rather than the gross of all films. If you play on the soundtrack for a Clint Eastwood film, as an acquaintance of mine did, you will be gleefully amazed at the size of your re-payment check.

The chart on the next page summarizes some of the other advantages and disadvantages of union affiliation.

Radio and Television Commercials

Under union agreements, commercials pay residuals, i.e. repeat payments for extended uses. These payments are made every thirteen weeks, and are governed by agreements between the union and advertising agencies. Local commercials recorded under AFM agreements used in a single market are allowed to run for as long as eighteen months with the payment of residuals. Local commercials have a markedly lower payback than national commercials because: 1) there is a great deal of recording going on in the secondary music markets, and the union had to modify the rules to compete with non-union producers, and 2) the union has recognized that the budgets for recording local commercials, and the money involved in buying time on local TV or radio is relatively small. A small bank in rural Nebraska cannot afford to make the sort of re-payments that a national beer company regards as part of the cost of doing business.

How significant is the income from residuals? In New York, the center for recording commercials, studio players estimate that two-thirds of their income comes from residuals, and only a third from new commercials.

(I have had the pleasant experience of earning as much as $2,000 in re-payments from a single one hour recording session, and have had commercials that have run for as long as ten years.) Other re-payment schemes govern the use of film scores on television.

Singers belong to either the American Federation of Television and Radio Artists (AFTRA) or SAG (the Screen Actors Guild.) Singers receive much higher residuals for their work than musicians get, and their union contracts are much more complicated. They have many categories of use, including local, regional, national, prime time, and so-called "wild spots" that allow for unlimited use in a specific period of time. A single national campaign for a major product that includes both radio and television and runs for an extended period of time may earn a singer tens of thousands of dollars.

Returning to the subject of the AFM, most musicians do relatively little recording. What about the players whose bread and butter comes from free-lancing or from performing in clubs?

The Musicians' Union as a Source of Work

When you live in a city of some size, 250,000 people or more, there are usually traveling shows of various kinds that come through your town. Among them are ice shows, touring artists who require small or large groups to augment their performances, the circus, and traveling companies of Broadway

Advantages of Union Affiliation	Disadvantages of Union Affiliation
The union provides you with a standard form contract.	You pay work dues of 1–3% on all jobs played. These work dues are based on the local Union minimums.
Comissions are limited by the Union.	You are not supposed to work for agents who are not franchised by the Union.
The Union sers the minimum wages.	Too many groups are willing to work for the bare minimum and some agrents are all too accustomed to negotiating minimum wage.
The Union may recommend you for jobs. Many locals have a job availablility book and will also help you to hook up with other players.	Some union locals make rock or country players feel unwelcome.
In the even of a breach of contract, you have some legal recourse. Some Union locals will even pay you the minimum wage and help you to institute legal proceedings to collect the rest, if the wage is "over scale."	
You can get unscrupulous employers put on the Union blacklist. A emergency phone number, (800) ROAD GIG, provides 24-hour assistance for traveling musicians.	
The owner cannot fire you without notice.	
The Union local in your town may participate in the AFM pension plan. It may also occere access to a credit union, discounts on such items as musical supplies, tires, etc.	
Meet other musicians.	
Musical instrument insurance, low cost recording.	

shows. In every town there are musicians called "contractors" whose function is to put together bands for such touring entertainment. In return for performing this service, the contractor earns from one-and-a-half to two times the union wage that is paid to the other musicians. Contractors usually play the job with the rest of the band, although in the larger towns they may not play, but simply supervise the proceedings. Contractors call rest breaks, see that everyone arrives on time with the proper instruments, and supervise the union paperwork and the collection of tax forms. The employer relies on the contractor to handle any emergencies, such as dealing with absent or late musicians or any other personnel problems.

Almost all of this highly professional work is funneled through the local Musicians' Union. If you are serious about trying to find this sort of freelance employment, you will need to join the Musicians' Union, unless you live in a right-to-work state. A right-to-work state is one that has passed legislation stipulating that membership in a union may not be a condition governing employment.

Even in such states, there is nothing to prevent a local contractor from "accidentally" hiring a band that consists entirely of union members. This procedure may sound unfair to you, but it is the Musicians' Union that has established the wage scales and working conditions covering these jobs. This often has required long and extensive negotiations, and even strikes or arbitration. If each musician had to negotiate with the employer, as individuals, they might be at a disadvantage. Few musicians are aware of the expenses of mounting a show, its possible gross, or any special conditions that pertain to a particular production or venue. This is where the union comes in, negotiating the agreements on a national or local basis, and protecting musicians against capricious actions.

For instance, because the conductor of a traveling show is unlikely to see you again, he may make unreasonable or peculiar demands. The union contract is designed to protect musicians against such eventualities, or at least to set up an arbitration process whereby your employment cannot be arbitrarily terminated.

In the case of the circus, the wage scale depends upon the population of the city. Cities are categorized as A, B, or C, according to population. The A or larger cities have a higher wage scale than the other categories.

When you join the union, you should inquire about local contractors. If you spend a little time with the secretary-treasurer of your local, you can learn how the freelance business functions in your town. A contractor may be retiring, or she may be replaced because the client was unhappy with the last band she hired. Once you have found out who the contractor is, try to get a recommendation to her from someone who knows her. At that time you should be ready to present a demo tape and resume to her. You may get hired initially as a sub—someone who is hired when the regular player-of-choice is sick, on vacation, or unavailable to work. If you play well and act like a professional, the contractor will probably call you again. It is also quite possible that other musicians on the job will call you when they in turn are in a position to hire musicians.

Your teacher may be just the right person to refer you to a contractor, but sometimes teachers are reluctant to refer a student for fear that their lack of experience or professionalism will create problems on the job.

Dealing with employers can be a tricky process. You need to be friendly and willing to take direction; yet it can be a mistake to be too be either too pushy or to be a pushover. Don't make too many suggestions or behave flamboyantly.

Be sure that you have an answering machine or voice messaging that can take calls when you are out, e-mail on your computer, and a calendar book in which you keep all of your bookings and commitments. Not showing up for a job on time, or at all, can ruin your career before it ever starts. Be sure that you have written down when and where the job is, what you are supposed to wear, and what instruments you were asked to bring or rent. If a contractor needs you to play an unusual instrument which you do not own, they should be willing to pay for or split the rental cost.

One of the advantages of union jobs is that they usually pay extra money for doubling on other instruments. A wind player may end up playing three or four instruments in a show. The additional money can really mount up.

Don't expect immediate results in dealing with contractors. The contractor may want to see you play before hiring you, but they often don't bother to seek you out to observe your playing. Your best recommendation is through word of mouth by other professionals.

Making Contacts Through the Union

It's already been mentioned that most of the freelance gigs that are major bookings, such as traveling Broadway shows, require union membership as a condition of employment. However, if you're a local country, casual, or rock group, is union membership meaningful, for you, too?

First, in all honesty, there are locals of the union that are indeed run by ex-accordion players, or by musicians who will seriously argue that the Glenn Miller Orchestra was the last great music organization. How do you combat that kind of attitude?

Two suggestions: First, play the best shows that you can, and impress these dinosaurs with your professionalism. Some union leaders really do think that rock musicians are animals that have temporarily been let out of cages, and that country musicians are people with boots and sideburns who learned how to play guitar in between milking the cows.

The other step is a bit more extreme. Not only should you come up with the cash to pay the union's initiation fee, you should think about becoming active in your home local. *Don't* join the union with the attitude that they have your money, now it's time for them to change their attitudes. Help to turn your local around to the place where you want it to be. The worst kind of union members are the ones who join and complain about the organization, but can't be bothered to lift a finger to change it.

Why bother to join the union if you're a rock or country musician? There are a number of locals in the union that are run by rock or country pickers. Locals in various areas of North America have officers who are tuned in to the music business in the twenty-first century.

On a more mundane but very practical level, as a rock or country musician, you are in a wonderful position to get employment referrals from the union. The union invariably gets calls for musicians to play weddings, dances, conventions, luncheons, birthday parties, store openings, political campaigns, nightclubs, etc. If you are the only union rock band in town, so much the better for you. Go down to the office of the local and get to know the secretary-treasurer. Explain to her what your band does, ask for to any appropriate job referrals, and give her a promotion kit and a demo. Ask to play MPTF jobs and even find charities or malls that want to hire your band. Encourage them to apply for MPTF funds, and make sure that the secretary-treasurer gets their application.

Many young bands often set up a sort of antagonism between "our" music and "their" music that often exist only in their own minds. All older musicians don't hate rock and roll, although it may not be the main ingredient for their major musical meal.

Is it really possible to change anything in an established group like the AFM? *Yes!* I was an inactive member of Local 802 in New York for about ten years—a union couch potato. I paid my work dues, collected my recording checks, and played a few live gigs. I even went to one or two meetings of the local. I didn't care for the autocratic and old-fashioned leadership of their union, but I figured I had better ways to spend my time than to get involved with the opposition.

When I moved to Denver, I became quite active in that local of the union. I received many job referrals (I never got any in New York), and went to most of the meetings. I ran for office and was elected to three terms on the Executive Board. I lobbied in the local to fight for the creation of local jingle scales because the national scales were unrealistic for the employers in our market.

About twenty-five years ago, I originated a concept that provided for lowering the wage scales on limited pressings of records. Although this proposal was not accepted at that time, the union adopted this idea a few years later. By then it had achieved the support of the RMA, the Recording Musicians' Association. The RMA is an organization of top studio musicians who work in the major recording centers.

The original limited pressing agreement provided for reducing wages for pressings of 5,000 or fewer records. In 1995, the union expanded the agreement in providing for another scale for budgets of $90,000 or less. These two agreements have enabled music in specialty areas to be recorded under union agreements, with the musicians enjoying benefits as well as reasonable wages. (The

$90,000 scale is about two-thirds the normal union minimum, and it includes pension benefits, and credits for the Special Payments Fund

This example indicates that rules are subject to change, if the people who desire that change have the commitment to fight for what they believe in, and the factual material to back up their feelings. You have the ability to turn your whole union local around. You can propose ideas, get on committees, run for the executive board, or you could even be president of your local in a few years. You can change the way your union acts and the way it is perceived in your marketplace.

Filing a union contract is as important for your welfare as it is for the union. It provides you with a convenient form without needing the services of an entertainment business lawyer. A violation of the contract gives you ammunition to sue the non-paying employer in small claims court, or in a regular court of law. If an employer stiffs you, the union will pay you the scale wages, and take the matter to court to get any amounts you're due over the union minimum. I once played in the band for a theatrical piece in Denver, where the employer stiffed us, and the local paid each of the six musicians the $1,100 we were owed.

Implementing innovative ideas in your local is as simple as formulating a creative idea, and having the staying power to fight for it. For instance, get your local to build a small recording studio available to members at bare-bones cost, or convince them to produce a sampler of local groups on a CD. Parlay that cassette into a recording deal for your own group.

Use the union to network with other musicians, songwriters, contractors, and recording studio producers or engineers. Be sure to tell the secretary-treasurer of your local that your band wants to receive referrals for gigs. Some locals have even started to *book bands*. Other locals send e-mails about gigs, or have Web sites that include employment opportunities.

Musicians who live in an area equi-distant between two locals often are unsure which local to join. You should be aware that there are some restrictions on your ability to work in a local other than the one in which you're a member. Work covered under national contracts, such as recording jingles or television scores, can be done with a union card from any local. However, you may not play a steady job, one lasting more than two weeks, or a number of consecutive weekends unless you are a member of the local in the town in which you are playing. Some locals have residency requirements of up to six months before they will allow membership in the local.

Smaller union locals often charge less in quarterly dues than the larger locals. However, if you or some of your band are members of a local different than the one where you are now working on a regular basis, the union is unlikely to toss MPTF jobs your way, or to refer work to you. They will generally adopt the attitude that work coming through the local's office should go to their own members. Many musicians who refuse to join bigger locals because of the additional expense find out that this decision has cost them lost referrals and MPTF jobs. On the next pages are some union local contracts, and a page out of the Denver local's availability list (open to any current members).

AMERICAN FEDERATION OF MUSICIANS OF THE UNITED STATES AND CANADA

(HEREIN CALLED "FEDERATION")

CONTRACT
(Form L-2)

FOR LOCAL ENGAGEMENTS ONLY
(NOT FOR USE IN CANADA)

Whenever The Term "The Local Union" Is Used In This Contract, It Shall Mean Local Union No. _____ Of The Federation.

THIS CONTRACT for the personal services of musicians on the engagement described below is made this _____ day of

_____, 19 _____ between the undersigned purchaser of music (herein called "Purchaser") and the undersigned musician

or musicians.

1. Name and Address of Place of Engagement: _____

Name of Band or Group: _____

Number of Musicians: _____ Number of Vocalists: _____

2. Date (s) of Engagement; daily or weekly schedule and daily clock hours:

3. Type of Engagement (specify whether dance, stage show, banquet, etc.): _____

4. Compensation Agreed Upon: $_____
(Amount and Terms)

5. Purchaser Will Make Payments As Follows: _____
(Specify when payments are to be made)

_____ *(Continued on reverse side)* _____

IN WITNESS WHEREOF, the parties hereto have hereunto set their names and seals on the day and year first above written.

X _____
Print Purchaser's Full and Correct Name
(If Purchaser is Corporation, Full and Correct Corporate Name)

X _____
Print Name of Signatory Musician — Home Local Union No.

Signature of Purchaser (or Agent thereof) — Signature of Signatory Musician

Street Address — Musician's Home Address

City — State — Zip Code — City — State — Zip Code

Telephone — Telephone

Booking Agent — Agreement No. — Address

Names of All Musicians	Local Union No.	U.S. Social Security Nos.	Direct Pay
			$

Form L-2, Rev. 9/15/95   59-C   Rekord Printing Company, Shamokin, PA (717) 648-3231

6. No performance or rehearsal shall be recorded, reproduced or transmitted from the place of performance, in any manner or by any means whatsoever, in the absence of a specific written agreement with or approved in writing by the American Federation of Musicians ("Federation") relating to and permitting such recording, reproduction or transmission. This prohibition shall not be subject to any procedure of arbitration and the American Federation of Musicians ("Federation") may enforce this prohibition in any court of competent jurisdiction.

7. This contract, and the terms and conditions contained herein, may be enforced by the Purchaser, and its agents, and by each musician who is a party to this contract or whose name appears on the contract or who has, in fact, performed the engagement contracted for (herein called "participating musician(s)"), and by the agent or agent(s) of each participating musician, including the Local Union. It is expressly understood by the Purchaser and the musician(s) who are parties to this contract that neither the Federation nor the Local Union are parties to this contract in any capacity except as expressly provided in 6 above and, therefore, that neither the Federation nor the Local Union shall be liable for the performance or breach of any provision hereof.

8. A representative of the Local Union shall have access to the place of engagement covered by this contract for purposes of communicating with the musician(s) performing the engagement and the Purchaser.

9. ADDITIONAL PROVISIONS: _____

Names of All Musicians	Local Union No.	U.S. Social Security Nos.	Direct Pay

(IF ADDITIONAL SPACE IS NEEDED, ADD SEPARATE SHEET (S).)   (Form L-2)

REFERRAL SERVICE INFORMATION SHEET

Date_____

1. Name of purchaser:_____

2. Address:_____ Zip_____

3. Phone: Day_____Evening_____

4. Type of engagement:_____

5. Date:_____Time:_____

6. Place:_____

7. Style of music:_____

8. Number of musicians:_____

9. Budget:_____

10. Number of people attending:_____Age:_____

11. Where did you hear about the Union_____

12. **PLEASE LET US KNOW WHEN YOU FILL THE REQUEST!!!!!!!**

13. Special instructions/requests:_____

    _____

    _____

    _____

14. Referrals:_____

    _____

    _____

AMERICAN FEDERATION OF MUSICIANS REPORT FORM
TELEVISION AND RADIO COMMERCIAL ANNOUNCEMENTS

RP № 026255

Date:_____

ORIGINAL SESSION:

Recording Date: _____ No. of Mus. _____

Recording Studio: _____

City: _____ State: _____

AFM Local: _____

Hours Employment: _____

RE-USE, DUBBING, NEW USE OR OTHER:

Original Report Form No.: _____

Original Recording Date: _____

Producer: _____

Producer's Address _____

Signatory of Record: _____

Employer of Record: _____

Employer's Address: _____

Payment Type
- ____ Original Session
- ____ Re-Use
- ____ New Use
- ____ Dubbing
- ____ Dubbing (Longer/ Shorter Version)
- ____ Short Term Use
- ____ Spec Factual Info
- ____ Local Info
- ____ Mech Edit
- ____ Sideline Session
- ____ Other

Medium
- ____ TV
- ____ Radio (13 weeks)
- ____ Radio (8 weeks)
- ____ Foreign
- ____ Non-Broadcast
- ____ Other

Rates
- ____ National
- ____ Regional (Nat'l Adv)
- ____ Regional (Reg Adv)
- ____ Local (Nat'l Adv)
- ____ Local (Loc Adv)
- Indicate region or local area in memo box.

Check here if:
- ____ Commercial made for cable only
- ____ PSA status confirmed by AFM
- ____ Session performed solely on synthesizer

ADVERTISER _____

PRODUCT _____

ADVERTISING AGENCY _____

ADDRESS _____

LOWEST NO. OF REPORTED HRS W'KD_____

NO. OF ANNOUNCEMENTS CLAIMED _____

IDENTIFICATION Titles and Code Nos. (Include track lengths for original sessions only). When identification changes give prior and new.

	Original (or Prior) Identification	TRK LGTH	New Identification
A.			
B.			
C.			
D.			
E.			
F.			
G.			

First Air Date _____

Cycle Dates Being Paid _____

MEMO

The Producer understands and agrees that the terms and conditions of the engagement covered by this Report Form include the terms and conditions of the AFM Commercial Announcements Agreement in effect at the time of such engagement.

Producer's Signature _____   Leader's Signature _____

EMPLOYEE'S NAME (AS ON SOCIAL SECURITY CARD) LAST FIRST INITIAL	CARTAGE	LOCAL UNION NO.	SOCIAL SECURITY NUMBER	HRS W'KED	NO. OF D'BLE PER SESS. ION	SPOT ID BY LETTER ABOVE	ID. OF SPOT PER DOUBLE	SCALE WAGES (1)	PENSION CONTRI- BUTION	H & W WHERE APPLIC- ABLE
1 (LEADER)										
2										
3										
4										
5										
6										
7										
8										
9										
10										
11										
12										
13										
14										
15 ARRANGER										
16 ORCHESTRATOR										
17 COPYIST (SEE PAGE 2 FOR ADDITIONAL COPYISTS)										

(1) Insert X if wages being paid are overscale

FOR FUND USE ONLY:

Date pay't. rec'd _____ Amt. paid _____

Date posted _____ By _____

Total H & W Contributions _____

Total Pension Contributions _____

REKORD PRTO.

AMERICAN FEDERATION OF MUSICIANS' and EMPLOYERS' PENSION FUND
(AFM & EP FUND)
733 THIRD AVENUE, NEW YORK, N.Y. 10017

Report Form

There are 6 copies of this Form.

Original (first) page, send to AFM and EP Fund, 733 Third Avenue, New York, NY 10017, with Pension contribution check made payable to AFM-EP Fund.

Retain one copy for Producer's files.

Send one copy to advertising agency where applicable.

Send remaining three copies to the applicable AFM Local where one copy will be retained by the AFM Local and:

(i) one copy will be sent to the American Federation of Musicians, 1501 Broadway, New York, NY 10036

(ii) one copy to the Leader

Pension Contribution Rate:
Commercials produced on and after 2/7/79 .... 9%
Commercials produced on and after 2/7/82 .... TV-10%
Commercials produced on and after 2/7/82 .... Radio-9½%

ORIGINAL FIRST PAGE COPY TO BE SENT TO THE AFM & EP FUND,
733 Third Avenue .... New York, N. Y. 10017

Arts Councils and Grants

Another source of help, and sometime money, is your state's arts council. In addition to the AIR programs described in Chapter 4, there are other grants for which you may be eligible. Some states offer individual grants programs for artists. In music, these programs are typically open to composers. Most arts councils are supportive of musical explorations. Grants offer an opportunity that is often not readily available in the marketplace. The grants are judged by a group of panelists who have expertise in the field of composition. They tend to favor "artistic" rather than commercial projects. Many of the panelists are deliberately chosen from other geographic areas to eliminate favoritism in awarding the grants. Call your state arts council to find out if they have a grant program for individual artists. An alternative is to get a commission from an organization that received a grant. This is the option you need to adopt if the arts council only funds non-profit organizations. Sometimes the sponsor will receive a portion of the grant in return for administering the program and assisting you with the paperwork. Possible sponsors could be local symphonies, a mayor's Arts Commission, or a local arts council. Usually the organization must be a 501 3C category non-profit organization under the federal tax code.

By using your imagination, you may be able to find a community organization, such as a facility for battered women, to sponsor you in a program of songwriting or music performance. There are also an increasing number of cities that offer grants to individual artists, so be sure to check with your city government or a local arts magazine to see if your town is one that supports the arts with its wallet.

There are many workshops that are offered on the subject of grants person-ship, which is the art of writing successful grants. Your state arts council may offer free workshops several times a year. There are also professionals who charge fees to impart similar information. (See Resources at the end of this chapter and the Appendix for books on grants.)

The key to writing successful grants is clarity, and the ability to match your proposal with an organization that wants to fund grants like yours. It is vitally important that your project description be understandable to an intelligent person who may not have a music background. Your budget and the means of implementing your project must also be clear. Be sure that your resume, which is usually required along with your grant application, clearly supports your capability to execute the project. For example, if you are applying for a grant as a composer or s songwriter, provide as much supporting evidence as possible that shows successfully completed work. For this sort of grant, teaching experi-ence is not necessarily a plus, and should not be stressed. On the other hand, if you are doing an educational project, it is wise to provide as much documenta-tion as possible that will indicate your teaching skill and experience. It is a good idea to have a friend who is not a musician read over your grant proposal. If she doesn't understand it, you need to re-work it.

The National Endowment for the Arts (NEA) and the National Endowment for the Humanities (NEH) are sources for a great variety of grants. NEA offers grants to jazz and classical composers and to specialists in the folk arts. They even have a grant program for small record companies. NEH gives grants to college teachers and independent researchers for critical studies in the arts.

NEA and NEH grants can offer a considerable amount of money. The College Teachers' Program, for example, pays up to $30,000. Consequently, the competition is liable to be tougher for a national grant than for a grant in a small state. Don't be afraid to apply. The state or national arts councils often can answer your questions about aspects of the application. Call and ask them, or visit the office of your state arts council for in-depth information. Although NEH and NEA budgets have been cut by Congress in the past few years, private foundations offer another possible source of funding.

NARAS, the National Academy of Recording Arts and Sciences, offers grants for projects that relate to the history of recording and American music. Membership in NARAS is a useful tool for information and networking. Active membership is restricted to those who have recorded six cuts of an album in national distribution. Categories of membership include singers, players, record producers, engineers, album note writers, songwriters, spoken word artists, video and music arrangers, comedy album artists, and album cover artists. The category of associate membership is available for those who do not qualify as active members. Current chapters of NARAS are located in Austin, Atlanta, Chicago, Los Angeles, Memphis, Miami, Nashville, New York, Philadelphia, San Francisco, Seattle, and Washington, D.C. Active members of the Recording

Academy get to vote in the Grammy Awards process, and are able to order records at an appreciable discount. (A list of chapter addresses is located in the Appendix.)

There are also private foundations that offer grant money. Check with your local arts council or with the reference librarian at your local library to see what is available in your state.

Specialized Casual Work

Referrals for casual playing jobs can be obtained through local music stores, other musicians, caterers, and happy clients spreading your name around. Another performer may find herself unable or unwilling to take a particular job, so don't be shy about letting other professionals in town know about what you do.

Sometimes casual jobs will require research into some specific subject matter, like music of the American Revolution. It is customary to charge the client a fee that will cover extra time that you may need to research and rehearse this material. Be sure to explain to them why you are charging something above your normal fee.

Some of these may involve your normal performing group, others might require you to put together a group for this performance only. Use the Musicians' Union or the local college's music department as a resource to meet your needs.

Don't be afraid to set a reasonable price for your skills. The average person doesn't realize that a musician doesn't work a forty-hour-a-week job, and must practice regularly to sustain his talent. One hundred dollars for a solo artist may seem like a lot to a client for a one hour evening performance, but it may be your only job during that particular weekend, and it will probably prevent you from taking another job on the same evening. Since Friday and Saturday nights are prime times for musicians, you need to factor that into your price.

Remember, too, that a single $100 job is actually better than two $50 jobs. You'll only have to drive to one location, and you'll only have to set up and take down your P.A. system once. If you don't respect yourself by setting an appropriate price, your employer probably won't treat you with respect either. Find out what the local union scale is, and charge above it. Scale is a minimum wage and should not be the upper limit of your income potential.

The same general principles apply to negotiations with agents. Set a minimum fee and never go below it. There must be some room for negotiation between the wage you'd prefer to get and the one you will reluctantly accept. If you go below your own minimum, you will probably resent playing the job, and not perform up to your abilities. This can hurt you and prevent you from getting further job referrals. Set a fee, negotiate to a point, and then stick to your guns. You will lose some jobs, but they are probably jobs that are not worth your time.

Through unions and other professional music groups, you can make useful contacts that will influence the direction of your career in a variety of benefit your musical growth and be financially beneficial as well.

Open Mikes and Jam Sessions

Many clubs dedicate one night a week to open microphone. This is a good opportunity to try out new material or to get performing experience. Usually the master of ceremonies is the only person that gets paid. If you are trying to make a living in music, it is best to limit the number of open mike sessions that you participate in.

Other clubs have regular jam sessions, where they either pay a rhythm section, or no one at all. If you contribute too many free services, people will be reluctant to pay you when other performing opportunities come up. It is imperative that you place a value on your musical services.

For the same reason, be careful of performing situations where the only way you get paid is by passing the hat, or using a tip jar. Does your lawyer or dentist solicit tips?

Chapter 6 Resources

Unions

Most of the books about the music business have brief discussions about the Musicians' Union, but I can't think of any that offer enough details to be worth your time.

Grants

Your best bet to exploring the world of grants is to contact your state arts council and the reference librarian at your local college or central branch of the public library. There are numerous books about grants and lists of grant opportunities in the library. It is also a good idea to find someone in your town who has developed a reputation as being successful at writing music grants. Chances are there is someone at your local college who has developed this skill.

CHAPTER 7

Expanding Your Recording Opportunities and Developing Skills

No matter where you live and whatever work you are currently doing, there are probably opportunities to earn some money doing recording work. In this chapter, you'll see how you can utilize these opportunities to increase your income and to develop your abilities as a composer.

The rate of technological change in the music industry has developed with amazing rapidity. Recording equipment is now affordable, and the equipment is relatively portable.

At one time, if you wanted to make a demo tape of a song you had written, you would have had to hire a rhythm section and rent a local studio. Studio time may have cost you from $25 to $65/an hour for eight-track recording, or slightly less for four-track time.

Anyone who has ever been involved with any kind of recording project knows that it invariably takes more time to complete the project than you expect. An instrument may be out of tune, singers may be tired or not phrasing in the way you wish, or other musical or technical problems may occur. In today's music world, you can buy a small four-track cassette studio, a synthesizer, and a drum machine for $1,000 or less. Or you can buy an eight-track A-DAT machine for about the same amount. These machines are designed to be easy to use, so that even a novice can quickly master them. If you have basic keyboard skills, you can literally be a one-person band, playing keyboards, electric bass parts on the synthesizer, and drums with a drum machine. You can perform similar feats with a guitar synthesizer. If you are also a good singer, you *are* the chorus and orchestra. Your major investment will be the limitations of your patience, as you record track after track to refine the song to your own taste.

If you have a MIDI set-up—a computer and a sequencer—they will adjust for any rhythmic problems. If your own timing is less than perfect and you don't own that gear, you should record a click track on one of the tracks as your first step in the recording process. A click track is simply a constant beat, and you can use a metronome to provide it. When you have filled up the other tracks, you can erase the click track and use that track for an additional vocal or instrumental part.

Rick Moss

There are several books by qualified engineering experts that can help you to manipulate home gear to its maximum potential. Some of these books are listed in the resources section at the end of this chapter, and more are in the Appendix. There is also a list in the Appendix of some regularly published magazines that will assist you in developing your engineering skills and keeping abreast of the latest technology. The following page provides an example of a small, home-studio set-up.

Jingles

What other local recording opportunities exist in the marketplace? If you are able to write songs, there is really no reason why you shouldn't attempt to master the art of writing jingles. As a matter of fact, the current trend in commercials is toward capturing the contemporary sound of recordings. If your aim is to do "commercial" pop music, what better way of learning to write a "hook?"

How can you crack the local jingle market? Virtually every city in the United States has advertising agencies. Listen to local radio and television ads first, and then call your local advertising agencies. If possible, make an appointment to see the creative director of the agency. What kind of jingles are being recorded in your area? Find out who is writing them. Often, the agency's creative people write the lyrics for a commercial, or at least come up with the concept for it. They usually hire other people to do the music. If you have a good demo tape, leave it with the creative director of the agency. You can find agencies listed in the Yellow Pages. In larger cities there may be a local advertising organization that brings local agency people together for meetings or lunches. Take a look at the map, and check out agencies within a fifty mile radius of where you live. Some major ad agencies are now headquartered in medium-sized cities, like Weiden & Kennedy in Portland, Oregon, or Crispin, Porter & Bogusky in Miami. Some of these agencies service national accounts, not just local and regional work.

With your home studio and synthesizer, you should be able to turn out good sounding demos for commercials. Most commercials are done in demo form before the agency and/or the client actually approves the work. Do not invest too much in a demo, unless the agency is willing to pay the costs that you may incur, such as hiring musicians or singers. Most agencies will not be willing to pay a creative fee for doing a demo; in fact, they may be shopping around and asking several other production companies to make demos, too. You can see the advantage of having a home studio, since renting a studio to produce five or six unsuccessful demos could quickly put you out of business.

It is also possible to deal directly with an advertiser, instead of an agency. Some small manufacturers or service outlets may not use agencies. If the advertiser is dealing with an agency, it is unwise to go directly to the client. If you try to bypass the agency they may bad-mouth you, and they certainly won't hire you to service other accounts. Agencies get commissions on all the work that they do for a client, and they will mark up your bills to get their portion of the take. If you bypass the agency, you're cutting into their income.

When the advertising agency receives a demo, they take it to the advertiser who will approve, disapprove, or ask for a revised version of the jingle. On a number of occasions I have witnessed a client spending considerable money by adding additional instruments or vocal parts to a demo, only to reject the "improved" product and return to the demo.

In order to maximize your profits and protect your own interests, it is best to record under union contracts. Locals of the AFM are empowered to create their own wage scales for commercials that are used in a single market. If your jingle is played in more than one city, it is considered a regional or national jingle, and you must pay higher wages to the musicians and singers. Consult your local AFM and AFTRA offices for the correct local or national wage rates. The leader of the band, who is often the producer-composer, must sign a contract for each recording session worked.

When the same commercial is used on radio and television, the musicians need to be paid separate fees for each use. Under union contracts, a musician receives a session fee, currently $110/an hour. When the commercial is broadcast, there is an additional payment of $31. Reuse payments on national and regional jingles are subsequently paid every thirteen weeks of broadcast use. On local jingles, these residuals are paid every eighteen months. Consult your local union for the correct current union minimums. In addition to your union wages as a musician, you are entitled to a creative fee for writing the music and/or words for a jingle. The amount of this creative fee can be anything from a few hundred dollars to thousands. It depends upon the client and the nature of the campaign. In order to know what to charge, you need to have some idea of how much money will be spent in buying time on radio and television, and how long the campaign is expected to run. For example, if your client has budgeted $100,000 for time buys on local radio and television, a creative fee of $250 is much too low. It is a good idea to set a minimum creative fee for your services, and to adjust that figure upward if you work for a major client or if you are required to perform extra work. Extra work might include an excessive number of conferences with the advertising agency, or rewrites based upon disagreements between personnel at the agency itself. Some of your clients will choose not to deal with issue of a separate creative fee. They will simply ask for a budget for the project, and it is up to you to include your creative fee in the total package. (See the sample budget on the next pages.)

If you sing on any commercials, file contracts with AFTRA, the American Federation of Radio and Television Artists. AFTRA has regional offices rather than local ones, and you will be surprised to find that their wage scales, and especially their residuals, are much higher than those that musicians get. These contracts are also more complicated in the ways that they deal with reuses. Most major jingle writers insist on singing on jingles, even if they are only lip-

Brand X Super Toys (Home Studio)	
Hours of Recording Time at $25.00 per Hour	_____
Instrument Tracks to Include Guitar, Bass, Drums, Keyboard—Musicians Fees:	_____
Union Scales:	_____
Pension & Welfare:	_____
Health Payments:	_____
Cartage—Bass Amp and Drums	_____
Doubling Fees:	_____
Singer's Fee for Jane Doe:	_____
Singer's Pension & Welfare:	_____
Singer's Health Insurance:	_____
Tape Costs:	_____
Creative Fees:	_____
TOTAL:	_____

Brand X Super Toys (Professional Studio)	
Studio Time: RPM Sound 24-Track:	_____
Tape Costs: 24-Track tape, 2-track Final:	_____
8 Radio Station Tape Dubs for Agency:	_____
Creative Fee:	_____
Musicians:	_____
Guitar, Bass, Drums, Keyboard, Flute, Synthesizer, Bongos—Union Scale:	_____
Cartage Fee for Drums, Bass Amp, Guitar Amp:	_____
Doubling Fees:	_____
Pension Fees:	_____
Arranging and Copying Fees:	_____
Health Payments:	_____
AFTRA Fees for 3 Singers:	_____
Pension & Welfare:	_____
Health Payments:	_____
Other:_____	_____
TOTAL:	_____

Other costs might include legal fees for contract with advertising agency.

synching, in order to collect these juicy reuse fees. Sometimes an agency will not pay a creative fee, but will allow the composer to appear on the contract as a singer even though he didn't sing.

In order to file union contracts, someone must be signatory to union agreements. It is to your advantage for the advertising agency to be the signatory; otherwise, it is your obligation to police and administer the payment of residuals and do all the paperwork. Major advertising agencies are all signatories to the union agreements, although their local branches may prefer that you sign off on the contracts. Try not to do this, because it then may involve you in disputes between the singers and musicians and the agency.

If a small-budget client who is not using an advertising agency insists that you be the signatory, the local union can show you how to get a franchise that will enable you to sign union agreements. When you sign these agreements, they require pension and health payments, payments for cartage of certain musical instruments, and doubling fees. Be sure that you have included all of these fees in your budget to the client or agency.

Do you really need to do these sessions via the union? My opinion is that you are foolish if you don't use union agreements. The wage scales are good, the repayments are beneficial, and you can build up pension credits by using the union agreements. If the employer defaults on payment, you can often get the union to assist you in collecting the money, and, as a last resort, put the employer on the unfair list to protect other musicians in the future. The reason to do commercials is to make money. Songwriting projects or records may have many emotional aspects involved in their conception and execution, but jingles are done for the "big bucks."

Sometimes a client will object to repayments, but not to the union minimums. Try to get your local union officials to help in explaining the rationale behind residuals to the client. Many clients are somewhat paranoid about some mythical monstrous repayment scheme. The truth is that if the campaign is successful the client will probably record new versions of the jingle. The chances are that the repayments to musicians and singers will amount to considerably less money than the client spends on buying radio and television time.

A few words of advice about the advertising business: don't try to get into the jingle business unless you can write well under very short deadlines. Sometimes a client will give you only a couple of days after they have approved a demo to complete the final product. They also think nothing of making lyric and even musical changes during the actual recording session. Don't expect a great amount of loyalty from an agency or client. You may save an account for an agency, and four weeks later not be able to get in the door to bid on another job. Remember that many agencies are virtually revolving doors, and the person who worked on the account you saved may be working at another agency. Another possibility is that the client moves the account to another agency because the client's own personnel shifts, and the new kid on the block has other loyalties.

Be sure that you bring your project in at or under the estimated budget. A good idea is to add a 10% to 20% over-ride or contingency fee to resolve any unpredictable problems. It also should be clearly stated in the contract that if the agency or client makes changes in the content of a commercial on or after a session, they will be responsible for any additional costs.

Even if the recording session takes place in your own home studio, you should still bill the client for studio time. They will expect this charge, and after all, you did invest money to create your own recording facility. If you are renting a studio, you may be get reduced rates by using off-hours, or by buying large blocks of studio time. Most studios have a written rate card, but will deal with clients based on how busy the facility is, and how much work they feel the client can bring into the studio.

Hiring a Sales Representative

If you want to get into the jingle business, but don't want to handle the selling of your own talents, there are three possible options:

1. You can hire an agent to represent you, in return for paying her a percentage of whatever work she brings in. You will be responsible for her expenses, which may include business cards, lunches, trips, and many tape dubs. You must negotiate with your prospective agent to determine whether her percentage comes off the top of the budget, or simply comes out of your creative fee. You should expect to pay between 20% and 33⅓% if you want a salesperson to spend much time representing you.

2. Your second choice might be to find a partner who is responsible for the selling. You then go into business together and share all costs and income.

3. A third option that might work in a smaller market is to utilize a booking agent and to pay him a fee, just as you would for a band booking. Be sure that the agent understands the jingle business, because it is a different ballgame than selling an act to a bar. A good agent should be able to sell your services for more than you would charge.

The third option is a bit unusual. Choosing between the first and second options depends on the people involved and what motivates them. Would you rather have a partner or be in control and be the "boss"? An agent is not apt to do a good job of representing you unless he is making a sufficient amount of money to justify his time and energy. On the other hand, many partnerships, like many marriages, end in bitter separations, and even legal actions.

Writing to Pictures

How can you develop your skills for writing music to picture for film, television, or commercials? Classes in TV and film scoring are offered at some colleges, like the University of Southern California in Los Angeles or the Berklee College of Music in Boston, among others. You can also experiment on your own by writing music to existing videotapes. You will need to develop an awareness of the relationship between music and the visual aspects of a production. Some composers foreshadow events about to happen on the screen, some mimic them, and others choose to work counter to the visual events in order to create an element of surprise. Generally, a client will present you with a finished video, and usually the music is recorded after the filming is done. There are exceptions, especially for dance sequences, which may be too complex to synch the music with the dancing after the fact. all of the visual events in the film commercial.

Get the agency to put a window on the screen with a running clock. This will save you many hours of demarcating when each step of the action is happening. If they can't or won't do this, you need to prepare a cue sheet for yourself that describes all of the visual events in the film commercial. A simple cue sheet for a three second commercial might look like this:

Time (in seconds)	
0.00 to 1.50	Tennis match
1.50 to 4.00	Women player smashed ball at net
4.00 to 6.20	Players walk to veranda
6.20 to 10.00	Two players ecstatically sip tea
10.00 to 14.10	Voiceover touting wonders of Playglo Tea
14.10 to 19.00	More tennis scenes
19.00 to 28.50	Jingle with product tag

If you own a sampler, sequencer, and synthesizer, you may be able to do some film/video projects and commercials without using other instrumentalists. If you own your own studio, this is a very practical alternative, but if you have to rent a studio, much of your savings will be eaten up with additional studio time.

It takes a certain amount of experience before you can readily estimate the amount of studio time that a project may require. If you are hiring other musicians, look for musicians who can master a part quickly, and have quality instruments that play in tune. Utilize musicians who can take direction, but who will also offer constructive, intelligent ideas when called upon to invent a part, or suggest a solution to a musical problem. A creative but even-tempered musician can save your session, or bring it to life by virtue of offering an idea. Sometimes a subtle little musical fragment can make a track sparkle.

Occasionally, feature films are produced in a local market, and with luck and a bit of sleuthing, you may get to score one. If the creative fee is low, try to retain the publishing to your original music. While this is difficult in Hollywood, it is sometimes possible to pull off in a small town with a producer who realizes he is not paying you a Hollywood price.

Some of these locally produced features may never be distributed locally, let alone nationally. It seems as though every local market has a "rich kid" whose parents have financed all or part of a film. It is usually poorly executed and produced, and will die a quick and merciful death. On the other hand, don't be surprised if some of these dogs show up on cable television at 3:00 A.M. on a Monday morning. If you are lucky enough to score a feature that gets on local or cable TV, you should realize some income from one of the performing rights societies. (Details about these performing rights societies can be found in Chapter 17.)

One of the growing sources of income for songwriters is to have their work used in films or on television shows. Twenty years ago most films only contained one or two songs, but nowadays it is not unusual to see a film that utilizes a dozen or more songs. If you are a songwriter, be sure that your publisher submits your work to music supervisors for film and television shows.

You can also utilize your composing reel to solicit work as a player or singer from local record producers. Studio work isn't stressed in this book, since fewer and fewer musicians will be employed in this capacity, because of increasingly sophisticated and reasonably priced samplers, sequencers, and synthesizers. This is the age of the composer-musician, the person who can fulfill both roles successfully. Nevertheless, you can never tell what sort of work might be available at a particular place in time.

If you are deeply involved in local productions, the chances are that few of your competitors will want to hire you as a player or singer. They will generally be reluctant to expose their clients to the competition.

Don't overlook the possibility of renting your home studio to other musicians to do demos of their songs. You may also want to look into opportunities to produce records for other artists. This is discussed further in Chapter 9.

Final Thoughts on Advertising and Film

Don't be surprised when bizarre events occur on film and jingle sessions. I once played on a session in New York for Gleam Toothpaste. The jingle was one of the best-written pieces I have ever played on, with a beautifully written contrapuntal rhythmic duet between an oboe and a soprano saxophone. The client didn't like it, so Mitch Leigh, the composer, went back to the drawing board gave them some mediocre Stephen Foster parodies which ran for nine months or so.

On another occasion, I did a score for a horrible film in Colorado. Another musician and I played about fifteen instruments. The client became very angry because even though he was paying badly, he expected to see a large orchestra at work in the studio.

Chapter 7 Resources

It is a good idea to subscribe to *EQ, Mix,* and recording magazines to keep up with new developments in recording. Some references on jingles appear in the Appendix, but a fairly current book is Jeffrey P. Fisher's Scoring *Soundtracks and Jingles.* The book was written in 1997, published by Mix Books, and distributed by Hal Leonard. Steve Karmen, a renowned jingle composer in New York has written a fascinating book on why vocal jingles are currently out of fashion. It is called *Who Killed the Jingle?,* and it was published by Hal Leonard in 2005.

CHAPTER 8
Working in Multiple Contexts

Working in multiple contexts means that you can find employment in more than one musical organization, even if you are a member of a group that performs on a regular basis. If you are capable of playing a number of instruments and have mastered several musical styles, you can probably find opportunities to work in a number of ways.

By this time, it should be apparent to you that your ability to work as a soloist can be a tremendous boon to your income. You should recall that on union jobs, the leader of a group gets double or one and a half times union scale. Even if you are not a union member, it is still possible for you to charge quite a bit more than you would make as one-third of a trio. The way that groups can split income has been outlined in Chapter 2, which covered the role of leaders, co-op groups, and side musicians. If you play in more than one group, you may assume more than one of these roles.

Suppose, for example, that you play electric bass in a trio called The Red Elephants that plays 1950s rock and roll. The three of you have played together since high school. You work as a musical co-op, splitting the money and owning the sound system in common. You may also be able to play guitar and sing. In that role you work alone as "Henry Lewis, singer-songwriter." Since you are a solo act, you will certainly function as the leader. You also play decent bluegrass banjo, and utilize that skill as a side musician playing with the Blue Devil Bluegrass Band on the first Monday of the month at a club.

Another example of the same sort of musical lifestyle might exist for a versatile trumpet player. On Friday nights you are a side musician with the Ultimate Kicks Dixieland Band. Most days of the week you lead your own lounge combo, and you play modern jazz concerts on flugelhorn with a co-op group. Occasionally, you do freelance work for the ballet in a neighboring town, or play for touring Broadway shows.

The leader of a group takes the responsibility of dealing with a client or booking agent. Often, the check for the job will be made out to the leader, so she, in turn, must pay the rest of the group. She must keep careful tax records, because the earnings will be reported by the client as having been paid to the leader, not to the members of the band. At the end of the year, if group members have earned over $600, the leader must send Tax Form 1099 to all the members of the group, stating the earnings and whether any withholding taxes have been deducted.

Since the leader usually selects or rejects any jobs offered (with or without the input of other group members), there should be general agreement in the band as to what jobs the groups wants to play, and what is the minimum wage that they will accept. In some groups, the leader handles the negotiations without discussing the matter with the other members. In others, the majority opinion of the group prevails. The democratic option can be complicated if some members are difficult to reach, or frequently out of town. In Chapter 7, there is an example of a standard union contract for a one-night casual gig. If you are a member of the AFM, you are expected to file a contract for each engagement that you or your group plays. If you are not a union member, you still need some sort of contractual agreement with your employer. The contract should cover days and times of employment, the length of shows, wages, and any special considerations, such as having a piano tuned on a regular basis. You should also have a letter of agreement with the club manager that sets forth whether the band is entitled to free or discounted food and drink.

On convention gigs that last for three or four hours, or require you to set up your equipment several hours in advance, establish an agreement with the client or the agent that sets forth whether you will get a meal. Sometimes the client is agreeable to feeding you, but doesn't want you in the dining room with a group that may be having a formal dinner or a business meeting.

Be particularly careful when dealing with convention gigs that are out of town. You may be asked to come early, and literally have no place within driving distance to grab a sandwich, let alone eat dinner. It is a good policy to demand (and receive) extra payment if you must arrive early and sit around for several hours before you play.

As we have already discussed, some agents have a peculiar attitude about the dinner issue. They seem to feel that musicians are socially inferior to the client, and should never mingle with guests in a social situation. In fact, the guests often enjoy talking to the performers because most business people are curious about musicians' lifestyles. It is also true that if you are the leader you should make an effort to see that the musicians don't eat so much food as to make pigs of themselves. It is best if the band limits or, better yet, avoids drinking alcohol during the gig.

It is important that the band and the client both honor the starting time, within reasonable limits. "Reasonable limits" could be defined as within ten minutes of the contracted starting time. Breaks should also be worked out by the agent or leader with the client. When a client wants continuous music, it is often possible to split the breaks so that that no one in the band has to play for two or three straight hours without a break. Upon the band's arrival, the leader should arrange where the band will dress, if they need to change clothes. He should also ascertain where the band can go to relax during breaks.

It may seem like an obvious point, but if you are going to work in multiple contexts, you will need a variety of suitable clothes. A bluegrass band doesn't dress like the combo at a debutante's ball.

Working for "The Door"

Some club managers will try to induce you to work without a guaranteed set fee, and instead recommend that you take a percentage of the money collected at the door. They may tack on a cover charge, and give you 50%, 75%, or even 100% of the door charge. This is usually a poor idea, unless you are playing a house concert. First of all, you may not get an honest count of how many people were actually there. You can place a friend or your road manager at the door to count the patrons, but your friend's count may not agree with the manager's numbers. This may be because your friend counted some guests who got complimentary tickets, or because you are getting a "short count." It is difficult to resolve this kind of dispute because it's an "are you calling me a liar?" type of situation, and it can get ugly.

Be aware that the union strictly prohibits a band playing for the door charge alone. You can, however, affect a sort of compromise: play for the minimum union scale, plus a percentage of the door. If you follow this plan, when the owner makes money, you will share in the profits, and at least you'll go home with some money in your pocket. You can also create a situation where the band builds a following. Your income and the club's profits can then both escalate each time you appear there.

For some years now, an outrageous custom has arisen in Los Angeles and New York. In some of the clubs in these cities, acts actually have to pay money in order to play at a club. This is a sort of perversion of the notion of playing for the door. The club manager polls the audience as they come in, and the band is awarded some of their money back, based on the number of people the manager says they have drawn to the club. Not only do the bands often end up with no money, they may actually have to pay to work. Another way some clubs handle this is to make the band sell tickets to the club.

The Musicians' Union has tried to prevent such practices. They have even picketed "pay to play" clubs, but often bands are their own worst enemies. Not only should you never accept such a deal, you ought to use any influence you have over other bands to keep them from working under these outrageous conditions.

How can you keep a client from bouncing a check on you? You can specify in your contract that payment must be in cash or certified check. This is particularly desirable with out-of-town jobs, where collecting bad checks can be an extremely difficult chore. A certified check is one that a bank has issued or guaranteed. Your agent should share your feelings on this issue. You can't pay commission on a job that hasn't paid you any money.

The Musicians' Union has established an 800 number—1-800-ROAD GIG—for bands that are stranded on the road when a club owner stiffs them by refusing to honor a contract. This number is staffed twenty-four hours a day, and the union will provide emergency relief, pay the band minimum scale, and pursue legal action against the club. The band must operate with a union contract, and if the wage specified is above scale when the union wins the lawsuit, they will pay the band the balance of the money.

Contracts

Under no circumstances should you play a club or a concert without a signed contract. "Casual" jobs, such as weddings or parties, should all be treated the same way. A contract for a casual should always specify that you get paid upon completion of the job. The happy couple at a wedding may disappear on their honeymoon, and a month later they will barely remember the name of your band. If you are the leader of a band, it is a good idea for you to introduce yourself to the client immediately upon your arrival. Arrange for a place where you can meet the client after the job is over. There is nothing more annoying than playing a four-hour gig, and then having to wait another hour to find the person who is supposed to write the check.

Leaders and Side Musicians

If you are using a union contract, remember that the leader of the engagement is required to file a copy of the contract at the union local *before* the engagement. If you have played the job without a union contract, it is difficult or impossible to get the union to assist you in any dispute over unpaid wages.

Since you may be working both sides of the leader/side-musician fence, here's another angle of the leader issue: many groups actually split the extra money that a leader receives in a union contract. If you play with the same group of people on a regular basis, that may be a reasonable idea. It avoids any jealousy or arguments about "who does more for the band, whose car the band is using," etc.

If one person truly does the biggest share of the work, is clearly the featured star, and invests more in the group's future, then it is reasonable for him or her to take the leader's fee. The whole concept of leaders goes back to the big band era, when a band consisted of a leader, like Benny Goodman, and the musicians he hired. The leader was usually the featured musician, and provided the P.A. system, the music arrangements, which were often specifically commissioned for the band, the music stands, and even the band bus and the costumes. The side musicians brought themselves and their instruments.

Anyone who has invested in all of these items obviously was entitled to a healthier share of the receipts than the guy who simply blew his trombone on the gig. Today's music is usually played by combos rather than big bands, and so the situation described may not be apropos. Ultimately, you will need to make your own decisions on how to distribute money and authority.

Old-style bandleaders often followed another quaint custom. They would hire a ten-piece band for minimum scale, perhaps $50 per person for a night, and sell the group for $1,000 to the club. This meant that the leader pocketed $500, or exactly ten times what the side musicians received. If an agent was involved the leader might net *only* $300.

As long as a leader pays union minimums, there is not much the union can do about the situation, but the band members should explore what their services are worth to the leader. There is no law that says you can't charge a wage above the union minimum!

If you happen to be the leader on a particularly juicy gig, it is a wise practice to let the band share in your good fortune. For example, in the ten-piece-$1,000 situation described above, if each musician had been paid $75, the leader still would have gone home with $325, more than four times the wages of the band members. All of this may come as a surprise to some rock and country musicians, but many of the old-time dance band musicians never received a dime above scale wages.

Each local of the union sets work dues, which must be paid after any engagement. The leader of the band is responsible for employing only union musicians, and it should be understood up front who is going to pay the work dues: the leader or the musicians. Some musicians prefer that the leader deduct work dues from their paychecks, because they are apt to forget about them. Others prefer to take care of their own business.

One problem that can occur in a band where all of the players work in many contexts is that one person getting an outside gig may interfere with work opportunities for the rest of the band. It is impossible to totally solve this problem. The band should have a clear agreement that certain dates should be set aside for the group, and some sort of minimum notice should be given if one member decides to take a two-week gig with a touring Broadway show. If too many conflicts arise, then it may be necessary for the offending member to leave the group. There is a fine line between taking what musical opportunities you want, and being responsible to three, four, or more other musicians. Finding competent subs for your position in a band can give you more flexibility in accepting other opportunities, while fulfilling your responsibilities to you regular group.

Chapter 8 Resources

The Buttwinick, Gibson, and Levine books referenced in Chapter 2 and Chapter 3 cover some of this material.

CHAPTER 9
Producing and Marketing Your Own Record

Today's Record Business

As we briefly mentioned at the beginning of this book, there have tremendous changes in the record industry since our last edition. Besides the amalgamation of Sony and BMG, and the increasing expansion of Universal, BMG has also acquired Zomba, which was the largest independent record label in the world. For the moment we will leave the matter of the Internet aside because Chapter 18 covers that particular aspect of the business.

Before we discuss independent record labels, and artists producing and marketing their own albums, we need to take a look at how the business models that govern record deals have changed. Up until a few years ago, artists received a small piece of the pie—usually royalties of between 5% and 10% of the retail selling price of an album. Few artists actually got into a royalty situation, because record company contracts contained so many deductions involving such matters as advances, independent promoters, videos, CDs given away to radio or journalists, tour support, and so forth. Moreover, foreign royalties were typically paid at 50% to 75% of the full amount, even though the major labels owned their own affiliates. Major label contracts were incredibly complex—documents of over a hundred pages were typical. Royalties were also reduced for record club sales, and for any new or forthcoming formats, even including CDs, not to mention digital and other new formats. Some record companies also attempted to own publishing and merchandising rights.

Several new wrinkles have transformed these procedures. Superstars like Madonna, Michael Jackson, and Bruce Springsteen began to demand ever larger royalty percentages, and record companies acceded to these demands by the superstars. Next, illegal file sharing of songs became a major headache for both record companies and artists. Younger listeners began to get used obtaining their music over the Internet without having to pay for it. Since it is fairly common knowledge among music fans that artists often don't receive any royalties anyway, these Internet "borrowers" rationalized their actions with the notion that buying albums often subjected the consumer to filler material in order to get the songs that they actually wanted and the artist often wasn't making money from the albums anyway.

A number of models have emerged that differ from the old-style record deals. One method is for record companies to fund labels that are owned by artists or producers. This has been particularly successful with some rap artists-producers, notably Puff Diddy or Russell Simmons. Madonna had a good run with her Warner Brother–funded label, Maverick. That company had tremendous success with Alanis Morrissette before eventually running out of steam. Artist imprint labels have had a mixed track record. Some of the artists started labels not for their own work, but to produce other artists. Record companies soon discovered that when an act like Hootie & the Blowfish, for example, lost their own sales credibility, their sponsorship of other acts became essentially meaningless.

Artists like Ani DiFranco, Bright Eyes, and Fugazi own and operate their own labels, and also recorded other artists. Amy Ray of the Indigo Girls started her own label to present acts that she felt deserved a hearing. Older artists, like John Prine and Arlo Guthrie, started their own labels either out of disgust for the practices of the major labels, or because they were no longer to get major label deals. Many of these artists have had considerable success with their labels.

Independent Labels

Meanwhile, some independent labels, notably Sanctuary Records, utilized a partnership model that had been pioneered by earlier independent rock labels. Instead of simply paying royalties, the album was looked upon as a partnership between the artist and the label, with shared expenses and profits. With that sort of a deal, artists began to be more prudent in what they spent on recording their albums. They began to grasp that if they could produce an album for, say, $50,000 instead of $300,000, under a profit-sharing arrangement, sales of 100,000 records could generate revenue, rather than being considered a failure.

Other Models

Some odd, new record companies have emerged in the last few years. Toyota, the automobile company, has started a record label in order to promote its Scion cars in the youth market. The label has made it clear that the purpose of the label is not to make money, but to promote the cars. As a result, artists retain ownership of their own albums. General Motors is pursuing similar options.

Starbucks Coffee has a record division, and with its thousands of stores all over the world it is well positioned to enjoy considerable sales of product in its own retail stores. Starbucks is also experimenting with record burners, where a customer can have a tailor-made CD made while drinking their latte! Putamayo, originally a store that imported clothes, started a world music label that has become so successful that the stores' founder quit the clothing operation to work full-time on the label. Barnes and Noble bookstores are experimenting with distributing an album exclusively in their 820 bookstores.

Clearly the record business is undergoing intense and constant changes in terms of the way records are recorded, distributed, and sold.

Record Distribution

The assumption governing this chapter (and this book) is that you do not wish to leave your local music market. If this accurately describes your current situation, then most likely you will not be in the running for a recording contract with a major label. In order for you to understand why this is, here's a brief discussion of the contemporary record business.

All of the major labels have branches that distribute their product to stores throughout North America. They also distribute recordings owned by other labels. At the close of the 1980s, many the largest independent labels were bought in whole or part by the majors, and this trend has continued today. For example, BMG bought Windham Hill, Universal bought Interscope, and RCA bought Zomba.

When rock and roll replaced the more middle-of-the-road musical styles that preceded it, there were quite a number of important small independent record labels, like King and Sun records in the 1950s. They distributed their records through independent record distributors. By the 1970s, the larger independent labels turned to the distribution divisions of their own competitors.

One of the primary reasons for this seemingly strange choice is that even the larger independents have always had trouble collecting money from independent distributors. Records have always been sold with return privileges, and up until recently there was never even a time limitation on the return of records. This meant that stores could return a large percentage of unsold product to the distributor who in turn returned the records to the label. Record stores were often late in paying distributors, who, if anything, delayed even further in paying the record companies. Supposedly this situation drove even the notorious Phil Spector, producer of a "million and one hits," out of business. How was this possible?

All of the people involved in recording and producing a record—studios, engineers, producers, studio musicians, arrangers, pressing plants, album fabricators and designers, etc.—expect immediate or rapid payment upon delivery of the product. The AFM contracts with record companies even specify that musicians who play on sessions must be paid within three weeks of the recording date. Many studios will not allow a master tape to leave the studio until full payment has been made.

Distributors are generally billed on a thirty- to ninety-day payment schedule, with small discounts given for early payment as an enticement to pay bills as soon as possible. At times, record distributors have taken the position that they would only pay quickly to companies that had consistent hit records. As soon as a company went into a "dry spell," the distributors would become increasingly reluctant to pay their bills. This happened because the distributor no longer cared if a company stopped shipping records. What good were a bunch of records that sooner or later would be returned? This left record companies in double jeopardy: they couldn't collect on monies owed, nor could they even get new product into the stores.

A company that owned its own distribution network did not need to concern itself with this problem. It simply paid the parent company on demand. Another aggravating factor was that a record company used to have a dozen distributors in different cities. Their willingness to pay bills and their aggressiveness in getting the records into stores varied accordingly. Although independent record distribution has a much smaller piece of the pie today (usually in the 15%–29% range), a few of the current independents, like ADA, Caroline, Koch, Navarre, RED, and Ryko actually distribute nationally.

The chart below outlines the way that record distribution works. Note that there are different categories of distributors. A rack jobber buys in huge quantities and stocks discount or department stores. Sometimes rack jobbers rent space in the store and utilize the store's sales personnel to stocking the shelves. A one-stop is an operation that carries labels of all manufacturers. It generally sells them to "mom-and-pop" record stores at a slightly higher price. The advantage to a small store is that they can do one-stop shopping for everything they need.

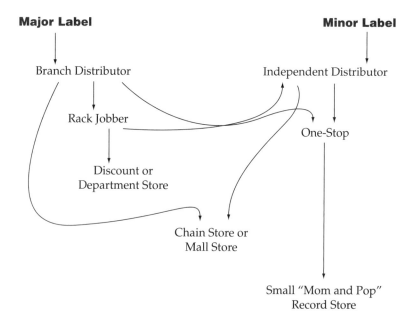

What do distributors charge? According to Todd Lathrop's useful book, *This Business of Music, Marketing, and Promotion*, the breakdown of independent label-distributor-retail store finances is that the distributor gets between 18% and 35% of the retail selling price. The retail store pays about $11 to $12 for a $15 CD. This leaves the label with about $7.50 for a CD. What the record company actually earns will depend upon the costs of making and promoting an album. Manufacturing costs are a small piece of the pie, with the easy and relatively cheap manufacturing costs of CDs. Even a thousand units of an album can be manufactured for $1 to $1.50 per album, depending on the packaging and graphics. Unit costs for larger pressings are much lower. You can count on your first CD being discounted at a high percentage to the distributor, as opposed to the work of a recognized artist.

When you look at how records are discounted at such retailers as Best Buy and add on the effects of file sharing, it isn't hard to see why independent record stores have a difficult time in today's marketplace.

It is important to understand the economics of the record business. A major record company expects to spend $250,000 or more on the creation and production of an album. In order to promote the record, they anticipate spending an equal amount on advertising and promotion. Along the way, they will give away more than five thousand copies of an album to radio stations, and music critics as well as copies given to stores for in-store play or listening stations.

Generally, records are sold through radio play, by videos on MTV and other TV outlets, and by play in the stores. Discos and clubs provide an outlet for dance music, and jukeboxes are still another way to introduce records to the public. However, a recording rarely appears in a jukebox unless it has already achieved hit status.

Singles

Up until the late 1980s, record companies made substantial amounts of money from hit singles (seven-inch double-sided 45-rpm records). These singles were the opening wedge for an artist's albums, which were plastered with stickers that said "contains the hit single_____." It was not unusual for hit singles to sell a million copies. Therefore, singles were regarded as a way of breaking an artist and promoting an album. They were also profitable in their own right.

Today, there are few singles that sell over 250,000 copies. The function of singles has come down to breaking an artist, and calling attention to her through saturation radio play of the single. Twelve-inch dance records provide a more profitable outlet for record companies. These records are singles that are re-mixed to be more danceable. Sometimes the length of the song is extended, and the rhythm tracks are highlighted. There are even producers who specialize in these re-mixes for the dance market.

The Apple iPod has created a substantial demand for singles that are legally downloaded onto these portable machines. The iPod is the legal version of file sharing, where consumers download free music from such former suppliers as MP3 and Napster, or current ones like Kazaa. The reader is certainly aware that record companies are involved in numerous lawsuits against frequent down-loaders, and they are also involved in legal actions against the companies that make file sharing possible. The ultimate result of these legal challenges is in doubt, and may take years to resolve. In the chapter on new technologies, I discuss some of the ideological issues behind these disputes.

Many people in the music industry have expressed concerns that the contemporary consumers' habit of down-loading individual tracks of an album, rather than treating the album as a whole represents a setback to the industry. It is an ironic development, because up until the 1960s the single was the basic medium of pop music, with the album almost an after-thought. Thanks to such artists as Dylan, the Beatles, and Led Zeppelin, the album became a much more significant factor, relegating singles to a promotional tool. Clearly, most artists have a vision that encompasses more than a single song, and for their part record companies make much less money when they sell one or two songs instead of an album's worth.

Getting a Record Deal

What do record companies look for in a new artist? They want the artist to tour, they prefer that she write her own songs, and that that she have professional management. Most of all, they feel the artist must have a "breaker," the song that can break the artist's career wide open. They are also looking for artists who are seemingly stable enough to write more than one hit, and who can survive the rigors of the business to record more and more hits.

Now to return to the situation in which most of the readers of this book find themselves. You have chosen not to tour all over the country, you probably (almost certainly) don't have the sort of high-level personal manager that will bring a smile to the face of major record company executives, you are not living in a major music market, and you don't have ready access to record companies.

There are still some strategies that you can employ to get the attention of a major record company, which are covered in Chapter 12, "The Urge for Going." However, the odds are heavily against you or your group finding a major record deal in your location and outside of the major music markets. Let's explore some alternatives.

Finding a Producer and an Engineer

The easiest way to get your recording to the marketplace is to do it yourself. You can use a home studio or rent one in your town. It is crucial that you spend a good deal of time selecting songs and working out the musical arrangements that you plan to use in the studio. This will save you a good deal of money, and will enable you to utilize your time in the studio in an intelligent way.

Try to find an experienced record producer to help you, since you are going to need all the help you can get! What should you look for in a record producer, what will it cost, and where can you find one?

Talk to other local musicians and bands and recording studio personnel about who they have worked with and what it was like working with them. Listen to some recorded examples of their work. If possible, visit some sessions they are producing. When you talk to a producer, pay careful attention to the interactions between your group and the producer. You don't have to agree with one another on all issues, but you need to develop a spirit of mutual trust. If this trust doesn't exist, you may waste expensive studio time, and end up with a product that satisfies neither you nor your producer. A good producer should be able to enhance the sound of your group without violating the spirit of the group's music. Above all, she needs to be someone that listens to the band, and understands what their vision of the project is.

Choose your recording studio and engineer as carefully as you chose the producer. Make sure that your producer and engineer work well together. It is best if they have already worked on some projects together. Be careful that both your producer and your band are happy with the engineer who will record your album. It takes a team effort to come out with a recording that is representative of your group.

Home studios may be adequate to record your album, but they usually don't have the capability or equipment to do quality mixing. If you are using a home studio, be sure that you have quality microphones, especially microphones that will be used for the vocals.

Beware of producers and engineers who seem to be trying to fit your group into a predetermined format. Are they really listening to the songs? Do they seem to have a sense of the direction in which you want to go, or do they jump to inaccurate conclusions? Do you feel that you are being hyped whenever you raise any serious questions? It is natural for the producer and engineer to want you to appreciate their knowledge of studio gear, but don't be snowed by the use of too many effects, or by playbacks of your music at deafening levels of volume. Do the producer and the engineer communicate well in the studio? If they do not, you will burn up lots of precious studio time. When you rehearse with the producer, what sort of suggestions does she make? Are they sensible and logical creative ideas, or she is trying to move your sound in another direction? In short, is she trying to manipulate you?

On a relatively modest local or regional project, you should expect to pay a producer from $1,000 to $3,000, plus a royalty of anywhere from 2% to 3% of the retail selling price of your recording. The royalty should not go into effect until you have recouped the amount of the original advance. For instance, if your producer has a 3% royalty, and you have paid him a $2,000 advance and your CD sells for $15, he will be earning $.45 per album, but he would not receive royalties until you have sold 4,444 copies of the CD.

You may think this is a lot of money to pay a producer, but your album probably represents at least a month's work, between preproduction, recording, and mixing. You should not begrudge your producer her percentage. If your work becomes a hit, why shouldn't she reap the profits of her work?

I recommend that you not hire a producer by the hour. It is much better to create an atmosphere where the only hourly charge you need to be concerned about is the rental of the studio. The producer needs to work as hard as is necessary without any concern for the hours involved.

Engineers are often included in the price of the studio and do not get any royalties for their work. (Engineers are among the most poorly rewarded people in the industry.) Only a few highly skilled practitioners in the major cities operate independently and enjoy royalty deals. That is why so many engineers turn to production, where they can get a piece of the action. Whenever possible, you should record and mix your product at the same facility, and use the same engineer. If you don't, the sound can be disconcertingly jumbled, and you will waste more money while the new engineer is figuring out exactly what is on the tape. The sound of your record is partly determined by the way the room is set up, what microphones are used, and how they are placed, the recording format (analog or digital) and the type of tape recorder and console you use. Don't take foolish risks.

Recording Formats: Cassettes, Compact Discs, and Vinyl

Since the last edition of this book, cassettes have disappeared as a viable recording medium. For dance records, vinyl is still an important option, but your primary choice will be whether to record an EP of four or five songs for a CD or a full album. Your choice should be based upon how much time you can spend in the studio, and your assessment of whether you are ready to do an entire album.

Mastering Records

Mastering is the process where tapes are converted to disc. Until recently, this process always took place in a separate recording studio, one that had a whole array of different equipment. Only a handful of major cities had this sort of facility. Today, there is an alternative to the use of a separate mastering studio. More and more, CDs are being mastered at studios that have a facility for cutting a master CD, called a CDR. The CD can then be manufactured directly from this CD reference disc. It is also possible to make a handful of CDs at these facilities for early play on radio stations or for sending out an album to a particularly important music critic.

It *is* possible to influence the sound of a record during the mastering process, whether it is done at the still-existent, high-priced facilities like Bernie Grundman's LA studio or Gateway in Portland, Maine, or a CDR-equipped local studio. This can be done through computer programs like Sonic Solutions, or by the use of re-equalization or outboard gear. The problem is that by the time you have mixed down a multi-track tape to a stereo tape, the changes possible tend to be gross. Re-equalizing the bass on the left channel will re-equalize the bass frequencies on any other instruments on that channel.

If you decide to use one of the mastering studios, I advise you to attend the mastering session. This will ensure that the engineer understands what you want, and gives you a voice in the decision-making process.

Budgets

Do a budget before you ever go into the recording studio. From your experience working in your home studio, you should have some notion of how long each song will take to record. Include time for instrumentals, vocals, mixing, and some provision for possible re-mixing. The smaller the group of people involved in the mix, the faster your production will move.

It's difficult to estimate how long it will take to record a song. Some people are very nervous in the studio, and seem to take forever to do their best work. Others enjoy the freedom from audience response that is part of the studio experience. Just as with rehearsals, don't allow a bunch of visitors in the studio, particularly those who feel compelled to give you the "benefit" of their often useless opinions and suggestions. If you have friends whom you feel obligated to involve in the sessions, invite them at the very beginning or end of a session, and make it clear that you don't expect them to hang out there. Visitors can also be a nuisance to producers and engineers by asking incessant and often foolish questions. You hired these people work, not to entertain your friends.

In working out your budget, consider hiring additional musicians who are not regular members of your performing group. A group doesn't need to be able to duplicate every sound on their record. Generally, what the listener will latch on to is a particular sound that represents a sort of trademark that identifies an artist. It can be a vocal sound like Sting's or Bob Dylan's, or an instrumental sound like Phil Collins's drum sound. The average listener won't care if Sting adds a flute to one track of his album, but if his vocal in performance differs radically from the sound of the recording, it will annoy many people.

Don't radically change the way your group sounds in a performing situation on your tape. If you don't have a mandolin player in your band, don't use mandolin on eight cuts of the album. Remember, also, that the listener is probably more aware of your group's vocals than any other component of your sound. Don't hire three or four great background singers and substitute them for your regular vocalists. In short, use studio musicians or singers to enhance the sound of your group, but don't use them in such liberal doses that the public becomes confused about what your sound truly is.

You should go into the studio with some notion what your CD ought to sound like. Use the following track sheet *before* you get into the studio as a guide to what you are going to do. Typically, in a twenty-four-track rock set-up, drums occupy seven or more tracks of the tape. By filling out a track sheet, you will develop a notion of what each song will need, and whether, for example, too many of the songs have an identical instrumental set-up.

Track Number	Instrument	Name of Player or Singer
1	Click Track	
2	Snare Drum	
3	Snare Drum	
4	Bass Drum	
5	Cymbals	
6	Tom-toms	
7	Overall Drum Set	
8	Electric Bass (with Amp.)	
9	Electric Bass (Direct to Console)	
10	Keyboard (Low Strings)	
11	Keyboard (High Strings)	
12	Rhythm Guitar	
13	Lead Guitar	
14	Synthesizer	
15	Lead Vocal	
16	Background Vocals	
17	Background Vocals	
18–23	Other Lead Instruments Special Effects	

Note: Tracks 1 and 24 are often the last used. It is generally thought that the outer tracks are more apt to produce technical difficulties. Be sure to allow two to four hours to mix each tune down, more if you are a perfectionist.

A group that has a single lead vocalist, guitar, bass, and drums is going to have trouble varying their sound enough to come up with an interesting album. This is where versatility becomes important. If the guitarist has several nylon-, steel-string acoustic twelve-string guitars, as well as jazz and rock electrics, and if the drummer is also a decent percussionist, you will be able to achieve a variety of textures even from a group this small. You should also avoid the temptation of overwhelming your audience with your versatility. Neither consumers or record companies are able to cope with popular music artists who have a dozen vocal sounds, and sing or play in three different musical genres. This may be a sad reflection on popular taste, but it is true. Even in jazz and classical music, the public usually identifies artists with particular musical styles or periods.

Financing Your Project

How do you raise the money for your project in the first place? If you can't afford to do it yourself, you need to find other funding sources. The group itself may be one source of funds. Projects can be financed by friends and family of the artists, by loans or outright gifts, and even by selling stock in an album. To avoid any hard feelings, you should make it very clear to anyone investing in the project that they are very unlikely to make a profit on this investment. In fact, they may never get their money back. Whether you will pay interest on loans, or give investors a percentage of your profits is up to you, but remember, anytime you give someone a piece of the action, you may regret it later. If Sony picks up your album, and you have to pay someone 10% of your royalties because they lent you $100 three years ago, you will regret making such an agreement.

Sometimes a manager or agent will invest in a project. Because they are professionals with experience in the business, they may want a larger piece of the action than you wish to relinquish. Any deal is possible as long as all the parties understand their obligations.

How can you budget for your sessions? The next pages shows a sample budget for your CD, including expenses for artwork and promotion.

Choosing a Studio

The first budget decision will be to determine what type of studio you should use. Many cities have twenty-four-track A-DAT studios that are not expensive to rent. Some of these small studios with up-to-date gear cost as little as $35 to $50 an hour. A-DAT tape costs are minmal, about $40 to $50 for forty minutes of tape for three interlocked A-DAT machines. Analog tape is much more expensive, costing $125 to $150 a reel for fifteen to thirty minutes of tape. It depends on what speed you choose to run the analog recorder at: 15 pr 30 IPS.

With care and planning, even if you use analog tape you should be able to make an album using three reels of tape. It is possible to rent used tape reels for less, but this used tape can lower the quality and brilliance of your sound. That should be part of what you are selling.

Another analog option is to rent a sixteen-track studio that uses one-inch tape. If you are recording rock, this is the absolute minimum of tracks you will need. It is also possible to "ping pong" your recording on a four- or eight-track machine. This will require constant re-mixing to create open tracks. This is time-consuming work. It can ultimately degrade the quality of your product, and may actually end up costing you more money because of the re-mixing than you will save in the per hour studio charges. One-half-inch tape of these machines should run you about $35 a reel.

Small hard disk studios also rent for $25 to $50 an hour. Since the material is recorded onto the computer, there are no tape costs involved. Hard disk is easy to edit on. Artists and engineers have varying opinions about the sound qualities of

Recording Budget (CD)	
Each Song:	_____
Name of Song:	_____
Basic Tracks (instrumentation):	_____
Vocals:	_____
Vocal and Instrumental Overdubs:	_____
Fees Paid to Musicians or Vocalisting, including any Pension and Health Payments	_____
Mixing Time:	_____
Tape Costs:	_____
Studio Hours (total hours at _____ an hour):	_____
Total Cost of Ten Songs:	_____
Mastering Costs:	_____
Pressing Plant:	_____
Album Art—Photo or Art:	_____
Design Costs:	_____
Printing of Labels:	_____
Delivery Costs:	_____
TOTAL:	_____

the different recording formats. If your product is keyboard-generated and doesn't require additional instruments, it may be convenient and cost-effective for you to record on a hard disk. Through multiple keyboard parts, the use of computers, MIDI files, and sequencers, you may be able to come up with a respectable product with a great expenditure of time and energy, but few dollars. This works particularly well with dance rap and techno music projects, where there may little or no need for live instrumentation in either recording or performance.

Many artists know audiophiles, high-fidelity hobbyists and amateur musicians who will happily donate their time and equipment for the cost of the tape. Whether this is a good idea depends on the quality of the studio, and of the engineer. Sometimes what appears to save money simply ends up wasting time.

If you are recording in the analog format, trying to limit the amount of tape that you use forces you to make quick decisions. Some artists never erase anything in the studio, figuring that they may use some amusing snippet at a future time. You won't be able to bask in that luxury, especially if you are using the analog format. If you are in doubt as to whether a take is good, your best bet is to trust your producer and engineer. That is why you hired them, isn't it?

Time Lines

It will probably take you about a month of full-time work to record an album. This is a general guideline. It depends on what sort of music you are recording, how many instruments and vocals are on the tracks, and how much of a perfectionist you are. Don't try to record music that is at the very edge of your technical abilities, unless you have virtually unlimited time in the studio. It takes too long to get a good performance, and you may not be able to perform the material live.

Cover art and fabrication are likely to take another two months. Try to find a graphic artist who has already designed CD and/or cassette covers. There are many technical and special specifications for these types of art layouts. Increasingly, this design is done with the help of computers. Be sure that the artist you work with talks to the people who will actually print the covers.

Promoting and Selling Your Album

Now that you have completed an album, it's time to market it. Start by writing a press release that tells about the concept of the album, where, and how it was recorded, and your plans for distributing it. If it is feasible, induce a local television station to come to the studio to report on the progress of your project. In local markets, this can be an excellent human-interest story.

Your press release should be simple and direct. Send it out to radio and television stations, daily papers, entertainment weeklies, and to neighborhood or suburban newspapers in different sections of your town, or its suburbs. You should send a copy of your CD with the press release, and an extra copy of the album cover. This can be expensive, but you are trying to build interest in your music. Be sure to send out the release (and the CD) to similar media in any neighboring cities where your band has worked.

Most record stores or distributors expect you to include a one sheet with the album release. A one sheet is a quick summary of the album with a brief bio of the artist, and some explanation of the rationale behind this particular project. This first and most obvious way to bring in some cash to pay for all of this is to sell the recording every time you perform. Depending on the type of venue, this can be done by the band itself, by your road manager, friends or even the club manager or her staff. You should offer a commission to the club if they handle the sales, although they may not accept it. Anything that spreads the word about your band and makes it seem more professional will help any club where you play regularly. Announce the availability of your recording during each set that you perform. Don't gloss over your product; you want people to remember it. By the same token, don't be a nuisance and overhype it. Be sure to perform some tunes form the CD in each set. The club may even want to host a record party when your product is first released. Invite any local media people, fans, friends, or people on your mailing list. This is the perfect time to sell them your product. If possible, have a friend at the performance sell your product before the show and at intermissions. You should also announce that you will be happy to autograph the album at the end of the show.

I have known some musicians who play in the streets primarily in order to sell their albums while they are performing. Make sure that your city doesn't require a license to do this and be prepared to pay sales tax in your city or state.

Your largest single profit center consists of selling your CD at shows. If you want to put a recording in local stores, they may accept it on consignment, or buy it from you. On consignment deals the store usually wants 20% to 25% of the retail selling price of the album. If they pay up front for the albums, you can expect them to want about a 40% discount off the retail selling price. Be sure to give the store copies for in-store play. Posters, flyers, and T-shirts are also useful promotional tools.

Although it's a good idea to consign records in stores, you will need to keep an inventory of how many records are in each store, and collect the money when the albums are sold. This will entail the use of your time and gas in your car, together with an endless round of phone calls. There is often only one person in the store who is authorized to pay you, and sometimes it will seem as though they are never there. If your records are consigned in stores out of town you will find it even more difficult to collect the money in a timely way. It will also be more expensive to check on sales when your calls are long distance.

It is also possible to work through independent record distributors. They will have to contact individual stores to sell your product. You will not get paid by the distributors until after they have collected from the stores.

Why bother putting records in stores at all? Improved distribution will broaden the sales potential of your product. If you know a store employee, he may be willing to give your CD some in-store play, or even display your cover on the wall. If you are getting airplay, the radio stations will virtually compel you to have your records available in stores. When people like a record they often call the station to get the name of the artist and the album, and if they can't find the record in stores they tend to get irritated at the station. When Windham Hill Records began, their first recording was never intended to be a nationally distributed item, and was pressed in a very small quantity. When the album began to be played regularly on a station in Seattle, they received many calls from annoyed listeners who couldn't find the record in stores. The station notified Will Ackerman, the company's founder and first artist that he either had to get the records in stores or they would stop playing it. This is how this large and quite successful record company actually started!

Realistically, you have a smaller chance of getting your CD into chain stores. These large-scale operations have taken over a big piece of the business from old time mom-and-pop stores. The chains often do their buying from one national warehouse location. They get high discounts and operate with computerized buying programs. It is a nuisance for them to stock local or regional product. However, depending upon the policy of the particular chain and who is managing the local store, you still may be able to get your album on the shelf.

You should send your recording to every radio station within a hundred miles of where you work, along with a full press kit of the group. (See the excellent press kit example that follow this section.)

Some stations like to do interviews with artists. Try to induce them to interview your group. Public record stations will even sometimes play cassettes, but most commercial stations are unwilling to do so. By the way, when you are sending review copies of your product, whether they are going to radio station people or newspapers, always find out the name of the proper music critic, music director of the station, etc. Otherwise your product addressed to *New Jersey Gazette* may end up in the trash. Public radio stations and more adventurous free-form commercial stations may allow disc jockeys to do their own programming. If this is the case in your town, find out which people might be apt to play your record. It's worth giving away a few more CDs to get some airplay. Also ask reviewers if they want extra album covers. Sometimes they'll reprint the cover in their newspaper or magazine.

What about radio stations in areas where you haven't played? Unless your product is in record stores, most stations will be reluctant to play it. There are books that list alternative radio stations and suppliers who will sell you appropriate labels. They are listed in the resource section at the end of this chapter and in the Appendix.

Find out what stations are actually playing your record. It's not a bad idea to send out prepaid envelopes or postcards to stations outside your area. If you discover they are playing your album regularly, you may be able to parlay that airplay into a booking at a club or college in that area.

Another way to attack the record market is to put out a vinyl dance single or a CD single. Although the manufacturing costs won't be drastically different than the cost of producing an entire album, the cover art is usually pretty basic, and the recording costs should be much lower. You can get into trouble if your song starts to hit and you don't have an album available to capitalize on this success.

You can hire local or regional promotion people to help get airplay for your product. In Shad O'Shea's book, *Just for the Record*, he points out that you can force airplay in your town by deliberately concentrating on towns fifty to one hundred miles away. He suggests all sorts of gimmicks, such as mobiles, T-shirts, teasers sent to music directors, etc. You can create your own list of radio stations by going to the library and consulting *Broadcasting Yearbook*. O'Shea also suggests that, when possible, you personally deliver the recording to the station, and that you take the time to write personal thank-you notes to stations that play your recording. You can hire local promotion people to assist you in getting airplay, but this is an expensive ploy.

Loretta Lynn achieved great success by personally visiting small stations all across the country, as she points out in her book *Coal Miner's Daughter*. Not only did the stations play her records, but they continued to do so after she became a big star.

How far you want to go in promoting your product is a function of how much you believe in it and how much time and money you have to spend. If your recording sells heavily in a city or region, you may be able to get a distribution deal with a major label, or they may even sign you to an exclusive contract and re-release your record.

Another way to promote your recording is to build up a strong mailing list through your performances. Many touring acts keep such a list on a computerized data base, broken down into categories of whether the fan has ever bought any recordings of the group. They keep the people on these lists abreast of new recordings and performances in their area.

Don't consider making a record until you have a well-formulated plan for how you will promote it and some method of distributing it. Merchandising involves its own sort of creativity. Shirts, matchbooks, pens, jackets, and mugs are all readily available if you can afford them. Advertising can also be effective, especially if you can identify a group that has a particular affinity for your music. For example, New Age music would obviously appeal to the people who subscribe to a journal on holistic healing. The late Chris Le Doux was an ex-champion rodeo cowboy, and he built his core audience among people who follow the rodeo. If you have songs that appeal to particular groups, whether they are jet pilots or baseball players, find the magazines or newsletters that go out to those people. You may be able to play their conventions, and in turn sell more albums.

Web Sites

These days it is important to have a Web site to promote your music. Don't bother unless it is attractively designed, managed by someone who changes it frequently (so that viewers stay involved), and features links to other sites— other bands, a record company, etc.

Bar Codes

Record companies use bar codes on each album. Soundscan computes record sales from the bar codes, and it if you are seeking a record deal with a label, it's great to be able to say that Soundscan picked up five thousand sales of your album in Boise. Many record manufacturers will give you a bar code, or charge a nominal fee for you to use one.

It is doubtful that a self-distributed album will make you rich, but stranger things have happened. George Winston became a major player in New Age music on the then barely known Windham Hill Records label. Hootie & the Blowfish had an independent regional album that did well on the beaches of the Carolinas and Virginia before they achieved major success and a major label deal. The same thing happened to the Colorado-based band Big Head Todd and the Monsters. All of these artists were ready and willing to do national tours. National exposure can fuel the success of a record, or it can follow from a successful album. If you don't plan to tour extensively, then don't expect national impact from your CD.

Producing and merchandising your own recording validates your professional standing to club owners, concert promoters, agents, and even the general public. It also provides you with a permanent landmark of where you are musically at the time that you recorded the album.

Publishing and Performance Rights

If you put out a tape or CD, you will need to copyright the songs and the performance. You will also need to join ASCAP, BMI, or SESAC, the performing rights organizations that monitor the payment of royalties for airplay and public performances to writers and publishers. In Chapter 11, "Making Inroads on the National and Regional Scene," the ins-and-outs of publishing, song-writing, and performing rights organizations are discussed.

If you don't write your own songs, or have used some songs composed by others, you will have to pay the statutory royalty rates of 9.1 cents to the writer and publisher of each song.* This is usually arranged through the Harry Fox Agency. (See Appendix.) If you are recording songs written by friends, you may be able to publish the songs yourself, which cuts the royalty payments in half. **

* As of the printing of this book. It varies from year to year.
** For futher information on this process, see my book, The Music Business: Career Opportunities and Self-Defense, third revised edition, 2003.

Fyah Wyah

Includes press kit cover with color photo, information sheet, press clippings, music award, flyers, photo on this and the next page.

Chapter 9 Resources

There are a number of books on making your own record listed in the Appendix. My favorite one is still Diane Sward Rapaport's *How to Make and Sell Your Own Record*, published by Prentice Hall, fifth edition, 1999. There are several books out that discuss record producers. Also check out Veronica Kalmar's *Label Launch*, St. Martin's Press, 2002, and the revised edition of Dayelle Deanna Schwartz's book, *Start and Run Your Own Record Label*, Billboard Books, 2003.

CHAPTER 10
Polishing Your Skills

Many musicians and singers who work in local markets find that, after doing much of the same thing over a period of years, they lose interest in music. Some become bitter about the music industry, and constantly compare their skills to that of some popular music superstar who they regard as an untalented fake. This is a fruitless pursuit. Although it is not possible to predict whether an artist will be successful or not, it is clear that in the field of popular music, image, physical attractiveness, and other non-musical qualities have a major role in the public's rather fickle tastes. (On the positive side, networking and good business relations have also helped these people.) Some musicians become so obsessed with the idea that people who have little musical talent become successful that they leave the music business and look for a more "stable" profession.

There are two ways to counteract the drudgery of playing music in the same or similar venues. One concept already discussed was that of developing enough musical versatility to pursue other musical opportunities in areas such as recording work, writing music, or freelance playing or singing.

Studying Music

Another way to retain a fresh approach to music is to seek out a new area of music, perhaps one that has always interested you, but one you have never taken time to pursue. This might entail the study of arranging or composing, taking vocal or instrumental lessons, or finding classes in audio engineering or video production.

To find the best teachers in your area, talk to other musicians, music store owners, and teachers at local colleges. Consult musicians who you respect and whose opinions you value. Most cities have stores or repair shops where the best players hang out. The proprietor of this type of place has usually spent many years in town, and has a good idea of who the best teachers are. Another resource is the Musicians' Union.

Sometimes, there's an underground network or grapevine from town to town about who the master teachers are. These people may be unknown to the general public, even in their hometown. Some rarely perform, but enjoy the stability of passing their skills on to motivated students.

It is possible to take music lessons at most colleges without enrolling as a degree student. This is usually handled through a department of "continuing education" or "extended studies." In some instances, continuing education lessons are taught by graduate students. Check out the teacher, his skill level, and his experience before you sign up. Be sure to keep in mind that great players don't always make great teachers, and some great teachers don't themselves play all that well. What a great teacher does have is a profound knowledge of their instrument, a strong dose of patience, and a real love for music.

Colleges also offer classes in arranging, composing, electronic music, songwriting, music on the personal computer, jazz history, and classes about the music industry. Try sitting in on a class before you sign up. This will give you an idea as to whether the teacher will be teaching things that are useful for you.

Many community colleges or four-year schools have jazz bands. If you wish to improve your sight-reading or doubling skills, or simply want a chance to play in large ensembles, they can provide you with new challenges. Similar opportunities exist in vocal ensembles and orchestras.

A music-arranging course provides you with a good opportunity to explore the sounds of other instruments and to learn to write for them. Similar courses can teach you the basic skills for writing music for film or TV. Provided that some of the musicians with whom you are working read music, you may be able to utilize some of these arranging and composing tools writing for your band.

World music, or music of non-Western cultures, is another fascinating study. Although learning about the music of Africa is not apt to give you specific ideas that you can immediately put to use at the local Holiday Inn, it can result in your learning some things about percussion that you can use in your band. (I have a friend in Denver who picked up a steel drum and took a few lessons while he was visiting a relative in the West Indies. He now gets additional work playing calypso music.) The study of exotic music from other parts of the world will broaden your perspective about the role of music and musicians in various cultures and contexts.

Jamey Abersold, Music Minus One, and Hal Leonard Publishing Corporation are companies that provide recordings that have fine rhythm sections. Sheet music is supplied with the CDs and you jam or read written music along with the band. Materials are available in most styles of music, and for vocalists as well.

Sight-reading

If you want to play freelance gigs, it is a good idea for you to develop superior skills at reading music at sight. When you are a rhythm section player, like a bass or guitar player or a drummer, you may be able to get away with being able to follow a chord chart. If this is the case, you will be expected to make up (improvise) your own part. No matter what instrument you play, you are going to need a basic knowledge of chords and chord progressions, and you need to be able to respond instantly to chord symbols. Even in a recording situation, you may get a chart that consists of a group of chord symbols with a particular rhythm pattern indicated. You shouldn't have to stop and think before playing the correct chord.

The late Tommy Tedesco was one of the outstanding studio guitarists in Los Angeles for many years. His in-print method books for guitar describe how a guitarist develops studio skills. He suggests that when someone hands you a difficult part that you not try to play every note the first time through. Rather he feels you should try to grasp the essence of the part, and play a bit more of what is written during each run-through. It is essential that you keep your place rhythmically, because being ahead or behind the rest of the band is an obvious tip-off that you are having trouble with a part.

The rationale behind Tommy's approach is that by playing a sort of *Reader's Digest* version of the part, you will give the arranger and producer the basic sound they want while you become accustomed to the nuances of the music. During the first few rundowns, the engineer is usually working on instrumental balances, so that no one is apt to be listening to your complete part.

Many good sight-readers point out that it is important to read slightly ahead of where you are actually playing. By doing this, you psychologically prepare yourself for any truly difficult passages, rather than coming upon them by surprise. The best way to become adept at sight-reading is to spend time each day reading new music. Read the most difficult parts you can find. This will help prepare you for anything that you might see in a show or at a recording studio. It is also a good idea to buy yourself legitimate (legal) "fake books." A fake book is a collection of melody lines, lyrics, and chords of hundreds of popular songs in every conceivable style—rhumbas, rock tunes, country ballads, etc. It is a very useful tool on jobs like weddings where the audience is liable to request virtually any musical style. Fake books also provide a common source of music between players who don't know one another well and may not have a common repertoire. Anyone with even a basic knowledge of music notation and chord symbols can play out of a fake book.

Songwriters' Organizations

A list of songwriters' organizations is in the Appendix. What can you get out of such groups? You may be able to locate a collaborator in the ranks of your local songwriting group. Today's collaborations are not usually separated between lyricists or composers, but involve input in both areas. Two writers may sit around trading ideas in a small room. They may have a couple of guitars, a keyboard instrument, and a drum machine. The process consists of two people coming up with ideas and hammering them out until they hone their song to a point where both parties are happy.

Some people deliberately write with more than one collaborator in order to explore fresh influences in their writing. Some writers excel at creating rhythmic grooves; others have a talent for chord alterations and substitutions. Some lyricists focus on story songs; others may work best on love ballads. By writing with different collaborators, you develop the opportunity to attempt different musical and lyric styles.

Songwriting groups may also sponsor contests that afford the winners the opportunity to perform at a public event in front of a large audience.

Songwriting organizations offer writers the chance to honestly critique each other's work. Most people are not sufficiently objective or analytical to see the limitations or defects in their own work. This is particularly true of people who write songs that are based on current or recent emotional experiences. These songs may be extremely meaningful to the writer, but may not hit home to a casual listener. You may resent receiving criticisms of songs that are close to your heart, but it may be very helpful for your development as a songwriter.

Many songwriting associations sponsor seminars. They bring professional songwriters, producers, and publishers in from a major market who can provide you with some insight on what is happening in these larger markets. Some of this information may be about the business copyright matters, how songs are recorded, or what song contracts should offer the writer. A speaker may take an interest in a local writer and actually publish her music, or take it to an artist or a producer. Some of the seminars are workshops led by outstanding songwriters from one of the major music markets. This can give you some insight into how the contemporary songwriting business operates.

Try to attend as many of these seminars as you can. Listen carefully to what the speakers say, and then evaluate the information in terms of your own goals and development. It is sometimes a mistake to accept advice without being critical of it.

Many of the speakers at songwriting seminars live in the major music markets. Their advantage over you is that they have access to who and what is currently viable in the marketplace. The disadvantage is that in a city like Los Angeles there is a plethora of would-be writers and artists. They all go to the same seminars and hear the same lectures. It is quite common for lecturers to deal in generalities that may or may not apply to your particular situation. Sometimes a writer develops a viable style because of his isolation and individual experimentation. Many of the best songs or musical styles would have never been accepted if they had been born in a major music market. The "suits" would have termed such work uncommercial. Is Bob Dylan, for example a "commercial" writer?

Local colleges or community colleges sometimes offer seminars or classes in various aspects of the music business. Such classes can be quite useful, but be sure to find out who the teacher is and what she has done. Is the teacher currently active in the business, or did she produce hits fifteen years ago? The fact that someone is teaching a class doesn't prove that what they have to offer will be relevant to today's music.

There are several songwriting organizations that can be helpful. The Nashville Songwriters Association International (NSAI) plays an important role in the Nashville songwriting community. It sponsors numerous seminars, and provides a source of contacts with publishers and record companies in Nashville.

The Songwriters Guild of America (SGA) is a source of help by providing suggested contracts that tend to favor the writer, as opposed to what most publishers will tend to offer you.

BMI and ASCAP sponsor seminars in different parts of the country that cover various aspects of songwriting, recording, and the music industry. These events provide local writers with an opportunity to meet top pros who come in and donate their time to teach about the business. To find out about such seminars, contact BMI or ASCAP directly, or talk to the music professors at the college nearest you that offers any programs in the music industry, audio engineering, or music merchandising.

If you pursue some of these suggestions, they may also open up some new employment opportunities. This may include teaching at a local community college, scoring local television commercials or industrial films, or even doing workshops on songwriting.

If you are trying to sustain a long-term musical career, don't get locked into one musical style or set of musical mannerisms. Music is an ever-changing world, and you should strive to be involved in its evolution.

Improving Your Skills as a Songwriter

In order to polish your songwriting skills, there are some things you can do without taking classes. There are a number of books about songwriting that explain how songs are written and merchandised. Many of these books are concerned with the actual structure of popular songs. Some of these books are marred by an over-emphasis on the song forms of the 1930s and 1940s—forms of limited use today, except in the writing of Broadway shows. Many of these authors have trouble acknowledging that in today's music it is often difficult to separate a song from the production of that on a recording. For some recommended books see the resources section at the end of this chapter.

I particularly recommend Bill Flanagan's *Written in My Soul*. Flanagan has an encyclopedic knowledge of contemporary songs, and his interviews with songwriters transcend the generalities usually found in books where major songwriters are interviewed. The writers that Flanagan interviewed express somewhat opposing views on the question of craft versus inspiration. For some, songwriting is a workaday operation, requiring time, effort, attention, and re-writing. Others, like Van Morrison, adopt a more freewheeling approach, largely ignoring commercial considerations and viewing themselves almost as a vehicle to express ideas and feelings that are in the air. Flanagan's book makes you want to go back and listen to many of the songs you may have taken for granted. More importantly, it will inspire your own work with a broader perspective. Meanwhile, here are a few more songwriting tips:

Melody Writing

Method	Advantages	Disadvantages
Play a series of chord progressions. Extract the melody notes from the structure of the chords.	Easy to get started.	Can the melody stand alone without the chords?
Write a melody in your head. Don't play it until the melody is completed.	Avoids any limitations caused by your lack of instrumental skill.	You may find the need for the rhythmic pulse that playing an instrument provides.
Write with a new isntrument, in an unfamiliar key or rhythm, or in a different tuning on guitar.	Can take you to new musical terrain.	You may feel insecure because you have no idea where this process is going.
Explore new chord patterns through books or play-along records.	Avoids feeling deadening feeling that your songs "sound the same."	May not make musical sense to you.

Lyric Writing

Lyric Suggestion Method
1. Write a story song about an actual incident.
2. Write several songs that have absolutely nothing to do with your own experiences.
3. Write about something you have read or seen on TV.
4. Write several songs that relate to the same concept. If this seems productive, develop a complete concept album.
5. If you have a good melody but don't like the lyric, rewrite the lyric entirely, as though it were another song. (This will work if you have a good lyric but don't like the melody.)

Chapter 10 Resources

If you are trying to polish your songwriting skills, there are some things that you can do without taking classes. There are a number of books about songwriting that explain how songs are written and merchandised. Michael Kosser's book *How to Become a Successful Nashville Songwriter* conveys a good sense of atmosphere as he takes you through the chronic writer's problems of rewrites, developing craft, dry spells, and intermittent success.

Most of the other books about songwriting are concerned with the actual structure of popular song. A few of the better books are Kasha and Hirschorn's *If They Ask You, You Can Write a Song*, Stephan Citron's *Songwriting*, and Sheila Davis's *The Craft of Lyric Writing*. (See Appendix D.)

For country writers, Tom T. Hall has a book called *The Songwriter's Handbook*. Hall sees himself as sort of a human tape recorder, and his antennae are always up, seeking the right phrase or feeling that will lead to a song. His song "Old Dog, Children, and Watermelon Wine" emerged from a conversation with a bartender in a dingy bar.

Another excellent resource is the revised edition of John Braheny's *The Craft and Business of Songwriting*. It is worthy of your attention for his discussions of the craft of lyric and melody writing, and it has excellent information about making demos and dealing with music business attorneys.

I have a book out called *Songwriting: The Words, the Music and the Money*, which has one of the few extended treatments of how melodies are written.

CHAPTER 11

Making Inroads on the National and Regional Scene

In every group, there are specific questions of goals and responsibilities that should be resolved. It is best for all group members to share common goals and common work schedules outside the confines of the band. If two people in a quintet have nine-to-five jobs and the others don't, the ability of the group to work late night jobs, or jobs that involve extensive driving, is going to be a source of conflicts and compromises.

When groups stay together for long periods of time, band members may develop a variety of commitments that go far beyond what they had the age of twenty. Marriage may reduce a person's eagerness to work weekend evenings, and persuading him to do so may result in compromising or destroying his marriage.

Any band seeking a national career needs to feel secure in its goals and identity. This cannot be accomplished if players wander in and out of the group whenever the mood suits them. One of the first areas a record company considers is whether a group will stay together long enough for the company to successfully promote and sell the group's albums. Group members should be honest with each other and maintain regular communication about their goals. It may become necessary for a person to leave the group, if her day job makes regular rehearsals impossible or difficult. If this situation is handled directly and without equivocation, there shouldn't be any hard feelings. If it is ignored, it may result in the ultimate breakup of the group and lingering bitterness between the people involved. It is a reasonable idea for the group to actually have a legal agreement that details who owns the name of the group, and the disposition of royalties and equipment if the group breaks up.

Keep a constant watch over the activities of the booking agent or agents who supply you with jobs. Sometimes an agent becomes stale or complacent, and is not interested in doing the necessary legwork that will keep you working on a regular basis. Stay aware of who the new agents are in town, and what sort of acts they are seeking. Breaking connections or old contacts is painful, but it must be done if your career is to grow. You may be moving in different and incompatible directions from your agent. An ambitious agent may have the connections that will catapult your group out of a local market into the national scene. If you are signing with a relatively large agency, and are relying on one particular agent to work with you, it is a good idea to utilize a "keyman" clause in your contract with the agency, as was discussed earlier in terms of management and record contracts. Since agents often leave to start their own agencies, this clause gives you an insurance policy against being tied up with an agency that doesn't know or care about your work.

Your own band may move in contradictory directions. Many musicians become boringly predictable or stop practicing. Sometimes a member of the group experiences personal problems that make him impossible to tolerate. Often one person in a group may want to move the group in a musical direction that is not acceptable to the rest of the band.

Regional Geography

The geography of your home area make have a profound effect on the nature of the regional scene. In the Rocky Mountain states or most of Canada, for example, distances between cities are great. This can make it impractical for your band to pursue out-of-town weekend jobs. The travel involved may eat up far more time than the job itself. It can also be a problem if you need to get to work on Monday morning, or if you have to take off on mid-Friday afternoon to play a job that is 180 miles away.

As the core cities of the United States expand into sprawling suburbs, the length and breadth of a metropolitan scene can extend for scores of miles, or in the case of Los Angeles, hundreds of miles. Living in Trenton, New Jersey and working weekend gigs in Philadelphia is not a major problem because the two towns are only thirty miles apart. A city like Philadelphia has so many suburbs that, with careful planning, you could work in the many surrounding areas of New Jersey, Pennsylvania, and Delaware for months without any anxiety about being overexposed at a particular club or with a specific audience. If you live in a smaller town with a relatively small metropolitan area, you need to be careful not to play too often in a particular venue or section of town. Many local bands end up breaking up because they never tour, and people develop the feeling that if they don't see the band this week or this month they will be playing in the same place later anyway.

Making National Contacts as a Songwriter

Probably the most promising way to crash the national music scene without moving to a major music center is to try to break in as a songwriter. It is possible to live in a secondary market and to make deals with big-city publishers who can push your material to major recording artists. How realistic is this scenario, and how can you make it happen?

The existing literature about the music business is often at odds on this issue. Some writers and lecturers maintain that if you are serious, you must move. Nashville writer Tom T. Hall suggests that you should stay where you are, and make occasional forays into the big city jungle. There are successful songwriters who have done it both ways, and there are even major recording artists active on the national scene who deliberately live outside the major music centers. Dan Fogelberg has lived in Colorado for some time, John Mellancamp lives on a farm near Bloomington, Indiana, and successful "New Jack City" producer Teddy Riley headquarters in Virginia Beach. Bill Danoff, writer of "Afternoon Delight" and co-writer of "Take Me Home, Country Roads" has pursued a lengthy writing and recording career from his base in Washington, D.C. Hit country writer Steve Seskin handles the situation by commuting from the Bay Area of California to Nashville. Other successful writers (and artists) have joint residences in a major market and such cities as Aspen, Colorado, or Santa Fe, New Mexico.

If you have national ambitions, but want to stay in your hometown, you should be aware of what you may be sacrificing. You are not apt to get motion picture assignments living in Buffalo. If you are not on the scene, movie or television producers are not likely to think of you when an assignment comes up. On the other hand, if you have succeeded in developing a national reputation, you may get opportunities for work that would normally require you to live in New York or Hollywood. For example, Bill Danoff has done some writing for TV producer Norman Lear. However, even someone with national credentials, like Danoff, will probably not get the call if there is a tight schedule for a project. The old cliché "out of sight is out of mind" is apropos in such instances. Efficient communication can be pursued through phone calls, fax machines, e-mail, and fiber optics makes simultaneous recording in different cities possible. Still, there is much to be said for face-to-face communication and getting to know the people that you work with.

How can you make national contacts? One way that works is to have your business taken care of by a personal manager who lives in a major music business center, while you stay where you please. That is why I recommend that your manager not be too "local." If your manager is "on the street," then she will know what TV shows are coming up, what publishing companies are hot, who is looking for staff writers, and what sort of dollars they are paying. This kind of information can be accessed from a secondary market, but it requires much more diligence and hard work if your representative is not on the scene.

Most staff writers work out of offices in one of the major music centers, but there are a few examples of writers who are paid a weekly salary or "draw" and live in their hometowns. Staff writers are paid weekly salaries of $300 to $500 and up, as an advance against future royalties. The only major music center where a writer might be able to exist on that kind of money is Nashville.

How to Access Artists from Your Home

Making inroads in the national scene while living at home is best accomplished in the area of songwriting. Many recording artists get deals because they write hit songs for other already established recording artists. The people who decide what songs get on recordings are the artists and their record producers. Occasionally, an artist's manager or record company executive may suggest a song to an artist.

If you can gain access to an artist touring in your market, you can have a good chance of getting your songs cut. Bill Danoff had written a rough version of "Take Me Home, Country Roads" with Taffy Nivert when John Denver came to Washington to perform at a local club called the Cellar Door.

Danoff was running the lights at the time, and he and Denver became friends. One night Bill played Denver the tune, which was originally about an artist who lived on a commune in West Virginia. Denver zeroed in on what he thought could make the song work commercially. His recording became a career-building hit. Danoff and Nivert then received a healthy taste of writers' money coming their way. This led to a recording deal on Denver's record label for their group, the Starland Vocal Band, and their own major hit, "Afternoon Delight." The band was so loyal to Washington that they did a summer television show that was shot on the streets in the nation's capital.

On the other hand, a Denver writer once collared the late Waylon Jennings before a concert at Red Rocks Theater, and tried to hustle a song to him. Jennings wasn't in the mood, and simply told the writer to send the song to "Waylon Jennings, Nashville, Tennessee." The anxious writer asked if the song would really get to Jennings. He replied that everyone in Nashville knew him. This may have been true, to a point, but the songwriter most likely got the message that Waylon was not in the mood to be pestered.

Sometimes aggressiveness pays off. A writer who saw Melissa Manchester perform on the *Today Show* decided that she had the right tune for her. She promptly took a cab down to NBC, where she bribed the stage door guard to let her stay "in wait" for Manchester. When Manchester came out of the building the writer thrust a demo in her face, and, poof, the song got recorded.

For every story like the one about the *Today Show*, there are at least fifty stories like the one about Jennings. You have to develop a sense of when an artist is receptive to hearing a song, and when they don't want their privacy disturbed. You also need to be lucky. Songwriter Tim O'Brien had his first top ten country hits while living in Boulder, Colorado. He got a tape to Kathy Mattea, and she happened to notice that he was originally from West Virginia. She also was raised in that state, and this made her curious about his song. The song, "Walk the Way the Wind Blows," became a top ten country hit, and broke open Tim's career as a songwriter. Another great example of good fortune occurred when Nashville songwriter Pat Alger offered a young singer a place to stay for the night. The young singer was Garth Brooks, and he ended up co-writing songs that sold over fifty millions copies with Alger.

Some other ways of getting a song to an artist who is appearing locally are through a club manager, a concert promoter, or a local disc jockey. Don't overdo it, though, and never try to get more than one song to the artist. Remember to supply a typed lyric sheet and to place your name and address on the tape box and on the tape itself. Make sure that your song is protected by copyright before submitting it to artists or producers, especially if you don't know them personally. Don't give up part of your writer's credit to someone making this sort of contact for you. The chances are heavily against the artist picking up any one song, and you may have given away a valuable asset that will later be recorded by someone else without obtaining any benefit at all.

Making Publishing Contacts by Mail

There is another way to delve further into the songwriting business. Pick up a current copy of the annual book *Songwriter's Market*. It lists music publishers, some record companies, songwriters, music print companies, advertising agencies, producers of slide shows, and industrial films, managers, and agents. Generally speaking, it is a good idea to stay away from the publishing companies with offices in rural Kansas. Their industry contacts are probably no broader than your own. The book's listings usually describe some songs that the publishing company has gotten recorded, and what sort of material they are looking for.

Small-time Publishers

The economics of songwriting are fairly simple: for every song recorded, there is a writer and a publisher. They share the current statutory mechanical royalty for each song, which should be split on a fifty-fifty basis. This royalty is the one that comes from sales of the record. Many record producers and recording artists own all or part of a music publishing company. One of the incentives that you can offer them in return for recording your song is to give them the publishing rights. If you have already committed the song to a small publisher in Idaho, an artist may turn the song down because she can't own all or part of the publishing rights. This may sound unfair or callous, but is a reality of the business. Be sure there is a provision in your contract for the song's publishing rights to revert to you if the artist or producer doesn't actually get the song on the record. This is called a "reversion clause." It is not unusual for an artist to record more songs than will actually appear on a finished album. They can then pick and choose the best songs and the best performances.

If you've never heard of a publisher, ask what songs they have had recorded in the last two or three years, and the names of the artists and the record labels. If you have never heard of the artists or the record companies, or if all the recorded cuts were written by the owners of the publishing company, it is safe to conclude that they are not a factor on the national scene.

Note that some of the major music publishers refuse to be listed in *Songwriter's Market*. This is because they are not interested in getting tons of unsolicited submissions. In order to be admitted to their doors, you will need to be able to drop the name of someone whom the publisher knows and respects, like a hit artist, songwriter, personal manager, prominent disc jockey, or promoter.

Contacting Music Publishers in Person

If you have the time and are willing to spend the money, you can always head for a major music center to knock on the doors of publishers. You should pave the way by calling the publishers before you make the trip. Ask anyone in your town who has any possible contacts—record promotion people, disc jockeys, concert promoters, and other songwriters. Call publishers listed in the Songwriter's Market who seem to be possible prospects for your songs.

If you can, try to see the publisher in person. Some publishers will refuse to do this, because they feel they can concentrate better on the music when the writer is not around. They also are sometimes embarrassed because quite often they listen to only fragments of a song before moving on. If it doesn't capture their attention, they move on to the next tune. Some writers think that the publisher is being rude, and don't understand that this is a custom in the industry. Never put more than three songs on a demo, because publishers usually will not want to spend too much time on a new, unknown writer. If they like your work, they'll ask for more.

If you do get to sit with a publisher (actually it is usually the professional manager or one of her assistants who will be screening your songs), listen carefully to what they have to say. Don't become defensive about your work. Remember that almost every major artist and songwriter has been rejected by some, and often many, publishers and record companies. What you are looking for is some critical feedback that will place your songs in relation to what is currently in the marketplace.

If the publisher will not see you, leave a tape with his secretary. It will probably take days or even weeks to get the tape heard. Be sure to make a note of the secretary's name. John Braheny calls secretaries and others who serve as screens to keep writers away from publishers "gatekeepers." If you want to get the gate to open for you at a future time, it's a good idea to become friendly with the gatekeeper.

Here's another little tip that can save you a lot of money. When you use the telephone, try to find the cheapest phone rates that you can get. The lowest rates are usually before 8:00 A.M. If you live on the West Coast, you're two hours earlier than Nashville time and three hours earlier than New York. If you live on the East

Coast, try to call the West after 5:00 P.M., when the middle tier of rates is in effect. If you are serious about contacting publishers, you will be making dozens of long-distance calls, so the amount of money involved can become considerable. Some high-level executives stay in their offices after their secretaries go home, and you can sometimes contact them directly by phone because they will take calls directly after hours. Other executives come in at amazingly early hours to try to catch up on their work. The more you know about the lifestyle of the person you are trying to reach, the better chance you can get through to her. Once you establish a contact, you can also use e-mail to stay in touch. Some people prefer to use the phone, others like electronic communication.

In general, it's somewhat easier to see music publishers than record company people. This is because music publishers are at a bit of a disadvantage today. Although the majority of songs recorded in Nashville are still written by people other than the recording artist, in New York and Los Angeles the opposite holds true. Because music publishers are having difficulty getting their songs cut, they are always looking for that magical writer amidst the sea of talent out there on the streets.

On your first trip you probably won't place any songs with publishers, let alone get them recorded. What you will be able to accomplish, if your songs show promise, is that you will meet some publishers who will encourage you to keep writing and to submit new material to them. If a publisher seems encouraging, stay in touch with him. Remind him that you are the guy from Rawlins, Wyoming who visited him last month. Ask the secretary of the company when the best time is to call.

If you leave a CD at a publisher's office, be sure that your name, address, and phone number are on the jewel case and the CD itself. This procedure has already been mentioned, but it can't be stressed enough. Major publishers get hundreds of song submissions. Don't become a casualty of your (and their) carelessness.

Most music industry people prefer to have songs submitted on CDs. They are the most convenient format, and also the format most commonly found in cars. Many publishers listen to songs during their commuting time in their cars.

If you are trying to establish a career as a songwriter, the publisher doesn't really care what you look like. A photo is of no importance, but any previous writing credits will make you look more like a professional. Send them along with a brief bio, but don't mention your hockey trophies or the fact that you were third clarinet in the all-state marching band.

Demos

When a music publisher picks up your songs, unless your demo is of excellent quality, they will want to make demonstration CD (demo) of your songs. This entails hiring singers and musicians and renting a studio. The publisher should pay for these demos, or the costs may be shared. Your share will usually be considered an advance against royalties.

If you can do demos in your hometown, the publisher should pay for your recording costs and the costs of hiring any additional musicians or singers. The publisher will want to be present at your initial demo sessions, if this is geographically feasible. Unless you have quite a bit of recording experience, you may well find his presence helpful. It is a good idea to have worked out what sort of sound and style you and the publisher want on the demo before you enter the studio. The need for quality demos is increasingly important. So many writers have excellent home studios that publishers have become more aware of the need for a demo that is virtually a finished product. It is no longer unusual for a producer or artist to copy or even use a rhythm track, or a quality guitar lick from a demo on the actual record. A simple guitar or piano demo has a hard time holding its own in today's market, outside the country music genre. On the other hand, don't spend a great deal of money hiring musicians for demos. It's still the lyrics, melody, and essential groove that best convey a song's message. Make sure that these qualities are emphasized on your demos.

Tip Sheets

Small monthly periodicals called "tip sheets" provide another source for matching your songs with artists or publishers. These publications list artists looking for songs, along with a description of what they want and a time frame for when the songs need to be submitted. Tip sheets are usually quit expensive. If you do want to send songs out to the artists or producers that they list, you may want to split the subscription cost with a fellow songwriter or persuade your local songwriters' organization to subscribe. Tip sheets are a useful way of keeping up with who is recording, and who is producing the recording. Of course the more a tip sheet circulates, the more writers you will be competing against for a place on the album.

Performing Rights Organizations

ASCAP, BMI, and SESAC are performing rights societies that collect the royalties that come from the public performance of songs. The bulk of the money comes from airplay on radio or television. These rights can be quite lucrative, and often in country music, will bring much more income than the monies from the sale of recordings. Which performing rights organization should you join, and how can you contact their representatives? The addresses of these societies are in the Appendix. Generally, these people are interested in talking with you only when you have material that is close to being recordable. As a new writer, your best bet is to join the society where you have the greatest rapport with their director of Artist Relations, or whatever title they are currently using for the person who sees new writers, or where they show an affinity to your style of music.

What good can these people do you? Marv Mattis, former West Coast director of Artist Relations was instrumental in helping to build the music scene in Portland, Oregon, and Denver, Colorado. Ron Sobel, who held a similar position at ASCAP, grasped the importance of the Seattle scene as it was evolving. He signed several key acts to ASCAP, and their photos with grateful inscriptions are on the wall of his office. These people are shrewd professionals, and they will only go out of their way to help the dedicated and talented few among the dozens of writers whom they meet.

The reasons for joining a performing rights society are:
1. To receive performing rights monies
2. To help make valuable contacts with writers and publishers
3. To participate in classes or seminars

Your choice of a performing rights society should include thefollowing:
1. Are they responsive to your calls?
2. Do you have rapport with anyone in their office?
3. Have they provided you with any useful contacts?

ASCAP and BMI also offer classes for songwriters. They are usually small and intensive, and may focus on a particular aspect of songwriting, such as writing Broadway show material. It is not really possible to become involved in these classes unless you live in or will stay in the town where they are offered. The Broadway show Avenue Q resulted from a collaboration sparked by two songwriters who met at a BMI theater workshop.

All of the performing rights groups are involved in the major industry seminars and conferences, such as Austin's South by Southwest. Talk to their representatives, read their propaganda, and make your choice. Chapter 17 contains some information about the history of performing rights in America.

There are a few critical differences between the performing rights organizations. Because the logging of songs is still done in a fashion that resembles political polling, rather than an exact science, many regional and local writers rarely receive much money from ASCAP, BMI, or SESAC. SESAC will pay an advance for any song that is on a nationally released record. ASCAP has a special awards fund for artists whose performance or activities have not been picked up in the ASCAP surveys of performances. ASCAP then gives these writers awards, based on the extent of their activities, especially public performances of their music. No writer who has earned over $15,000 in a year is eligible to receive these payments. At present, BMI has no comparable program.

Accessing the Major Songwriters' Organizations

The Nashville Songwriters Association International can refer you to many of the publishers in town. They also hold large annual seminars that feature major writers and publishers. If you are headed to Nashville, try to attend one of these meetings, where you will hear writers and publishers talk about their craft and critique songs. If you attend the NSAI wingding, leave time afterwards for going around to publishers' offices. During the NSAI annual meetings, many of the publishers will be at the meetings, and not in their offices.

It is not realistic to go cold to NSAI and expect to blow everyone away. You are competing with highly skilled professionals. What you will get is some valuable counseling, information, and eventually, some access to the sort of publishers and producers who are both reputable and apt to be receptive to your work. Both organizations have many out-of-town members, and NSAI will even place your cassette in rotation from afar and send you a written copy of the publisher's critique.

NSAI and the previously mentioned Songwriters Guild of America all charge membership fees to support their vastly overworked staffs. They are probably the best single investment a songwriter will ever make in the music business. Oddly, New York has no similar songwriting organization.

Music Print Publishers

Steady and sometimes surprisingly good income can be earned by writing instructional materials for the music print publishers who print instructional and artist's folios. Contact one of the companies listed in the Appendix, and submit a table of contents and some sample pages. How does your work differ from material that is already available on the same subject? Don't be shy, but evaluate your strengths realistically and focus on the part of your approach that is innovative and may appeal to music teachers and musicians.

Publishers pay a royalty on each copy of these books that are sold. If you use copyrighted songs by other authors, you will have to share some of that royalty with the writers and publishers of that material. Consequently, many author use songs that are in the public domain (older than seventy-five years), or write their own original material. Not all music print publishers give advances, but those who do typically pay $500 to $1,000. A portion of the advance is paid upon signing a contract, and the rest upon acceptance of a completed manuscript. A typical royalty is 10% of the retail selling price, but a music publisher may pay slightly more or less than that amount. It depends on their enthusiasm for your project, current market conditions, and their normal business practices. The most popular instruments are keyboards and guitar, but these are also the instruments that have been covered in considerable depth by numerous authors.

It makes no difference where you live. The music print publishers are spread out all over the country. If you're an experienced arranger, there is also work available to write choral or band arrangements for school ensembles. There is also a great need for guitar transcribers who know tablature and have good ears. Arranging work includes no royalty payments, unless you include some original compositions in a folio. The publishers generally pay arrangers on a per page basis.

There are only a handful of important music print publishers. They include Alfred Music in Los Angeles, who recently acquired the print rights for Warner Brothers Publishing; Mel Bay in St. Louis specializes in guitar music; Cherry Lane Music in New York, who publish quite a bit of heavy metal and singer-songwriter folios; Carl Fischer in New York, who recently acquired the Theodore Presser classical music catalog; International Music Publishers, another classical music operation headquartered in New York; Neil Kjos in San Diego, who does a good deal of music for school bands; Hal Leonard, the world's largest print publisher, in Milwaukee; and Music Sales in New York publishes a combination of instructional methods and mixed folios of songs and instrumental pieces.

Summer Music Festivals

If you are a high school or college student and are free to travel during summers, there are numerous summer music festivals all over the United States and Canada. They provide instruction and performing opportunities in almost every imaginable type of music, and some them are held in wonderful scenic areas. The classical music world in particular offers some excellent summer music festivals.

The National Repertory Orchestra, located in Keystone, Colorado, is a major training ground for symphony musicians. Other such events are the Aspen, Banff, and Tanglewood music festivals. The Hollywood Bowl Symphony also offers opportunities for young musicians to play chamber and symphonic music. There is a real lack of symphonic training orchestras, and a graduate of a college music program will rarely have the opportunity to join a major orchestra fresh out of school. The stimulus of playing with other outstanding young musicians and under fine conductors can bring a young player to a higher level of performance.

Magazines like *Bluegrass Unlimited*, *Dirty Linen*, *Downbeat*, *Jazz Times*, and *Sing Out* list summer blues, bluegrass, and jazz festivals. At the annual Winnipeg and Vancouver folk festivals held in July, musicians come from all over the world to play. Workshops and instructional sessions are featured in addition to the major evening concerts.

There are numerous opportunities available in local and regional music markets. Some artists will prefer to test the larger markets, and others will acquire business reputations in those markets but remain in then place where they prefer to live.

Chapter 11 Resources

The annual *Songwriter's Market*, published by Writer's Digest Books in Cincinnati, is the best single source of information about music publishers. It is best to use the current edition, because companies and go in and out of business and change their names. Executives also often move from job to job. It is very embarrassing to write or call someone who hasn't worked for a company for two or three years.

Newly revised editions of books by Tim Whitsett and Randy Poe book on music publishing both provide useful information.

CHAPTER 12

The Urge for Going: Staying or Leaving

If you have ever played music professionally, somewhere deep within you, you probably harbor the fantasy that you or your group could be the next major star. Should you wish to pursue such a goal, here are some of the roadblocks and detours that await you, as well as the possibility of making it in the big world but remaining or returning to your hometown.

To be straightforward—if you are after national exposure, hit records, and the big bucks, the major music centers (see Chapter 1) are where you can find these things. It's where the major record companies have their headquarters, and where television, movies, commercials, and music publishers are all present in profusion. (See the charts on the following pages.)

If you decide to go, there are a few recommendations it would be wise to follow: have enough money to live for six months before you have to worry about becoming a bag person. It's helpful to have or develop some non-music job skills, especially some that offer flexible hours of employment. Waiting on tables is something you can almost always do and word processing skills can usually get you a job with a temporary employment agency.

My friend Ron Bergan, former national educator director for NARAS, broke into the music industry through temping at music publishers and record companies. This gave him an opening wedge, which ultimately resulted in his working for a music publisher.

Before you go to your city of choice, buy the Sunday newspaper. Check the want ads, and see if it is feasible that you can find some employment once you move. Los Angeles and New York have a fairly constant demand for temporary office workers. It is also possible to find temporary manual labor jobs in large cities, or odd jobs, like giving out telephone directories.

The major music business towns all have entertainment papers or journals, like *Music Row* in Nashville, the *Village Voice* in New York, or the *LA Weekly*, *BAM*, and *The Music Connection* in Los Angeles. These papers will give you a feel for what kind of live music is happening in town, and they may also help you to find an apartment, a songwriting collaborator, or even a job with a record company. Some of these newspapers will even be available in your hometown. Check with the largest newsstand or bookstore in town.

Opportunity Chart

Major Music Market	Local Scene
National exposure	Local exposure
Heavyweight personal managers and music attorneys	Few or no full-time managers or music business attorneys
Record companies galore	A few small labels
Network television	Local news and talk show, perhaps a variety show (depending upon size of city)
Major concert halls and stadiums	Varies, depending upon size of market
Hundreds of studio musicians and songwriters	A small corps of professionals, often with limited knowledge of musical styles
Major music publishers with worldwide contacts	A few music publishers; one or two may have some national access
Headquarters for music trade papers	Local correspondents for trades, maybe
Excellent music teachers of many kinds	A few select and experienced teachers
Major recording studios with state-of-the-art equipment	A few large studios; some competent studios with slightly-dated equipment
Access to a large pool of would-be band members, song collaborators	Easy access to a smaller talent pool

Let's assume that you took your two-week tour, and now with or without your band you've move to the Big Apple, LA-LA Land, or Music City. Where do you go from here? It's going to be apparent to you within a matter of weeks that you're not likely to crash the big time without any help. If you want to try to find a record deal, there are three possible directions in which to look.

Personal Managers with National Clout

The first and likeliest method to break through the big city barriers is to enlist the services of a personal manager. Of course, the personal manager that you want may prefer to represent an act that already has a record deal. (See more on this subject in my book *The Music Business: Career Opportunities and Self-Defense.*)

In the book *Entertainers and Their Professional Advisers* by Egon Dumler and Robert F. Cushman, there's an excellent article by Dee Anthony about personal management. Anthony has managed a broad range of talented and successful musicians and entertainers, from Tony Bennett to Emerson, Lake & Palmer. He

Upside of Staying Where You Are

Major Music Market	Local Scene
Very expensive housing and high cost of living (less true of Nashville)	Relatively reasonable housing (you know where the best deals are because you live here)
Los Angeles: constant car expense, must drive great distances in heavy traffic; New York: impossible to keep car in the city because of incredible garage cost	Manageable transportation
You must make new contacts: you know virtually no one; hard to make new contacts: you always seem to be "on hold"	You know who is straight and who is jive; if you're not sure, you have the contacts to help you check it out; you have friends or peers to consult; you have friends and family there
Large and impersonal	Small and friendly (because you know the turf)
Jobs are hard to access	You know where the gigs are, or can find out
Not too friendly; you feel that you're lost in a maze of impersonal and complex business decisions	You know everyone; you feel comfortable

points out that a manager not only obtains a record deal but also works with a music business lawyer to negotiate it. Later on, she must exercise gentle or forceful persuasion in order to convince the record company to spend money on publicizing the artist, funding videos, and offering tour support.

A manager should not represent too many clients, nor should he choose to represent clients who have skills that are directly competitive with one another. A big-time manager may be able to offer an immediate set of bookings to a new client alongside a better known act that the manager also represents.

An experienced manager can also help a group with matters such as pacing a set or establishing a lighting chart. She can get professional help in these areas if she doesn't have that sort of expertise.

Be careful when signing a management agreement that includes the manager handling your publishing and producing your records. Check that he is not also simultaneously taking commission on your earnings as a writer or recording artist. Try to build in some performance guarantees in your agreement, such as getting your group a recording contract, or earning a specific amount of money annually.

The contract should clearly state how much of the artist's monies the manager will be allowed to spend on the group's development. These include travel and entertainment expenses. If the monies owed to the group go directly to the manager, a special account should be set up to disburse this income. It should not be co-mingled with the manager's other income or expenses. There also needs to be some understanding of what continuing royalty income the manager may receive in the event that the group and the manager agree to separate.

Finding a Manager

It is difficult to find an honest and tireless manager. *Billboard* and *Pollstar* list managers in annual directories. *The Music Connection*, which is published every two weeks, lists managers every three months. Check with other musicians for recommendations, but be open-minded and somewhat skeptical. Not all musicians are sufficiently versed in the business to comprehend what a manager actually does.

To check out a manager, ask her for a client list of current acts that she has handled. Check out these credentials with these clients as carefully as you can. Ask how many people work in her office, and how many clients she represents. If the office has other managers working with the one who has signed you, consider the "keyman clause," the one that stipulates that if she leaves the office you can break your contract without penalty or payment of additional monies.

In choosing a manager, avoid relatives, romantic partners, and, generally speaking, friends. It is a business, and the reality is that many personal relationships do not last. Do you want to be managed by an ex-husband or wife? Another criteria is to pick a manager who is willing able to devote their full-time efforts to the job of managing you, and a handful of other acts. Without that commitment, you will not be properly represented. Expect to pay 15% to 20% of your gross income for these services.

Most management deals run from three (optimum) to five years, although a manager might try to sign you to a seven-year agreement. Never sign a managerial contract without consulting a good music business attorney to read it. Don't use the same attorney that the manager has (or recommends) to insure that your own interests are properly represented.

Agents

Unlike the situation that prevails in local markets, a nationally oriented booking agency will insist on an exclusive agreement with an artist or group before booking them into clubs or concerts. The choice of the booking agency can critically affect the group's finances, and the choice of venues that the group plays will have a profound influence on the possible sale of the group's records. The actual choice of bookings can also have a positive or negative influence on how the artists feel about their music. Some issues that are apt to surface include the amount of attention the band is apt to receive from a particular audience that, in all likelihood has come to see a well-known headline performer.

Other Paths to a Record Deal

If you cannot locate a competent manager, it is still possible to get a record deal through a music business attorney. Music business attorneys have frequent contacts with record people. They often have social relationships with them that include attending or participating in sports events and hanging out together. A lawyer can get you to the proper person at a record company, and he can also suggest an appropriate personal manager. If a record company is genuinely excited about an act, they can also provide leads to managers. Generally speaking, record companies prefer not to do business with acts directly, because it often leads to hard feelings on the part of the artist.

Music publishers sometimes will front the money for high-quality demos, and even produce entire albums. They then will try to market the records to record labels. Any active publisher has a wide circle of record company acquaintances through his normal song-plugging activities.

Another path to a record deal is through an independent record producer. If a producer has a good track record, that alone may be enough to convince a record company to take a chance on your act. Occasionally, a record company likes a group, but not the person who produced the demos. If you are under contract to the producer, this may destroy not only your chances of getting a deal, but of getting a true story out of the jilted producer.

Music Business Attorneys

Skilled music business attorneys are expensive. In a major music market fees of $200 to $500 an hour are not unusual. Sometimes the payments can be spread out, or based on your income. It is best not to give a lawyer a percentage of your income, because she will then earn money whenever you perform as well as record. If you have to give up a percentage to a lawyer, it is preferable to restrict that payment to the record deal itself. Some lawyers are willing to place a cap on a specific contract. This means that there is a maximum fee that you will be charged for the negotiation, regardless of the exact number of hours that the lawyer spends.In a number of cities, there are organizations of lawyers who perform legal services for artists at minimal cost. Whether this is really a good deal for the artist depends on the lawyer's experience and his negotiating skills. I certainly would not hesitate to show a single songwriter's agreement to such an attorney, or a local deal with an agent. I would be somewhat less comfortable at showing him a 120-page Universal Records contract that covers merchandising rights, publishing, producer royalties, etc. It is a good idea to see if your lawyer has ever negotiated contracts that are roughly similar to the one you are looking at. The national organization of these lawyers is called Volunteer Lawyers for the Arts, but each city has a somewhat different localized name for the group. (See the Appendix.)

Staying or Going Summary

You may want to make yourself a circular life diagram and figure out where you fit into the picture before you head for the major music market.Question marks are placed next to "aesthetic satisfaction" and "income" because for some people, these drives lead them to the national market. For example, if you want to compose feature film scores, it's hard to work that out when you live in southern Kansas. Others might do quite well at home without the additional pressures and expenses of big city living.

No one can tell you what you want to do. You must look at your life, goals, and dreams, and evaluate them in terms of your own needs, talent, and personality.

Going but Coming Back

It is possible to strive for success on the national scene while maintaining a goal of eventually returning to your hometown. Once you have secured big city representation, you *can* return to your original home base.

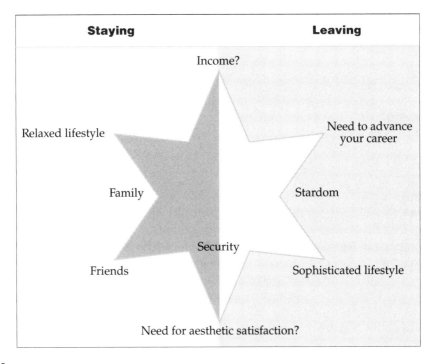

In any case, you're going to need a couple of years just to know where to go and what to do. If you're totally on your own and are moving in order to join up with other musicians, it's likely to take you three to five years.

You can try to get help by networking through the union or local music or songwriters' organizations, music stores, or entertainment publications, but essentially you're involved in a trial-and-error process. You are apt to audition for bands that you won't like, meet people who are flakes, encounter styles that are unfamiliar, and, in general, try to figure out what in the world is going on. You will hear endless horror stories from songwriters who had songs similar to the one you are looking at that were "stolen" from them by band members who were fleeced by record companies, records that came out without any promotional effort behind them, producers who were hype artists, and managers who didn't do anything for their clients.

Consider the source of this information. Many people who are not successful are always able to find an external reason for their lack of success. Invariable, that reason has to do with someone else who let them down. How many people have you met in the record business who told you, "The record company did a good job, but I blew it. I wasn't ready." Or, "Our manager was cool, but so many people in the band were drunk that we never did consistent shows." Or, "I had a good publisher, but I just couldn't deliver hit songs consistently because I was too young and inexperienced."

Anyone who always blames other people for her own lack of success is probably deluding herself. There are bad record companies, crooked managers, and thieving lawyers. But you are also responsible for your own actions. You weren't forced to sign a contract. Remember, most people who get recording contracts don't become stars, and most people don't get recording contracts at all. Most songwriters don't write hits, and most don't even get publishing deals.

Desiring success is undoubtedly one part of making it. Having some form of talent, whether it's singing or dancing well, or writing wonderful songs is another. Finding a good manager is a combination of thorough searching and luck. Getting a hit record involves luck and talent. There are artists who get their fair shot at success, but the public simply won't buy whatever they do. There can be any number of reasons for this—bad management, talent that never focuses properly, bad timing, bad luck, and, of course, poor record company promotion.

Money Isn't Everything

Success can be defined any way one chooses. Selling millions of records doesn't make a group musically profound, it just means that the public bought what the group had to sell. You may find that you are happiest doing something that is outside the mainstream of popular taste. It may be that your musical interests are esoteric or unusual, that you are musically ahead of what the public wants to hear or that the public is simply not interested in what you have to offer. Popular music often revolves around fads that bear no particular relationship to anything tangible. Take the accordion. There used to be thousands of accordion players and teachers throughout North America. Every time you turned around, there was somebody on a TV variety show playing "Lady of Spain."

During the 1960s, the guitar took over. Suddenly, the only accordions in sight were found in polka bands or oom-pah groups. The accordion didn't change, it simply took on the connotation of being square and old-fashioned.

Then, lo and behold, the accordion became "in" again. All sorts of hot zydeco groups featured it, as did the group Los Lobos in the movie *La Bamba*. The late 1980s adolescents never knew it was corny, so it outgrew its negative connotations. A similar thing has happened to the mandolin, once seen as kind of a parlor instrument, or one associated with Italian music. The popularity of David Grisman and the use of mandolin on Shawn Colvin's hit "Sunny Came Home" has made people see the mandolin in a different light as a contemporary instrument. So has the popularity of the contemporary bluegrass group Nickel Creek, which features the superb mandolin playing of Chris Thiele.

You need to identify the essential qualities of your music and to locate the marketplace where there are buyers for your musical wares. What you cannot do is to assume massive success will come from following such a path.

Some of the record labels that specialize in music that is not necessarily designed to appeal to the mass-market are located in secondary music markets. There is a good deal of New Age music coming out of Boulder, Milwaukee, and San Francisco, and specialty jazz labels are quite active in the San Francisco area. There are some important traditional jazz labels in the New Orleans area and blues labels in Chicago. Country and folk music labels are also found in such places as Boston and the southern part of the United States. Sometimes a label starts in a particular place because the owner lives there, or a strong regional musical style, like Cajun music, leads to the founding of a regional label that later expands into the national market.

There are several books that list dozens of record companies all over the United States. If you contact one of these labels, invest in a phone call or query letter before sending your tape to make sure that you know who to send your tape to. In general, these sorts of companies are friendlier to new talent than the major labels, who are besieged by submissions.

Small record companies offer an artist more personal service and access than a large label can provide. It is possible to remain in direct contact with the decision makers at the label, and to get a "yes" or "no" answer without having to wait for a series of committee meetings to consider your project. You are not apt to get any large cash advances from small labels, nor should you be surprised that your record will not necessarily be stocked by the massive chain stores that are spread across the shopping malls of North America. Many of these stores avoid minor label records because their stock doesn't turn over often enough to justify using the space.

Living Outside the Mainstream

There is no reason why a successful artist can't live outside the major music markets once her career has taken off, as long as someone in the major markets is taking care of her business affairs. If a musical group wishes to relocate outside the major markets, it is best if they all live in reasonable proximity to one another. If the bass player lives in Florida and the lead singer is in Iowa, there are going to be problems in establishing regular rehearsals and routing the band to and from jobs. This highlights the needs for people working in groups to continue to communicate as their careers build. It is a bit different when a group simply re-creates their own (or other people's) hits. If there is no new repertoire to learn or record, the need for regular rehearsals diminishes.

Groups need to retain a common sense of the musical direction that brought them together in the first place. Of course, there is room for personal and musical variations and explorations, but there should be some solid common ground for the group to continue.

Assuming that you do have the same general goals, and that you still enjoy hanging out and playing together, it is indeed quite possible to live almost anywhere you choose. You may even be able to record your product locally, which can prove to be a great idea or a poor one. You should know one another well enough by this time to be aware of what constitutes a valuable support group, and what provides disturbing distractions. Some people work better when their families are nearby, and some, like boxers, seem to require an isolated environment.

Of course, other factors may come into play. If you want to work with a hot production team like Jimmy Jam and Terry Lewis, you may find yourself freezing to death in their wintry home of Minneapolis, rather than sunning yourself in Phoenix while recording at a studio of your choice. (This is no longer necessarily true. Jam and Lewis now split their time between their studios in Minneapolis and Los Angeles.)

A new scene can be a stimulus to the creative process, and that is why some artists make a point of going to another town or even a foreign country each time they record. Some artists run through producers in a similar fashion, looking for new creative stimulation.

You know who you are and what works for you. If you don't, it's up to your manager to discuss it with you. Major groups tour most of the time, and they can live anywhere. It is different if the basis of your attempt to scale the heights of the music business is daily work on a TV show in Los Angeles, or if you're an established country star whose fans expect you to appear every Saturday night on the *Grand Ole Opry*. If you feel strongly about living outside the major music centers, then you and your manager should develop a plan that will enable you to realize that goal.

Developing Local and Regional Music Scenes

Consider a final possibility. You may want to leave the area where you grew up or went to school and go to a secondary music market in another part of the country. Portland, Oregon; Austin, Texas; and Minneapolis are all appealing cities, and each has a growing music scene.

Your choice of what town to live in could be governed by factors such as contacts, climate, lifestyle, family considerations, or a chance to visit a new locale. You may also change your mind about such matters as what sort of climate, lifestyle, and musical work you prefer.

Shifting opportunities occur as different areas become larger population centers, with increasing employment possibilities.

Chapter 12 Resources

There are a number of resources that can help to access independent labels. Musician publishes an annual *Musician's Guide to Touring and Promotion* that lists labels and includes the names of contacts. Rising Star Music Publishers of Atlanta also publishes an annual book entitled *National Directory of Record Labels and Music Publishers*.

If you use these books, be sure that you have the most recent edition available. People change jobs and labels change names and sometimes go out of business. Writing or calling someone who has not worked at a label for over a year marks you as an amateur.

CHAPTER 13
Playing Music Part-Time

The overwhelming majority of people in North America who call themselves professional musicians do not attempt to pursue a career in music on a full-time basis. Past surveys have shown that 80% of musicians who belong to the American Federation of Musicians work at music on a part-time basis. No survey has ever been taken that indicates what percentage of these people have made this choice because they can't make a living in music, and how many prefer the security of another more stable or lucrative profession.

There are a number of positive aspects that accompany playing music part-time rather than on a regular basis. First of all, you're less likely to become bored or cynical about music if you don't have to do it all the time. Many full-time musicians do not have the luxury of rejecting work, but take whatever playing jobs they are offered. Some must ignore the questioning of finding a job that fulfills their musical interests, and take the best-paying jobs that are available.

In all fairness, sometimes taking a musical job that you would never choose for reasons of your own stylistic preferences or prejudices can turn out to be a good experience. It can lead to the mastering new styles, change your approach to a particular instrument, and even lead to the development of new musical tastes and knowledge.

Most full-time musicians are forced to do some traveling, whether it may be a weekend commute to a ski resort or a club gig in a suburban location miles away from town. Traveling is expensive, and if weather conditions are unfavorable or the driver is tired, it can be dangerous as well. It tends to upset many marital relationships, because the spouse who is at home may feel abandoned for so-called "fun," while the musician feels that he is misunderstood.

When full-time musicians embark on a national touring career, the situation is even more difficult. Tours can last for months at a time and the traveling musician is subject to temptations of drug, sex, and alcohol, none of which tend to reinforce a marriage or improve the attitude of the touring musician. Long and tiring travel, working late at night, and the necessity of living for weeks in hotels with little human contact outside the members of your own band, can be very disruptive and bring on loneliness and depression.

The part-time musician has the opportunity to operate at maximal musical efficiency by turning down jobs that are of no musical interest. Many full-time musicians refuse to do this, feeling that if they refuse one job, they may stop getting any musical opportunities at all. To be released from financial dependency on unwelcome gigs can be an incredibly liberating experience. It means that you can direct your musical energies toward practicing and playing the music of your choice, rather than the music that a club owner, bandleader or other employer may require.

There are a surprising number of really fine musicians who make a living at some other profession. Ron Aldridge, a noted periodontist in New York, is equally well known to New York jazz connoisseurs as a superb clarinet player. Another part-time clarinet player is director Woody Allen. Denny Zeitlin is a psychiatrist and piano soloist of renown in the San Francisco area. Other musicians play part-time until they retire. Armed with a comfortable pension they then play primarily because they enjoy doing so.

Full-time musicians have a difficult time wresting with the demons of night work, keeping a practice and rehearsal schedule, and family responsibilities. For many talented people, this makes a career as a full-time musician incompatible with raising a family. Part-time playing can provide a welcome respite from the demands of child care, although it requires the presence of a cooperative spouse who will make evening commitments to child care.

Freelance dance band musicians often play dances just on weekends. They may be tea dances or singles mixers, which occur more often in larger cities. The average young musician may be totally unaware of such gigs. The repertoire is usually material that dates back to the 1930s or 1940s, and the players usually work for union minimum or even less. These are not show groups, but musicians who play for dancing. If the band plays well and the leader has some good charts, these jobs provide an enjoyable outlet for local musicians who do little or no performing during the week.

Some musicians satisfy their need for security by accepting jobs as school music teachers, or occasionally as teachers of other subjects. This leaves weekends, summer vacations, and holidays free to accept playing jobs.

It is up to you to determine what will make you happy, and to decide what options are realistic. Some musicians prefer to stop playing if they can't play at the level that they wish to attain.

The quality of musical life that a musician can sustain over the years is largely a function of his willingness to practice. There is the occasional brilliant player who doesn't practice at all. Usually these people have a regular club job, or do so much studio work that they are able to do their practicing on the job. I knew a superb New York percussionist who recorded constantly but didn't keep a musical instrument in his house for over twenty years. He literally got his practice on the gig.

Some musicians who are part-time players make a conscious choice only to play music that appeals to them. They use their other profession as a way of securing regular income and only play jobs that they know will be enjoyable. This group of musicians may be among the happiest and most fulfilled of musicians. They don't have to compromise their musical tastes or work with undesirable people, because they never allow themselves to get into a situation where compromise is necessary.

This is not to imply that full-time musicians are unhappy people, or that it is impossible to make a living playing music. These are only some of the many compelling reasons that cause some musicians to turn to music as a part-time profession.

As a part-timer, you can assume an independent freelancer attitude. Since no particular job is essential to your security, you can turn down anything that isn't worth doing. Full-time musicians are often confronted by contractors that make unreasonable demands. The implication is that if you don't take this job, they will not hire you again. A part-timer can simply laugh at such demands.

A very close friend of mine had a variety of reasons for dropping music as a regular source of employment. He found that when he tried to work as a full-time musician, he was unable to resist the temptations of hard drugs and alcohol. After he saw some very talented musician friends destroy their lives by taking drugs, he elected to quit both drugs and music. He moved to another town and got a job cleaning airplanes.

He never cared for his job, but the discipline that it required inspired him to pursue a part-time musical career as a disc jockey, songwriter, and arranger for a local gospel group. Since his bills were paid through a regular job, and he had flying privileges, he was able to spend the bulk of his free time in one musical pursuit or another. He was able to get some of his songs recorded by the Staples Singers by pitching them in-person, courtesy of the airline. He was also able to sustain family relationships, which he knew would have been destroyed had he continued his junkie life in New York as a would-be bebop trumpet player.

The Life of the Symphony Player

Playing in a major symphony orchestra is probably the most stable job that a musician can find. In the top orchestras, the minimum wage scale is as high as $2,000 a week, with medical, dental, and pension benefits; instrument insurance; and extra income available through freelance work, teaching, and recording sessions. For some one thousand musicians who play in the top North American orchestras, their career as musicians has attained the stability, respectability, and income level that more traditional professions enjoy, with guaranteed incomes of $100,000 per year or more. The more typical symphony player works in a ten-to-forty week season and earns from $5,000 to $40,000 a year.

Symphonic musicians are hired on the basis of auditions. It is not unusual to find fifty or more players competing for a single job in a minor orchestra. Naturally, the competition gets tougher when an orchestra like the Chicago Symphony or Philadelphia Orchestra is hiring. If you are interested in these jobs, the *International Musician*, the monthly publication of the American Federation of Musicians, has several pages of classified jobs each month advertising vacancies in various orchestras.

Other opportunities for classical musicians include playing in chamber music groups on a regular or informal basis. Some chamber groups become artists-in-residence at a particular college or music school, and often perform regular concerts together with teaching a relatively light load. Some of these groups, like the Juilliard String Quartet, do extensive recording work. Major cities usually have some sort of opera and ballet companies. They provide further employment for classical players. In the largest cities, these playing opportunities actually provide regular employment.

A very small number of classical musicians make handsome livings as solo recitalists. In Los Angeles, they play on film scores, and in New York may find work on commercials. In the largest cities, there is a pool of freelance players who go from one sort of job to another. The pay is good, but the competition is fierce. In secondary markets, these opportunities are more limited. Columbia Artists Management sponsors a Community Concert series that provides extensive performance opportunities in smaller cities for musicians whose careers are in the early to middle stages of development.

Because of the limited number of opportunities available in performance, many classical musicians and composers take teaching jobs at universities or colleges. For a composer, a school job offers several fringe benefits. Graduate students are available to assist with lengthy orchestration or the operation of MIDI equipment, and the college orchestras offer virtually guaranteed outlets for performances of new music. Moreover, this work can provide valuable experience for the student, as well as being useful to the composer. There is relatively little new music performed by professional symphonies, and when a composer is fortunate enough to have a new work performed, the orchestra often allots insufficient rehearsal time to learn a piece. It is far usually more difficult for an orchestra to perform a new piece than something that is a staple in the repertoire. When a composer is teaching at a college, she can rehearse a piece until she feels the college orchestra has reached a reasonable performance level.

There are virtually no full-time composers who don't moonlight as college professors. The lucky few are generally found composing music for films or television. Many colleges offer internal grant programs that encourage musicians and composers to write or perform music. As the budgets for state and national arts councils shrink, these opportunities become increasingly important. Grants can assist composers not only with money but by providing a formal or informal public relations support group.

Specialized Performing Groups

In certain cities, such as Boston or San Francisco, there is considerable interest in "early music" ensembles that play music going back as far as the twelfth or thirteenth century. These ensembles provide a steady living for a small number of musicians who have mastered these styles and who usually perform on authentic period instruments.

Songwriting

Songwriting, though still a long shot, offers attractive options for the part-time musician. Songs may be submitted to publishers, record producers, or artists through the mail, or through some of the songwriting groups already mentioned. It takes a great deal of persistence to continue developing one's craft and to continue to keep making demos and submitting tunes. If a part-time writer has access to a local performing group, then at least the writer can have the satisfaction of hearing his work performed in a professional manner.

Some part-time performing musicians even form groups that are outlets for their own original music. Other full-time musicians may be members of several groups or accept solo gigs, but have another performing group where they play original music. Often such groups self-produce their own CDs and sell them wherever they perform. The danger of this sort of arrangement is that a musician can't play at two venues at the same time. Consequently, a musician may find herself honoring a prior commitment to play music that she doesn't particularly like, rather than pursuing the music that she prefers.

Performing Full-Time, Part of the Time

Some bands perform music on a full-time basis part of the year, but devote a portion of their time to other musical projects. This can be because some of the group have family or teaching commitments, or that certain members of the band are interested in and perform music that other members of the group don't particularly like.

There are numerous summer jobs at outdoor venues and music festivals that may make it attractive for a band to play together in the summer, and to perform little or not at all during the rest of the year. Certain holidays like St. Patrick's Day, Christmas, or the Fourth of July may provide playing opportunities that are not available at other times of the year. A friend of mine from Denver named Charley Provenza played three winter ski seasons as half of a duo in Steamboat Springs, Colorado, but pursued other musical options when he returned to Denver each spring.

Dedicated Amateurs and Semi-Professionals

For dedicated amateur or semi-professional musicians, music is their principal hobby. Many such musicians devote many hours of practicing and listening in an effort to enhance their skills. Earning money from music is, at most, only a remote consideration to someone with this sort of orientation.

The dedicated amateur has one great advantage over the full-time musician. Since money is not a factor in the creation or performance of her music, she is free to do whatever she likes with her music. This may mean playing music for a church group, for family, friends, schools, or whoever she chooses. These enthusiasts often make the best students, as they continue their studies with full-time professionals. They put in long hours and spend a good deal of time researching the way music is created, and how it should be performed. There have been times, to be honest, when I was jealous of this luxury, as I was accepting musical jobs that were boring or stupid.

Many of these amateurs constitute the best audience for full-time musicians. They listen to and react to subtle musical nuances. They are the ones that ask a performer intelligent questions after a performance, as opposed to being concerned about hairstyles, hobbies, etc. There are dedicated amateurs in every form of music, from the weekend chamber music players, to the parking-lot pickers at bluegrass festivals, or the jazz fans who organize local jazz appreciation societies. Sometimes they offer financial support by helping a group to produce a record or tape, or serve as a formal or informal public relations group. Folk music fans may even provide their living rooms for informal house concerts for travelling artists.

Technology, the Composer, and the Schools

Electronic music technology, the proliferation of music software programs for computers, sampling devices that enable one musician to imitate the sounds of an entire orchestra or to create new sounds and colors make it possible for a composer to write and perform music in his own home studio. As the twenty-first century dawns, many full-time and part-time musicians will be able to devote long hours to realizing their musical compositions with the aid of these tools. Other musicians are terrified at this prospect, because they feel that it threatens the tradition of acoustic instruments that have dominated Western music for the last four hundred years.

More and more schools music programs are acquiring equipment that can offer the individual student useful information about the various aspects of orchestration. Self-programmed software frees the band director to concentrate on other matters as the individual player learns and rehearses her parts. Many schools are already combining acoustic and electric instruments to produce rich orchestral sounds. In a small town, synthesizers and sequencers can be utilized to fill in parts left out because of a lack or orchestral players. Some churches are pursuing similar musical paths.

It's important for school music programs to spend more time teaching children to listen, and to experiment with the new musical tools that technology has developed. This could greatly expand the prospects for music making in our society.

Musical Literacy

A friend of mine named Bruce Ronkin, who teaches at Northeastern University, has developed a re-definition of the term "musical literacy." He defines it as an awareness and understanding of all musical styles, instead of concentrating on the technical aspects of music. I think this is a very useful concept, because it places the emphasis on the student and teacher being open to many musical styles. The truth is that most of us are fixated on specific musical styles and techniques, and many of us don't listen to a variety of musical styles.

Bruce's notion also re-focuses the notion of literacy, removing it from the sheer ability to read and write music in notation. It isn't that these are not useful skills, it is rather that they don't necessarily define musicality. Many rock and country music players, and some jazz musicians are extremely musical and have developed advanced technical skills on their instruments. Such musicians should be encouraged to read music, but this encouragement is best presented as the development of additional tools, rather than presented in a condescending way. Many teachers would also benefit from a more open attitude toward a variety of musical styles. Invariably when I hear someone say that they don't like a specific form of music, like country music, I have found that they, in fact, have listened to very little of that music. They are not aware that country swing, country rock, and bluegrass, for example, are distinctly different musical styles.

Where Do You Fit In?

Now that we've looked at the various categories of professional and amateur musicians, locate yourself in these pictures. Determine what you want, what you dream about, and what it is that you find gratifying. Mix into this recipe the question of what is practical in your particular circumstance. What sort of stress fires you up, and what level of anxiety makes you incapable of functioning as an intelligent human being?

Evaluate how much music means to you, in what musical direction you want to go, how much effort you are capable of putting into your music, and how the demands or desires for a home and family life, economic security, and decent income fit into your personal crystal ball.

Place your life in an overall time frame. How much does music mean in your life now, and how much do you expect it to mean in fifteen years? Do you have career goals that can be fulfilled in a specific and realistic way, or are your musical aspirations simply unresolved fantasies?

These are difficult questions to answer, and the answers may lead to some tough decisions. One person may become totally dedicated to improving her craft, and another may set up a timetable for success with an alternate career option at the end of the experimental period. A third person may walk away from a musical career because it is too much of a long shot.

The purpose of this chapter, and to a certain extent of this whole book, is to help you to clarify your choices, not to give you pat answers. Take a long-term view of your career, and in that context, evaluate your choice of residence and answer the question of full-time versus part-time versus amateur musical career. Whatever you do, orient yourself toward realizing your goals in a creative and fulfilling way.

Chapter 13 Resources

Very little has been written about music as a part-time profession. I wrote one chapter about it in my out-of-print book, *Music Making in America*, published by Frederick Ungar in 1981. Books about careers in classical music are also scarce. A useful current resource is Ellen Highstein's *Making Music in Looking Glass Land: A Guide to Survival* and *Business Skills for the Classical Musician*, fourth edition, CAG, 2003. A good general career guide for music is Angela Myles Beeching's *Beyond Talent*, published by Oxford University Press, 2003. Randy Poe's *Music Publishing: A Songwriter's Guide*, third edition, published by Writer's Digest, 2005, is a reasonable guide to the business of songwriting.

CHAPTER 14
The History and Development of Regional Music Markets

From time to time in the music business, a number of secondary music markets have exploded, usually lit up by one or a few major talents. Some of these artists were able to build long-term careers, many of them disappeared, and most of the music scenes that spawned them (or was it the other way around?) have not shown the staying power over the years that characterizes the four major music markets of North America.

Detroit

One of the most spectacular and most consistent of all the regional scenes developed in the early 1960s around Motown Records in Detroit. Prior to Berry Gordy's efforts, the musical cachet that Detroit possessed came from the presence of such sterling jazz players as Kenny Burrell and Louis Hayes. Most of the jazzmen left at the first opportunity to go to New York, where the jazz scene was "really happening."

Motown records was built around the songwriting and production talents of Holland-Dozier-Holland, Mickey Stephenson, Smoky Robinson, and such artists as the Supremes, Martha and the Vandellas, the Temptations, the Miracles, Marvin Gaye, and Stevie Wonder. All of the work was supervised by the energetic business and creative perfectionism of Berry Gordy. There was a small but select group of studio musicians involved, especially the legendary bassist James Jamerson and drummer Bennie Benjamin.

Motown also had a talent management division that even schooled its artists to behave as ladies and gentlemen at any social occasion. The bulk of the hits were published through Jobete Music, the publishing wing of Motown. The management wing of Motown was responsible for the career advancement of its artists. All divisions of the company brought in revenues to keep Motown prospering. The company also employed choreographers to ensure that each act was carefully staged.

It seemed that the success of the company would never end. The Jackson 5 and the Commodores were signed, and the solo careers of Michael Jackson and Lionel Ritchie were also piloted by Motown. Possibly Berry Gordy simply became bored. He moved the company to Los Angeles so that he could become involved in the motion picture business. At the same time, he invested the company's money in Broadway shows. The star Detroit rhythm players were eventually replaced by Los Angeles studio players. When Motown left, the music business in Detroit vanished into thin air.

A few years ago I was in Detroit, and saw an ad in the local paper advertising that the "Motown All Stars" were performing at a local Holiday Inn. It was a sad commentary on the exodus of Motown. If there is a lesson here, it is that there needs to be more than one game in town for a local scene to develop and prosper. When Motown left Detroit, the music scene folded, because Motown was the pop music scene there.

An odd footnote to this store is the movie *Standing in the Shadows*. This movie, now available on video, details the lives of the Motown studio musicians. Gordy had a policy of not printing the names of the studio musicians who played on his records, and this video accomplishes its objective of paying tribute to these unsung heroes. It also has resulted in some gig and recording opportunities for these players.

In the last few years, several major figures have merged out of the Detroit scene. Eminem has become a major rap and movie star, as well as a record producer. Jack Black of the band the White Stripes has achieved a worldwide breakthrough as, not only with his duo the White Stripes, but by producing several Detroit bands.

Because records can now be made relatively cheaply using home studio gear, the possibility of artists emerging from dormant or non-existent music scenes is now present anywhere. The sort of records that involve the use of studio musicians, back-up singers and big-name producers is another story, but many of today's artists are not concerned with this level of production expertise.

The Philly Sound

In the late 1950s and early 1960s, Jamie/Guyden Records was born in Philadelphia. It developed around the talents of rockabilly idol and guitar hero Duane Eddy. Swan Records started at about the same time. Its most dramatic success occurred when Swan picked up the rights to a couple of English 45's by a little-known act called the Beatles.

The first major music scene in Philly was built around Cameo Parkway Records, the production and writing skills of Dave Appell and Kal Mann, and such acts as Chubby Checker, Bobby Rydell, and the Dovells.

Cameo's decline was caused partially by the success of the English rock groups and by the inability of the company to continue to come up with new acts to sustain their reign on the charts. Another factor in its demise was its attempt to expand into other areas of music, such as MOR and even folk rock. The founders of the company never really had a feel for these idioms.

Cameo's disappearance was followed by the success of the Philly Sound of writers-musicians-producers Gamble and Huff. They reigned supreme on the soul and pop charts in the 1970s, producing such acts as the O'Jays, the Spinners, Harold Melvin and the Blue Notes, Billy Paul, and others. Much of the Philly sound involved complex orchestral arrangements by the gifted arranger-composer-producer Thom Bell, who also wrote songs with lyricist Linda Creed. By the end of the 1970s, the Philly sound had run its course. However, Gamble and Huff continued to make records and experienced intermittent success. On the rock and roll side, the Hooters experienced some national chart success operating out of Philly.

Since the glory days, the town has experienced some successes in the rap and alternative rock fields. But Philadelphia is only ninety miles away from New York. This means that musicians and songwriters in the New York area are readily accessible to Philadelphia producers. However, the same proximity means that a large percentage of Philly-based talent heads for New York. It's also too close to New York to develop an independent corps of big-time managers, booking agents, or music business attorneys. It's too easy to get on the New Jersey Turnpike or hop on a train and head over to Manhattan.

There is something of a renaissance of chart-making black music in the Philadelphia area, especially the work of producer-writer-artist Missy Elliott. NARAS has established a Philadelphia chapter.

A recent article in the *New York Times* reported that a number of musicians and visual artists were starting to gravitate to Philadelphia from New York in search of lower-cost housing. If this development continues, it will certainly contribute to a revival of the Philly music scene.

New Orleans

New Orleans was the incubator for hit after hit in the 1950s. Fats Domino was the single most consistent hit-maker, but there were also hits by Ernie K. Doe, Huey Smith, Aaron Nevillle, Lloyd Price, and others. Many of these records involved the songwriting and arranging talents of Dave Bartholomew, and later on, the arranging, composing, and production talents of the legendary Allen Toussaint. Many of these hits were engineered in a thrown together studio by ace engineer Cossimo Matassa, but it didn't seem to translate into the modern multi-track world of white rock and roll. New Orleans lost its preeminence in rock, although the occasional superstar, like Paul McCartney, would go down to the Crescent City to work with Toussaint in his Sea Saint Studios. In recent years, Rounder Records, an important independent label, has recorded quite a few blues and Cajun records in New Orleans. These records have a modest but consistent sale, and do well in Europe. The Canadian producer Daniel Lanois had a studio in New Orleans, and produced some successful records with Bob Dylan, R.E.M., and Pearl Jam, among others, before moving on. The city retains its reputation as the home of traditional jazz, and the Marsalis brothers began their careers here. Rock acts Better Than Ezra and Cowboy Mouth are among a half-dozen acts with major label deals.

Rapper-entrepreneur-clothes designer Master P. has sold millions of rap and dance records on his No Limits label, and has also written and produced hits for various members of his family. Producer John Fischbach who has worked with Stevie Wonder and other hit artists now lives and works in New Orleans.

The annual Jazz and Heritage Festival is a major event, drawing hundreds of thousands of people from all over the world to the Crescent City. New Orleans has a temperate climate, and there is also quite a bit of jazz played outdoors, in the parks as well as in the clubs around the French Quarter. The versatile guitarist-singer Snooks Eaglin often performs locally. Because of the recent hurricane, it is difficult to predict the future of the New Orleans music scene. It is impossible to guess how many of the musicians who were compelled to leave will be able or willing to return.

Memphis and Points South

Memphis has its own story to tell. The first important pop records cut in Memphis were produced in a makeshift studio by the late Sam Phillips. Phillips started out recording black bluesmen in the early 1950s, but had in his mind the sound of a white man who would sing the blues and popularize it to the American teenager. He finally found that man in Elvis Presley. During the early Presley years, Phillips also successfully recorded Johnny Cash, Jerry Lee Lewis, Carl Perkins, and others. Phillips sold Presley's contract to RCA for $35,000, which he used to expand his recording operation. Presley went on to become an authentic superstar, and the early Sun Session recordings are still prized items among Presley fans. They were re-released by RCA (now known as BMG). Phillips had hoped that Carl Perkins would succeed Presley, and the Perkins recording of "Blue Suede Shoes" was a big hit. Unfortunately, Perkins got into a serious auto accident, and his career languished during his long recovery. Phillips drifted out of the record business, and was one of the early founders of the Holiday Inn.

Just as there were two generations of Philadelphia pop success, Sam Phillips's exit from the record business was followed by the meteoric rise of Stax and Volt Records. Throughout the 1960s and 1970s, a group of studio musicians who recorded under the name Booker T. and the M.G.'s. turned out numerous hits for themselves and other Stax artists. The same group was hired by producer Jerry Wexler to play on many Atlantic Records sessions. Successful Stax artists included Rufus and Irma Thomas, Sam and Dave, Otis Redding, Isaac Hayes, and the Markeys.

The company had a long and involved artistic and business history, much of it detailed in Peter Guralnick's excellent book *Sweet Soul Music*. An exhaustive study of the company is detailed by Rob Bowman in *Soulsville, USA*. This book offers a detailed view of the company's rise, evolution, and decline. Bowman points out that by 1973 the music industry was generating about $185 million per year, making it the third-largest commercial activity in the town and the fourth largest recording center in the world.

During this time, Willie Mitchell, an independent producer with his own record label, had considerable success with an instrumental group called the Bill Black Combo, but hit even richer paydirt with soul superstar Al Green. Green turned to gospel music, and although he's been quite successful in that field and at time worked again with Mitchell, the glory days are long gone.

All of Stax's success wasn't enough to nourish a permanent music scene, despite Memphis's long musical roots in the W.C. Handy blues tradition, and its role as a focal point for the bluesmen of the Mississippi Delta. After Stax folded, most of the scene went with it. However, Ardent Recording Studios hosted a number of the successful Z.Z. Top sessions, and there are other up-to-date studios in operation. Beale Street was considered one of the key centers for blues, and it currently is experiencing a sort of blues revival. The city has promoted the area as a major tourist attraction, and its annual W.C. Handy Awards are a sort of Grammy Awards of the blues.

The legendary Chips Moman also played a considerable role in the success of the Memphis sound. He cut some 120 pop, rock, and rhythm-and-blues hits at his American studios in Memphis. Many of these records were cut with co-writer Dan Penn. Both of them were also involved in the music scene in Muscle Shoals, Alabama.

Memphis developed into a regional jingle center, but nothing has replaced the preeminence of Stax. The town remains an active music community with a healthy deep-rooted respect for roots music. Memphis State University even has a record label that specializes in gospel and blues music. Some of the Stax artists, like Memphis Horns trumpeter Wayne Jackson still live here, as do producer Jim Dickinson and songwriter Keith Sykes. It's just that the glorious past was so dramatic that it all pales by comparison.

Another "happening" music area in the 1970s was in Muscle Shoals, Alabama. The town exists around a population base of about 100,000 people in four neighboring cities in Northern Alabama. In its heyday, the scene featured three thriving recording operations. Rick Hall's Fame Studios, Muscle Shoals Sound, formed by a group of rhythm players who left Hall to go out on their own, and the neighboring Wishbone Sound.

The Muscle Shoals rhythm players were considered among the best in the nation. They recorded hit after hit with such artists as Paul Simon, the Starland Vocal Band, and a long list of rhythm-and-blues-oriented acts, including Aretha Franklin. According to Charlie Gillette, writing in his book *Making Tracks*, the

Muscle Shoals players were willing to consider one song a single union recording session, whether it took ten minutes or ten hours to record the song. Jerry Wexler was one of the prime users of the Muscle Shoals rhythm section. When he moved to Miami he offered them a regular job as his rhythm section. They refused the opportunity, and the Muscle Shoals scene started to dissipate. Barry Beckett, the ace keyboard player of the section, moved to Nashville, and started playing on and producing country and western records. Some of the other players followed him to Nashville or to Memphis, and Wexler found himself another rhythm section.

Later, Muscle Shoals has experienced an odd revival. Country artists like Sawyer Brown and Earl Thomas Conley have cut records at Rick Hall's Fame Studio. There was a certain irony in the changeover from funk to country music. Many of the Muscle Shoals musicians enjoyed financial success by refining what are essentially black musical styles, yet they themselves are white. The blues and gospel label Malaco bought Hall's studio and operated it for several years, but were unable to make a go of the studio part of their operation. At the present writing, it appears that the long and distinguished rein of the Muscle Shoals Sound has come to a halt.

Miami

Even before Jerry Wexler moved to Miami, a music scene was developing there. An excellent studio complex, Criteria, had already recorded Crosby, Stills, Nash and Young. Other records were being cut by producer/engineer Bill Szymcyk. Henry Stone, a music business veteran active in record distribution and production experienced great initial success in the disco years. His act K.C. and the Sunshine Band didn't last, nor did the several successive hits by the Cornelius Brothers and Sister Rose lead to a long-term career. Another local group, Gloria Estefan and the Miami Sound Machine was able to establish itself as a major recording act, with a string of hits and nationwide support.

Miami is a major importer and exporter to all of Latin America. In recent years all of the major labels have established branches in the area that are primarily aimed at jumping into the expanding Latin American music market. Chris Blackwell, former CEO of Island Records, has a studio here, and is reportedly going to start a new label. It seems certain that Miami will be the major center for Spanish-language recording. As the population base of the United States becomes increasingly Spanish-speaking, Miami has become a significant if not a major music market in the twenty-first century. Miami has a large population of Cuban immigrants, but it also is home to people coming to the United States from virtually every country in Latin America.

A recent article in *Billboard* stated that Miami is now the fourth largest recording center in the United States. Not only do artists come here from all over Latin America to record, but recordings are made in Miami that are specifically intended to be sold in Latin America. Many of the musicians have immigrated from various parts of South America, so that it is easy to get a sound suitable for any country there. It may well be that in future years artists who want to tap into the Spanish-speaking market will come here in droves, in the same way that when musicians want a "country sound," they are apt to go to Nashville.

Atlanta, Macon, and Athens

For years, the late Bill Lowry has run a significant publishing and recording operation in Atlanta. Over the years, he produced hit records by such artists as Tommy Roe, Joe South, and the Atlanta Rhythm Section. His company remains active today, primarily as a music publisher. Atlanta is also an important regional jingle center, and a significant city for post-production work for television. Ted Turner's television networks have their headquarters in Atlanta.

In the 1990s, Atlanta has developed into one of the centers of black pop music. La Face Records is located in town, and there are a number of other successful producers and label owners. An article in the *New York Times* Arts and Leisure section by Kevin Sacks referred to the music scene as "an heir to Motown." Sacks listed Dallas Austin of Rowdy Records, Jermaine Dupri of So So Def Recordings, and Rico Wade of the Organized Noize production group as being among the prime movers and shakers. The town has a strong black music radio scene and some major black colleges. La Face Records provides a major recording label outlet for local productions. Founded by L.A. Reid and Babyface Edmonds, it has survived a split between the two principals. Edmonds returned to Los Angeles, and Reid also left, working as the CEO of Arista Records, before moving to Universal Records. In the Sacks article, Reid estimates that the company had a value of $100 million in 1998.

Capricorn Records made Macon, Georgia shine via the success of the Allman Brothers and the outstanding soul artist Otis Redding. The company was revived in the 1990s, and continues to record new music and to re-issue leased product on CD. Athens is a thriving college town, home of the University of Georgia. The B-52's and R.E.M. emerged from the live music scene in Athens to achieve national fame.

I have more to say about the Georgia music scene in the next chapter.

San Francisco and the Bay Area

Another rich regional music scene was the fabled San Francisco sound, epitomized by such bands as the Jefferson Airplane, Moby Grape, the Grateful Dead, and Quicksilver Messenger Service. San Francisco was one of the centers of pop-folk music in the late 1950s and early 1960s, serving as the incubation center for the Kingston Trio and the Smothers Brothers. It has a long history as a good jazz town, and Fantasy Records has had its offices here for years.

It is an unusual town, characterized by charm, diversity, and sophistication. The area has a large student population, with several universities in close proximity. San Francisco itself boasts an ethnically mixed and diversified population. The area directly south of the city is Silicon Valley, the computer heart of the world.

In the 1960s, the town became one of the centers of the hippie movement, with its flower power, use of psychedelic drugs, and love-ins. Record companies jumped on the avant-garde image and found themselves in a bidding war to sign the hot San Francisco rock acts. These groups were drawing thousands of people at clubs with unique light shows. There were also massive audiences at love-ins and open-air concerts in the park. Promoter and sometimes-manager Bill Graham was a spark plug of the local music scene. Modern FM radio was born here, with the freeform efforts of KSAN. Prior to the birth of the rock format on this station, FM was the sort of radio wasteland that we find on AM radio today. KSAN featured a high degree of community involvement, live music on the radio, and disc jockeys who saw their work as being artistic rather than simply commercial.

All of the San Francisco bands noted above were signed by major record labels, and all did quite well, with the exception of Moby Grape, a brief shooting star for Columbia. The Grateful Dead had a enduring career that was distinguished by lengthy and successful concert appearances, supported by a fanatical group of fans called "Deadheads." The band's career ended in the mid-1990s with the death of guitarist Jerry Garcia, although various combinations of band members continue to tour.

Janis Joplin also burst on the San Francisco scene, and after a brief career with Mainstream Records, was a major artist for Columbia. Sly and the Family Stone also stemmed from the Bay Area.

Creedence Clearwater Revival brought phenomenal success to the local Fantasy Records. After a long dispute with the company, Creedence lead singer-songwriter John Fogerty has recently returned to the label after its sale to Concord Records.

Ultimately, the season of love ended, and so did the San Francisco sound, but other subsequent popular groups were grounded in the San Francisco scene, such as Huey Lewis & the News, Metallica, and jazz guitarist Charley Hunter.

There are certain parallels to the dilemma of Philadelphia. San Francisco is 450 miles away from Los Angeles—about an hour by plane. Many of the local people gravitated south. The acid-rock style also became passé as we moved into the funk era of the 1970s.

Engineer-producer Fred Catero started a record label called Catero Records in San Francisco, and David Rubinson and Narada Michael Walden are Bay Area producers with successful track records. The late 1970s saw the re-emergence of San Francisco on the national scene with the birth and success of the Windham Hill record label. The label began its life in Palo Alto, and achieved great success with "New Age" music. Windham Hill started with acoustic guitar and piano music, but has spilled over into more of a jazz and world music orientation. Today it is owned by BMG, and has no presence in the Bay area.

There is a strong local music scene in San Francisco in jazz, classical music, and to some extent in folk and New Age music. There are also dozens of small "alternative rock" labels in Berkeley and San Francisco. Many musicians are supported through the active club scene, and radio stations and some strong independent record stores, like Amoeba Music, make a point of featuring local music. The popularity of relatively esoteric music, such as classical or world music can be attributed to the sophistication of the San Francisco population and the presence of so many colleges. The annual NARAS-sponsored San Francisco Music Fair also fuels the local scene. George Lucas's Luke Skywalker Ranch has an excellent audio facility, and there are some opportunities for musicians to play on film scores. The late Bill Graham is gone, but his promotional activities continue through his company, Bill Graham Presents, currently a division of media conglomerate Clear Channel. The main problem is, once again, the comparison to past glories, and the easy proximity of that old devil Los Angeles.

Boston

The San Francisco sound exposed some authentic musical talents to the national music scene; this was not the case with the MGM Records–promoted "Bosstown" (Boston) sound. Apparently, MGM realized that Boston was a college town too, and had its own share of crazed hippies in the late 1960s. So MGM signed a group of forgettable Boston bands, and under the guiding hand of producer Alan Lorber, dumped thousands of dollars into what proved to be a vacuum. Nothing came of the Boston sound except a large tax loss for MGM and discouragement for a group of unhappy bands. Before Lorber's folly, there was an extremely active folk scene in Boston, which included Joan Baez, and Jim Kweskin and the Jug Band, promoter-manager Manny Greenhill, and a considerable number of singer-songwriters, many of whom still live in the area.

Boston is home to an extraordinary number of colleges, including the Berklee College of Music and the New England Conservatory. There are local jingles and fairly lucrative opportunities for local musicians to play in shows that are trying out in Boston before heading for the Big Apple. During the 1980s, Maurice Starr found and produced the archetypal teenybopper band New Kids on the Block, but he has left town without further comparable successes. The world is still waiting for a "Boston sound." The lesson to be drawn from the Boston debacle is that a regional music style must have some integrity. Simply selling artists on the basis that they are from Des Moines is not going to induce thousands of record buyers to flock to the stores to support the Iowa sound!

Austin

Austin, Texas, represents a different sort of musical atmosphere. The night-club scene has always been a significant part of the Austin musical canvas. When the Texas Music Conference sponsored its first South by Southwest musical gathering in 1986, it flew in dozens of music industry folks from both coasts to view two hundred bands playing in clubs during a four-day period. At that conference, twenty record company offers were tendered to the bands and soloists who performed during the festivities. The festival remains one of the most significant regional music festivals in North America, attended by dozens of record company personnel, music publishers, bands, fans, and "wannabes." SXSW has also added a film and media festival the week before the music confab, and has franchised similar events in Toronto, and briefly in Portland, Oregon, before the locals took control of one themselves.

Austin has always been a center for young, single people who have the energy and interest to go out at night. There is the huge University of Texas campus, and also the state government, with its large number of employees. A variety of musical interest groups are present in this varied population. It is interesting that many college towns, such as Athens, Georgia; Bloomington, Indiana; Ann Arbor, Michigan; Madison, Wisconsin; and Durham and Chapel Hill, North Carolina, have some sort of active music scene. Many of these scenes are derivative folk-influenced scenes, not necessarily ones that reflect main-stream pop music values.

Part of Austin's appeal for musicians has to do with its role as a sort of cultural refuge for the person who doesn't feel at home in Dallas, Houston, Lubbock, or El Paso. By the end of the 1960s into the early 1970s, Austin experi-enced a great influx of musical talent. There was Steve Fromholz, a consummate writer and entertainer who achieved local and regional fame, Rusty Weir, the ultimate bar musician, B.W. Stephenson, with his one big hit "My Man" for RCA; Jerry Jeff Walker, the transplanted New Yorker who wrote "Mr. Bojangles"; the sardonic rock madness of Kinky Friedman and His Texas Jewboys; and there was Michael Martin Murphy, with his hit, "Wildfire." Murphy invented the Cosmic Cowboy and then drifted north to Colorado to escape his image, and south to Taos, New Mexico, to become a pioneer in the revival of "Western" music. Most of all, there was Willie Nelson. More than any of the other Austin performers, Willie Nelson had the ability to bring the entire music scene together. Everybody was a Nelson fan, from ladies with beehive hairdos to truck drivers, ropers, freaks of all descriptions, and the university crowd.

In the same way, Nelson brought different aspects of the music together as well. His band was a mixture of old and new. He could play old-time country songs, his own ballads, or the up-tempo honky-tonk style of music that could bring a bar crowd to its feet. Nelson had his beard and pony tail, and he looked more like a hippie than a cowboy, but he talked more like a cowboy than a hippie. His performances at the famous club, Armadillo World Headquarters, became legendary, as did his Fourth of July picnics, where every social class in Austin got together to drink beer and party in the hot Texas summer.

Musically, Nelson was the original "outlaw." He and Waylon Jennings defied the Nashville establishment with their long hair and their insistence on retaining control over the artistic components of their records. Nelson eventually built a studio called Lone Star, where he sometimes recorded and where other local musicians cut sessions. He also befriended some of his local buddies by recording their songs, probably earning these writers far more money than their years of nightclub performances had reaped.

Austin was not a racially mixed music scene, in the sense that Stax Records had been. Its obvious country roots were represented by Kenneth Threadgill. He was a "hillbilly" singer who ran a bar in the early 1960s that provided, among other things, welcome shelter for a young and troubled Janis Joplin. However, the Austin scene did cover plenty of ground outside of country music. It drew on such Texas bluesmen as Mance Lipscomb and Lightnin' Hopkins.

From the mid-1970s, Antone's became the home of live blues music in Austin. The Fabulous Thunderbirds with Jimmy Vaughan were the houseband, and Jimmy's brother, guitar idol Stevie Ray Vaughan, cut a lot of his musical teeth there. Blues singers Marcia Ball and Angela Strehli were other local favorites. Not content with his nightclub and record store, Clifford Antone started a record label that enabled some of his artists to achieve some national recognition.

In 1976, the *Austin City Limits* television show appeared for the first time. The show was nationally syndicated, and became one of the most popular shows on public television. The first season showcased only local Austin performers, but over the years there has been a mix of the Austin fixtures, along with visitors like Chet Atkins, Jimmy Buffett, and Merle Haggard. For the most part, the show has been country-oriented, and this probably fueled the notion that Austin is a country and western music scene.

What the Austin music scene has that so many local music scenes lack is the ability to constantly re-invent itself with new talent that feeds and extends the music. Singer-songwriters have always comprised the heart of the Austin music scene. Willis Alan Ramsey, author of "Muskrat Love," and the late Townes Van Zandt, who wrote "Pancho and Lefty," were important participants in the 1960s. More recent singer-songwriters include Nanci Griffith, who wrote "Love at the Five and Dime," and the talented and quirky Lyle Lovett. Neither of them record or live in Austin, but the town is an important aspect of their musical and psychological roots.

The city of Austin has lent its support to the music scene by hiring a liason to the music community who works on such prosaic but real problems as creating proper loading zones in the congested Sixth Street nightclub area, so that musicians don't have to trek for blocks carrying amplifiers and P.A. equipment. In general, Austin seems to want to promote itself as a music town, just as Nashville calls itself Music City, USA.

Because Austin has a warm climate, and because virtually all pop musicians know about the South by Southwest Music Festival and the Sixth Street club scene, musicians have been visiting Austin for thirty years now. Often they end up staying there. By virtue of this longevity, the Austin music scene has proven itself in a more significant way than virtually any of the other local or regional scenes. Other music communities may have started out bigger, or peaked higher, but they also suffered precipitous declines.

In order for Austin to sustain its musical scene, there needs to be an emasis on more locally recorded product. Watermelon Records has provided some of that impetus, and Arista-Texas had its headquarters in Austin. Arista-Texas was a visionary attempt to capitalize on the Austin–San Antonio scene, releasing both singer-songwriter and Tejano music recordings. Unfortunately, when CEO Tim DuBois left Arista-Nashville, his brainchild did not survive. San Antonio, less than a hundred miles south, has a major Tejano music scene, and Austin would probably benefit by more direct interaction with that community. There is a music-business program at Austin Community College, but the University of Texas music department has no direct connection with the popular music community. The university media programs have been more generous. *Austin City Limits* is televised at the university, and there is a significant college radio station. There is clearly a need for more of an overall infrastructure to build the local community—personal managers, agents, music industry attorneys, record producers, engineers, and recording studios. There *is* a thriving advertising community here.

One of the keys to Austin's future is whether the major writers and artists who come out of this scene can be induced to stay there to record, and to invest their dollars in the local music community. As long as the talented writers and recording artists are going to Nashville and Los Angeles to record, and even to live, they are making a statement that something is missing in the local scene.

Austin plays a unique role in terms of the overall Texas scene. Texas is a huge landmass that is dotted by cities in different sections of the state that vary from being rather typical, suburbanite mall-infested areas to cities whose basic function is to provide a business center for a particular geographic and cultural area. It was acceptable to have long hair and a beard in Austin when there were parts of the state where doing so would subject the bearer to abuse or physical harm.

Since rock and roll, "outlaw" country and contemporary folk music have always had a rather thin alliance with society's "straight" values, Austin became a place of refuge for musicians and other artists seeking to escape an oppressive cultural climate. The Austin country writers followed Nelson's lead in the sense that they envisaged themselves outside of the Nashville mill that so efficiently organizes the composition, manufacture, and distribution of country and western music.

Houston

During the 1990s, Houston began to emerge as a major hip-hop scene. Such acts as Slim Thug, Mike Jones, Paul Wall, UGK, and Lil' Flip took up the mantle from the Geto Boys, emerging with major label record deals and strong music publishing affiliations. Only time will tell if this scene can sustain itself, but Houston is a major population center, and would seem to have great potential as a regional music market.

A recent *New York Times* feature article by Kelefa Sanneh, which appeared on April 17, 2005, details the success of Houston's rap scene, which Sanneh describes as producing "some of the country's best and weirdest rap music since the late 1980s." Local independent label Swisha House has developed a partnership with Warner Brothers Records. At the time the article was written, three solo rappers were about to make major label debuts, quite a feather in Houston's musical cap.

During the 1960s, local labels Peacock and Duke achieved national success, but the current scene seems to have evolved out of the work of a 1990s remixer named DJ Screw, whose mix tapes influenced and inspired the current set of rappers.

Minneapolis

Bob Dylan was probably the first music superstar to come from Minnesota, but because all of his recordings took place in the major music-business towns, his emergence was more of a general spiritual encouragement than anything else. During the late 1950s and early 1960s, Minneapolis was a regional jingle center, and also played a prominent role in the folk music revival. Koerner, Ray, and Glover were among the leading white blues singers on the coffeehouse circuit who helped to bring about the re-awakening of consciousness in America's blues roots.

Minneapolis has always been an important center for the sale and distribution of records. Target Stores are headquartered here with their own internal rack jobber division. This differs from most other department and discount stores who usually order from outside rack jobbers. Rack jobbers stock and service these outlets for a percentage of the store's record sales. They are, in effect, renting space in the stores K-Tel, the record oldies television outlet, and Pickwick International, another major record manufacturer and distributor, which is headquartered here.

In the 1980s, two significant developments influenced the Minneapolis music scene. First came the astounding success of (the artist formerly known as) Prince. He put together bands, arrangers, and a production team and opened a massive studio facility called Paisley Park. Other producers and arrangers like David Z. (Rivkin) and his brother Bobby soon emerged from projects that involved Prince, his band members, or acts that he signed to the WEA-distributed Paisley Park label.

Secondly, there was the brilliant and consistent record production team of Jimmy Jam and Terry Lewis. Originally associated with a Prince-controlled band from which they were fired, Jam and Lewis have won dozens of writing, and publishing awards to go with their 1986 Grammy Producers of the Year Award. The Minneapolis scene includes other musical idioms as well. Michael Johnson, who has achieved success in the pop and country-pop fields, lives there and has done some recording in the area. So does semi-legendary guitar guru Leo Kottke. Garrison Keillor has returned to broadcast the *Prairie Home Companion* radio show, after a brief hiatus in New York. This program provides a key forum for folk, country, and occasional jazz musicians in the area.

Prince's record label did not achieve success with the WEA group, and the label and Prince himself are no longer connected with WEA. There are many live outlets for music in the Minneapolis–St. Paul area, and Red House has emerged as a leading folk music record company. A thriving booking agency called the Good Music Agency has emerged as an important force on the local music scene.

Minneapolis also has a symphony orchestra, as well as a unique group called the St. Paul Chamber Orchestra, perhaps the most outstanding ensemble of its kind in North America. The presence of these ensembles makes quality string and woodwind players available for recording sessions. This makes it possible to do the sort of feature film and television work that requires good orchestras. The Guthrie Theater is a strong regional theater with a repertory company. It contributes to, and is a reflection of, the health of the cultural scene in the Twin Cities area. The advertising business has always been strong here, and the state film commission promotes the music community as well as seeking to induce Hollywood productions to shoot here.

The problem with developing an extensive music business mechanism in the Twin Cities is that the power centers of the music industry remain on both coasts. For a major talent management operation to work, the people involved would have to be willing to become virtual bicoastal commuters. Perhaps a better possibility is the establishment of Twin City offices for companies that headquarter in Los Angeles or New York. This is more likely to occur in Chicago. With the recent move by Jimmy Jam and Terry Lewis to open another studio in Los Angeles, it is open to conjecture how long they will retain their allegiance to Minneapolis. That loss would be a devastating blow to the Minneapolis music scene.

Chicago

The Chicago music scene has had a long and interesting story of its own. At one time, all of the major record companies had staff offices in Chicago, and the corporate offices of Mercury, now part of Universal, was headquartered here. Chicago had a hot rhythm-and-blues scene in the 1950s, sparked by producer Carl Davis. In the late 1950s and 1960s, Jerry Butler had periodic success as an artist, and other major success was enjoyed by Curtis Mayfield and his group, the Impressions. Chess and Vee Jay records were important producers of blues and rhythm-and-blues records through the 1960s.

Today, the major labels have gone, but there are several important blues labels based in Chicago. Blues giant Alligator Records and its friendly competitor, blues-jazz label Delmark, remain in the Windy City. Chicago remains an important center for jingles, with the giant Leo Burnett Advertising Agency based here. In recent years, Chicago has slipped behind Los Angeles as the number two advertising center for jingles, with New York remaining the top player.

There are several major recording studios here that do recording work for CDs, film, and television. Chicago had a big hand in the folk music revival, and spawned the talents of numerous folk revivalists and singer-songwriters, including Steve Goodman and John Prine. There was also an important gospel music community, with T.J. Dorsey and Mahalia Jackson bringing notoriety and attention to the gospel music scene. Recently, there has been an upsurge of successful recording artists operating out of Chicago, including Liz Phair and Smashing Pumpkins, and such rock alternative acts as Freakwater for Thrill Jockey Records. There are a number of small labels headquartered here but at the moment Chicago lacks a distinct musical identity, outside the blues clubs and record labels. Controversial indie rock engineer-producer Steve Albini is a fixture on the local music scene.

Bloomington, Indiana

The Bloomington scene is centered around the indie rock label Strictly Canadian. Currently the label has signed about twenty acts, and they own their own distribution, which carries over fifteen labels. The label's own records are distributed through Warner Music Group's Alternative Distribution Alliance. As is the case with Omaha's saddle Creek, artist Jason Molina has issued a number of albums for the label using different names and differing personnel. Label act Antony & the Johnsons has sold over 60,000 copies in England, underlining the current international nature of the music industry. The label's biggest domestic success has been with cult artist Sufjan Stevens.

Portland, Oregon

The Portland music scene has never had a single artist or musical style that has galvanized the musical scene here. It has been more like a steady proliferation of mainstream rock (with a touch of the blues) bands and acts, like Robert Cray, Quarterflash, Jeff Lorber, the Dandy Warhols, Cherry Poppin' Daddies, Everclear, the Decembrists, and Meredith Brooks making their way into the major record companies and larger music communities.

Portland talent has also periodically enjoyed support from local radio stations. Although this may not make a major difference in the big picture of national music exposure, it has provided a basic part of nurturing and developing for the Northwest music community. Quarterflash's record *Harden My Heart* sold ten thousand copies in Portland and Seattle before Geffin Records picked it up and helped it go platinum.

There is a very strong independent-record-store scene here, with Music Millenium at the top of the heap with two well-stocked outlets. They also operate a national record distribution company called Burnside. There are a number of small and even tiny independent record labels in the Northwest, spread throughout Washington and Oregon, including the Kill Rock Stars label in Olympia, Washington.

Another focus of the Portland music scene was an annual rock and roll charity ball. The proceeds go to charities and some fifty bands perform throughout the evening. Bud Clark, the former mayor or Portland, was a big supporter of this event, formerly called the Mayor's Ball. Two mayors later, the ball seems poised to re-appear on the scene.

So far, Portland is yet to produce a musical superstar, although Art Alexakis has tasted considerable success with his band, Everclear. Local band Pink Martini is an underground sensation, with their first CD selling over half a million copies in Europe. Nevertheless, there is a steady stream of bands forming, maturing, performing, and getting recording deals and local airplay. Many of these bands have been able to tour nationally, and have sustained relatively successful careers without enjoying hit records. There is a strong local blues scene, with a massive annual Waterfront Blues Festival.

Other music-related enterprises have also begun to prosper. Weiden and Kennedy is a local advertising agency that created the Nike "Just Do It" campaign, and has expanded to the point where it has offices in Europe. *Willamette Week* is the local weekly paper, and it provides good music coverage in a generally well-written paper. *Willamette Week* is now the primary sponsor of the NXNW Music Festival that was originally brought here by the Austin SXSW people. Other music papers, including the *Two Louies* deal specifically with local music. Ex-Gang of Four bassist David Allen is a presence on the scene, and, as mentioned above, Pink Martini are extremely successful in Europe and are local celebrities.

Other Scenes

If you read the national music trades, like *Billboard* or *Radio and Records*, and look for the local music and entertainment magazines, you can follow the development of regional music markets. Practically every medium-sized or college town has a free local weekly paper with entertainment coverage.

There are always some music scenes developing in the most unlikely parts of North America. New Jack City musical guru Teddy Riley has his studio in Virginia Beach, the hit-making producers the Neptunes also headquarter in Virginia, rap producer Jay King continues to work in Sacramento and John Mellencamp records in a home studio on a farm near Bloomington, Indiana. Albuquerque has an interesting fusion of Native American and Chicano music, and Tom Bee has created a sort of Indian Motown there. The other leading producer of Native American music is Canyon Records, located in Phoenix. San Antonio is the major center for the recording of Tejano music. For years, Chip Davis has been crafting Mannheim Steamroller Records at his Sound Recordings studio in Omaha. Recently Omaha label Saddle Creek Records has established a national presence through the recordings of Connor Oberst (Bright Eyes). Many of these records have sold multi-platinum, and are an industry unto themselves. Recently, Vancouver and Toronto have developed into major television and film production centers, not just for Canadian productions, but for numerous American movies and television shows.

There are always certain fundamental ingredients behind the evolution of American popular music, at least in the rock and roll era. Rock music is a fusion of elements drawn from the roots of the blues, country and gospel music. On the country music side are old fiddle tunes, Appalachian Mountain ballads, and the sort of vocal style that Alan Lomax refers to as "closed-throat singing." This vocal style is an anguished nasal, pinched cry. The black or Afro-American tradition includes field hollers, work songs, call-and-response chants, an "open-throat" vocal style, and adaptations of European culture mixed with African elements, like bottleneck-blues guitar style. Blues employs the "metronome sense" of the African drummer. Bluegrass, by contrast, is notorious for its high, lonesome vocal sounds and the frequently used device of speeding up tempos during a performance.

Most of these regional scenes contain interesting fusions of black-and-white musical style, such as the peculiarity of Muscle Shoals with its all-white, but funk-oriented rhythm players. Memphis was unique in that the Booker T. and the MG's rhythm section was a racially integrated group.

The Philly and Motown sounds derived from black sounds were laundered with white musical mannerisms, such as string sections on the Philly records, and Motown's simplified four beats to the bar, devised to appeal to the white teenager.

Local Markets Ebb and Flow

In looking at the way that scenes start, grow, and change, there are a few similarities that emerge from these creative and business explosions:

1. **Overdependency on a single account or producer.** Since the average career of a record producer has been estimated to last five years, clearly a single producer cannot sustain a music scene's long-term growth. Even the most successful producers are apt to move to another locale to use a different group of musicians, studios, or arrangers or simply because they want to sample another scene.

2. **Focus on a single musical style.** American popular music is distinguished mostly by its unpredictability. No one knows what the next successful musical innovation will be, or where it may originate. Reliance on specific musical styles to the exclusion of experimentation and growth is almost a certain invitation to a scene cresting and meeting its demise, as the musical style goes through the stages of innovation, success, imitation, rust and neglect.

3. **Lack of overall music business development in conjunction with successful records.** Many of the towns discussed, like New Orleans, didn't have a full-time music business apparatus. These towns lacked a jingle, film, music publishing, or television business that could provide additional work for studio musicians, composers, and arrangers. The absence of music publishers inhibits the growth of a vital songwriting community. There also needs to be a music business community of lawyers, personal and business managers and accountants that can service the business of the music community.

4. **Financial ability to keep up with the latest technology.** Purchasing and exploring the latest recording paraphernalia and electronic musical instruments is an expensive and time-consuming process. Many regional scenes cannot support this aspect of development. As each new format appears, it may be necessary for a studio to totally abandon its existing equipment, or to create another recording room to house the new gear. In the same way that musical scenes rise and fall, recording studios become the talk of the business, and then may be forgotten.

5. **Presence of a vital live music scene.** There has to be some place for talent to emerge, polish its skills, get audience feedback, and develop a following. Some towns, like Philadelphia, historically had restrictive liquor laws that discouraged nightclubs. When the laws were finally changed, the scene had moved to surrounding suburban areas in another county or state.

6. **Government support.** Although government support cannot create a scene, it can assist in sustaining and expanding it. This support can be tied in to each state's film commission, but very few states have chosen to follow this path.

7. **Media support.** Media support includes music papers, better music coverage in daily papers, the presence of a college radio station that plays different styles of music outside the mainstream, and assistance from local record stores, unions, and the creation of viable local and regional music organizations. It is also important to try to convince existing privately owned radio stations to feature a local music show.

8. **Music business education.** There are an increasing number of colleges teaching classes that discuss the music business, and hands-on classes in music engineering. It is logical that some of the graduates of these programs will be the future spark plugs of their local music scenes. A number of these schools have even started their own record labels, a good way to provide hands-on experience.

To evaluate all of these factors, take a look at the chart on the following page. Clearly, the first ingredient for a healthy music scene is the presence of local talent that is worth recording. Next, there has to be a local studio that is

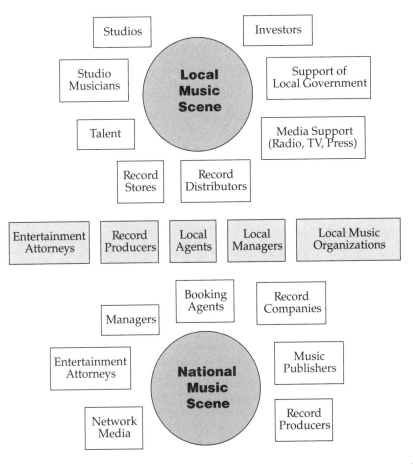

good enough to get that sound on tape. This, in turn, requires the presence of musicians, engineers and producers.

None of this can happen unless someone or some group of investors provide financial backing. The investors can be the band itself, a recording studio, a manager, family or friends, bankers lending money based on proven equity from a music publishing company, or a group of investors who buy shares in a recording project. To pare it down to the essentials there must be:

1. Talent to be recorded.

2. Money to complete the recording.

3. Talent in the studio that is capable of carrying out the production.

4. A manager to sell the product to a record company, or the group must have an alternate plan to put the record out themselves.

5. The local music scene needs to nurture the act, by providing local radio play and reviews from the local-music press.

6. Local music stores who carry and display the record.

7. Publicity apparatus in place to create excitement about the group.

8. Managers to help build careers, and agents to get work for the artists.

A key ingredient to the longevity of music scenes is the development of musical variety. Of all the major music scenes, only Nashville is still predominantly identified with a single musical style. Although this may be an unjust label in the sense that there really is a great variety of music available in Nashville, in the mind of the public and most of the music industry, Nashville is a country-music town. Country music brings in the artists, the fans, the songwriters and the dollars. Nashville has survived because country music has gone through numerous trends and fads, while retaining a core base of fans.

Nashville is an exception to the rule. The identification of Memphis and Muscle Shoals with rhythm-and-blues music may have made these towns but it also led to their eclipse. The same goes for the Philly sound. Motown is probably the other exception to the rule, but they left Detroit and some of their artists, like Marvin Gaye and Stevie Wonder, evolved in new musical directions far beyond the scope of the original Motown sound.

This has been a brief survey of how a music scene develops, the ingredients that reinforce the music, and where the process leads. It is my hope that this has given you some encouragement for helping to build a viable music scene wherever you may live.

Note: There are many other meaningful regional music scenes, such as the one surrounding King Records in Cincinnati, and the story of Peacock Records in Houston. Other product has emerged from Jackson, Mississippi; Cleveland,

Ohio; Sacramento, California; and the beach music scene of Virginia and South Carolina. We shouldn't overlook the alternative product coming out of Chapel Hill, North Carolina, from Mammoth and Merge Records, or artist Ani DiFranco's successes with her Righteous Babe label in Buffalo and Houston's thriving rap music scene.

Chapter 14 Resources

There are many books available on the music scenes in the towns discussed in this chapter. They are listed in the Appendix of this book. There is really no detailed general discussion of regional music in any other books that I have seen.

CHAPTER 15

Seattle and Denver: A Tale of Two Cities, with Excursions to Atlanta and Georgia

Now that we've mapped the fundamentals of how regional music scenes operate, let's take a look at two very different regional music scenes.

Seattle

The history of the Seattle music scene includes some early hits by a vocal group called the Fleetwoods. Their first hit, "Come Softly to Me," hit the charts in 1959. Shortly thereafter, the rock instrumental combo, the Ventures, achieved national success with their recording of "Walk—Don't Run." In the late 1960s and early 1970s, Paul Revere and the Raiders, dressing in Revolutionary War–styled costumes, made a number of hit records.

The first edition of this book was written in 1989. At that point, Queensrÿche was the best-known Seattle band. It was a sort of progressive heavy-metal band pushing the aesthetic borders of that style of music. Subsequently, a series of events occurred that evolved into the explosion dubbed "the Seattle sound."

A local label called Sub Pop began its life as a fan magazine in 1979. By 1986, it had turned into a record company. It then released a series of albums by several (then) obscure bands: Soundgarden, Nirvana, and a band called Mother Love Bone that later evolved into Pearl Jam.

Sub Pop was founded by two young punk-oriented fans named Bruce Pavitt and Jonathan Poneman. From the first it was their intention to create a regional music scene. Lacking the money that MGM had dumped into the ill-fated Boston sound, the two partners proceeded along somewhat different lines. They enlisted photographer Charles Peterson and producer-engineer Jack Endino to work on almost all of the Sub Pop products. The idea was to create a somewhat uniform look and sound, even though the bands signed were rather different from one another. They invested some money in flying Everett True, a writer for the English music magazine *Melody Maker*. True wrote a series of profiles and stories that established the credibility of the Seattle music scene. It worked beyond anyone's wildest dreams and, by the mid-1990s, there were some thirty bands in Seattle with national recording deals, plus many more on the dozens of local labels that emerged with the success of the so-called "grunge" bands.

Sony even hired an A&R rep to live in Seattle and provide the company with leads to the newest hot bands. By the mid-1990s, Sub Pop had sold 49% of the company to the huge Warner Brothers–WEA organization. This enabled the company to obtain substantial financing to sign acts, expand their catalog, and promote their product.

Initially, most of the record companies believed that Seattle's success was simply a temporary boom based on the sound of Soundgarden, the first of the 1990s bands to hit big. When Alice in Chains, Nirvana, and Pearl Jam all became major acts in quick succession, the boom hit epidemic proportions. New bands were created by the minute, and existing bands and unemployed musicians flocked to Seattle to inhale the magic elixir of grunge.

In fact, there was a stronger foundation to Seattle's music scene than these bands. Sir Mix-a-Lot achieved some major success in rap music, Kenny G. is a long-term resident, and for years Seattle, has had an important folk scene centered around two massive music festivals that occur during the Memorial Day and Labor Day weekends. In fact, Douglas Mays, a local booking agent quoted in Clark Humphrey's book *Loser: The Seattle Music Story*, has said that "Seattle has more different kinds of bands, and more studios per capita, than maybe any other city in America. We still need a pressing plant, but we have just about all the other elements to become a major music center."

One of the major catalysts for local music was a music paper called *The Rocket*, which appeared every two weeks. Browsing through its pages revealed an active recording scene and a passionate involvement with music (sadly, this paper no longer exists). The paper started as a monthly insert to the *Seattle Sun*, in 1979. The *Sun* was an alternative paper in Seattle during this period, in the style pioneered by the *Village Voice* in New York.

Recording Studios

Like a number of other cities, Seattle has experienced some attempts to turn it into a major center for film work and recording. This included a studio called Smith-Kaye and a temporary move to the area by Hollywood director Stanley Kramer.

Neither of these experiments worked out, but Seattle hit the media jackpot with the opening of Bad Animals Recording Studio. Bad Animals was a partnership between longtime Seattle residents the Wilson Sisters, lead singers of the band Heart, and multi-media producer Steve Lawson. The association with Lawson virtually guaranteed activity in the areas of film, television, and commercials, while the cachet of the Wilson Sisters brought in the rock and rollers and the record projects. Eventually, the partnership dissolved. Lawson operated the studio as a multi-media operation, and eventually sold out to some of his employees, who continue to operate it today.

Bear Creek is another large studio operation that is more of a CD project studio, with a rural farmhouse location. It tends to be blocked out for longtime periods for bands who are recording album projects. Soundgarden recorded their Superunknown project at Bear Creek.

A student of mine named Scott Liss did a survey of Seattle studios in the mid-1990s. He uncovered twelve relatively inexpensive studio operations that had recording capabilities ranging from sixteen to thirty-two tracks, and rates of $20 to $35 per hour. The mayor's office on film listed about four dozen such studios as of May 2005. Certainly, the range of studios is adequate to service the needs of everyone from garage bands who intend to produce their own records, to world-class bands recording with big budgets for major labels.

Personal Managers, Agents, Etc.

Part of the support system that builds major music scenes is the presence of a major music business infrastructure. This includes the various aspects of the business that are not apparent to the general public, such as management companies, booking agencies, and entertainment attorneys. Although Susan Silver Management handled Soundgarden and Alice in Chains, there is nothing here comparable to what is in Los Angeles. A single entertainment attorney, Neil Sussman, seems to be well known in the Seattle area, and he advertises in local music periodicals.

Live Music

During the mid-1990s, Clark Humphrey reported almost two dozen "over-twenty-one" clubs and bars that featured original live music in Seattle, Tacoma, Olympia, and Bellingham. As long as the Seattle economy, jointly fueled by Microsoft and Boeing, continues to boom, this trend will almost certainly continue. Downtown Seattle is congested and offers limited parking. This will certainly be a deterrent to the expansion and even continuation of an active live-music scene in the downtown area. Another negative is that the city seems disinterested in the local music scene, except for its attempts to ban concert posters. The state offers even less support. Local musicians have had to fight to keep the state legislature from passing offensive censorship bills. On the other hand, the presence of a number of college and universities in the area, especially the giant University of Washington in Seattle, provide a built-in audience for live music.

Other Aspects of Seattle Music

Paul Allen, the multi-millionaire co-founder of Microsoft, has built the Experience Music Project, a museum originally intended honor Seattle native Jimi Hendrix. It has been transformed into a rock and roll museum. Its location near the Seattle Space Needle has brought an influx of tourists which will almost certainly have a positive long-term effect on the government's attitude toward the rock music scene.

An odd sidebar to the Seattle music universe is the presence of background music giant Muzak. This resulted from a merger of the New York Muzak Company with the Seattle Yesco Foreground Music Company. All operations were moved to Seattle. Although the company has little relevance to the Seattle rock music scene as such, it does provide employment for programmers, engineers, and music editors. Among the ex-employees are Sub-Pop founders Pavitt and Poneman.

Seattle has an active folk scene, with a huge annual Folklife Festival, and a more rock-oriented festival called Bumbershoot. The world music scene includes a strong ethnomusicology department at the University of Washington. Quite a few important musicians, like guitarists Bill Frissell and Peter Buck from R.E.M., have chosen to live here, as has popular sax player Kenny G.

Record Companies

Clark Humphreys lists almost eighty active local record companies in the Appendix of *Loser*. This does not include labels that are really a single band putting out their own album. This is a very large number of companies for a city with less than three quarters of a million people. Naturally, many of these companies have primarily local distribution, but as the scene has developed, more possibilities exist for distribution deals with larger companies, or even the purchase of these labels. Sub-Pop is now owned by Warner brothers, but it still headquarters here, and is by far the largest of the Seattle record companies.

General Ambiance

Seattle is definitely one of the "magic" cities in the United States, where people like to come and visit, fall in love with the general atmosphere and quality of life, and decide to stay. There is the ocean, the mountain views, the houseboats, and a generally cosmopolitan feeling about the area reminiscent of San Francisco.

Another part of the lifestyle is the ever-present coffee and espresso houses, the colorful Pike Street Market, and the rain. The nearby presence of Vancouver (British Columbia) itself is quite a thriving and attractive city, and such neighboring or nearby towns as Tacoma, Olympia, Bellingham, and, not all that far away, Portland, contribute to the notion that the Northwest has a unique identity. Every one of these towns has a large college community, which provides an ideal audience for new and regional music styles.

Can It Continue?

Midway into the first decade of the twenty-first century, the Seattle music scene is no longer the flavor of the week. Soundgarden has broken up, Nirvana is no more, and although Pearl Jam continues, it is no longer the super group of the early 1990s. Nevertheless, new bands seem to continually emerge from the rain. Built to Spill and Tuatara are on Warner Brothers, Sub Pop has a bunch of new groups, and several other bands enjoy major label deals. Dave Grohl has merged from the wreckage of Nirvana with the Foo Fighters, and who knows how many other groups are woodshedding in garages and basements. Krist Novaselic, Nirvana's bass player, is still here, and plays music and delivers political lectures.

In 1993, the Christian label Tooth and Nail moved to Seattle, to add yet another ingredient to this eclectic scene. Certainly what Seattle does have is a viable music community that raises some interesting questions about the growth and longevity of a regional music scene.

Denver: Some Would Rather Be in Colorado

I moved to Colorado from the New York area in 1972. After ten years of studio work, songwriting, and record production, Colorado was quite a shock. At the time, it seemed everyone was moving there. Oil companies were booming at the time, and Western Colorado was supposed to become the oil shale capitol of the United States. John Denver was singing songs about the Rocky Mountain high. People thronged into the state from California, Texas, New York, and other places. The band Firefall was headquartered in Boulder, and they and Dan Fogelberg did some recording at a studio called North Star. Jim Guercio build a studio at his Caribou Ranch north of Boulder, and all sorts of major artists recorded there, including the Beach Boys, Elton John, and Chicago. Successful New York producer Bill Szymzyck moved here and started Tumbleweed Records. Barry Fey had already established himself as a major league promoter, and was putting on concerts not only in Denver and Boulder but in adjoining states. Recording studios opened and the Denver Center for the Performing Arts soon emerged as Denver's version of the Guthrie Theater. The population grew, and the music community was primed for the start of a major music community.

By the early 1980s, things started to slow down. Oil prices dropped and the oil companies started to leave Denver. They concluded that it was not viable to pursue oil shale as a natural resource. A regional music organization called the Rocky Mountain Music Association was formed and, in the mid-1980s, held several regional conferences that attracted music publishers and A&R representatives from major labels. In a period of about a year, local attorney Ed Pierson made a deal with MCA Records, made two major publishing deals for bands and writers, signed Jill Sobule to MCA music, and, after witnessing (and promoting) a bidding war, signed the Subdudes to Atlantic Records.

By the end of the 1980s, the economy had declined. It had gotten so bad that the large buildings that had changed the skyline of downtown Denver were like ghost towns. Space was available for $1 per square foot for the first year of a three-year lease, and other, similarly extreme deals were being made to rent at anyone at virtually any price they chose. Six multi-track studios in the Denver-Boulder area were out of business by this time. Firefall was long gone, and John Denver had become old news. It seemed that everyone was moving to California. That included me, and I lived in the Los Angeles area from 1987–1988, working for NARAS, the National Academy of Recording Arts and Sciences, the organization that created the Grammy show. I was its national education coordinator, and it was during this time that I began to write the first edition of this book.

After one year in California, I decided that I would rather be in Colorado. I came back to the Denver area just at the point when California suffered a series of catastrophes. The riots that followed the arrest of Rodney King were flowed by the closure of many military bases in California, some disastrous fires and rock slides. It seemed that everyone was leaving California, and thousands were headed to Colorado. Meanwhile, the studio business had quietly resumed, but this time the studios seemed to position themselves into different niches. Several multi-track rooms added automated mixing, the A-DAT format came in, and it seemed as though all the studios were reasonably busy. Barry Fey continued to be an active promoter, but MCA opened a huge outdoor facility south of Denver that held close to twenty thousand people. Several independent promoters emerged that specialized in rap, hard rock, folk music, and women's music. A couple of theaters in Denver became entertainment venues, as well as two in Boulder. By 2000, Fey was in semi-retirement and Chuck Morris was operating a venue called the Fillmore, near the downtown area. Morris had originally worked with Fey, and later was involved in managing several acts, including Leo Kottke, the Nitty Gritty Dirt Band, and alternative rock band Big Head Todd & the Monsters.

Denver has a strong Chicano population, and there is a semi-invisible Spanish language music scene that promotes concerts and performances that largely go unnoticed by the Anglo population. There are also record stores and small labels that specialize in music for the Spanish-speaking population. Denver was a center for Chicano activism in the 1960s, with a local activist, the late Corky Gonzales establishing an organization called The Crusade for Justice.

Colorado is the corporate headquarters for TCI and several other major players in the cable television business. Unfortunately for the local community, little actual production is done here. Every year, one or two feature films are cranked out, but so far none of them has proved to be a major success. Dan Fogelberg has moved to the western part of the state, and has a home studio. John Denver, who never did record in Colorado, died in a tragic airplane accident. Several of the Eagles have residences in Aspen, and Glenn Frey has a home studio there. Caribou Studios burned down, but Pat Leonard, who has produced Madonna, among others, has a small home studio operation at Caribou, and in a quiet way there are at least four acts with major label deals. The most successful has been Big Head Todd & the Monsters, with one gold album to their name so far. They initially recorded on their own label, and through extensive touring were selling some thirty thousand units of their self-produced CDs, before picking up a management deal with Morris/Bliesener Associates. This in turn led to their record deal with Irving Azoff's Warner-distributed Giant Records, now re-named Revolution Records. After their major label fling, the band is once again recording for their own label. Currently local band the Fray is signed to a Sony affiliate. Dressy Bessy is another successful Denver touring band.

The area also is the home of Silver Wave Records, which started out as a New Age label, and has now added more of a world music profile. W.A.R. Records moved to Boulder from New York, and they are the home label of the Samples, another act that tours nationally. The Samples have been in and out of major label deals with Arista and MCA, but seem happier as independent artists.

The Denver-Boulder-Nederland area is a breeding ground for acoustic jam bands. A number of touring bands have emerged from this area, including Acoustic Junction, Leftover Salmon, String Cheese Incident, and the Yonder Mountain String Band. They combine acoustic folk-bluegrass-roots music with a sort of folk-rock sensibility. String Cheese and Yonder Mountain have their own independent record label, which they own with their management company.

David Edwards is a Denver artist who has two groups that he performs in. The band 16 Horsepower is extremely popular in Europe, and did several albums for A&M. Edwards's other group is Woven Hand, and they too have recorded several albums. Edwards's unique songs are rooted in foot music with religious overtones, and although he is well regarded in the area, he seems more popular abroad.

Denver doesn't have a strong, regularly published entertainment paper, although new ones seem to sprout up or disappear each year. *Westword* is the local alternative paper, and they devote quite a bit of (sometimes controversial) coverage to music. Each issue usually includes a couple of articles about local bands. Barry Fey has sold his business to Universal, MCA remains along with some further possible competition from an alliance between manager Chuck Morris and the House of Blues. Contrary to the opinion of most local musicians, there is a fairly active live music scene. No one is getting rich, but the clubs do at least pay people. There is also a large convention business here, and other work is available at the state's various ski resorts, at least during the winter months. There are regional jingles here, and some musical work is available on local industrial or tourist films. A couple of people write jingles full time, but a large percentage of their work is done with samplers and synthesizers.

The Denver Symphony went under, but was fairly quickly replaced by a cooperative orchestra called the Colorado Symphony. Various players function as both labor and management. A local chamber music orchestra is a distant memory, although the opera and ballet do occasional performances.

Denver is a sports-crazy town, and there is a new downtown baseball field, with restaurants and clubs all around it, which usually have some live music during the season. A new basketball arena is also under construction, which will supposedly feature a full soundstage and the capability of doing film and recording. A new football stadium follows closely behind.

One of the problems of building a music scene in Denver is that the city is like an island in the Rockies. Salt Lake City is 500 miles to the west, Omaha and Kansas City are 600 miles to the east. Albuquerque is about 350 miles south, but it is a much smaller city. Colorado Springs is only sixty-five miles south of Denver, and it is a growing city, with a population of 300,000. It's a tough trip in the winter months, and Colorado Springs is a rather conservative town between the large military presence and its role as the headquarters for a number of right-wing religious organizations. It's difficult for musicians to tour efficiently with such large distances between the various venues.

Mark Bliesener, who used to be Chuck Morris's partner has pretty much inherited the managerial side of Chuck's business, and Ted Guggenheim, another manager, seem to interact with some record companies, but since Ed Pierson left to go to California in 1988, there are no "deal-maker" attorneys who have good record company access. There are no local booking agencies who book on a national level, outside Scott O'Malley in Colorado Springs, who focuses on cowboy poets and country-folk music.

Colorado has an active folk and country music community. The Swallow Hill Music Association in Denver owns its own building, books concerts by touring artists, and has a very successful acoustic music school, and there are several large country music clubs. The Boulder-Nederland area has an active coffeehouse scene for acoustic music. There are strong annual folk festivals in Telluride, quite a distance west, and in Lyons, a town north of Boulder that is much closer to Denver. In the mid-1980s through the early 1990s there were a number of soft jazz or jazz fusion bands with national deals.

After a number of successful releases on GRP Records, Nelson Rangell now records for Koch, and a band called Images has gone through several major deals before recording for a local jazz label called Fahrenheit. Another local band on the label that tours extensively is Dotsero.

One of the biggest problems for Denver musicians is that local radio has become extremely corporate. Two companies own the larger stations here, and there is no college radio station that can be heard outside college dormitories. In the last few years, an AM station and an FM station have begun to provide a broader listening palette for the radio audience. There are occasional local music shows that drift in and out of the airwaves, and even several of the NPR stations are tightly formatted. Several stations regularly play folk rock or soft rock, but they don't extensively program local artists. Nick Forster's E-town radio show is a syndicated radio show out of Boulder that features a considerable amount of acoustic music in the blues, folk, bluegrass, and singer-songwriter veins. There are a number of strong independent record stores, but a number of them have gone out of business since Tower Records moved in.

The school where I used to teach, the University of Colorado at Denver, is going through a significant expansion in its School of the Arts. The professional studies department has an active music and recording engineering program. It is an open question whether a college program can play a major role in creating a music scene, as opposed to reacting to an already existing scene. It certainly should be a goal of such programs to relate to the local music community in a dynamic and useful way.

In my opinion, it will be difficult for Denver to become a major regional music market. There is relatively little infrastructure, the local film commission is almost entirely ignorant of the presence of a music community, and Denver's location makes mounting touring clumsy. The best bet for Denver would be for a superstar artist or producer to decide to want to open up shop here. The few that have done so have not had any relationship to speak of with the local music community. Denver also lacks a specific musical style that it could represent to record company people. If a Pavitt or Poneman were here possibly they could invent that. The question remains, however, if there is enough significant local talent to follow the hype. Possibly Denver is better off assuming the role of a Portland, rather than a Seattle. There is plenty of music in and around the area, and there are good studios and competent engineers. Without a larger population base, and closer large cities, it is hard to sell records in quantity.

Atlanta and Georgia Today

The state of Georgia commissioned a study of the economic impact of its music industry in 2003. They turned up a number of interesting things that are relevant to our discussions of regional music scenes. The surveyors estimated that the impact of the music industry on Georgia's economy was $985,000,000 or just under a billion dollars. They turned up over three hundred recording facilities in Georgia. Because it has over a million African-Americans, Atlanta has the fourth highest urban radio scene in the United States. Record producer Jermaine Dupri has written and produced hit records for a number of successful artists, including Monica, Usher, Alicia Keys, and Jagged Edge. So So Def Recordings is funded by Sony Music. Def Jam South is another prominent record label on the scene.

The hip-hop duo Outkast have their record label and recording studio here, and a large number of major artists and producers, including Peabo Bryson,

Bow Wow, the Indigo Girls, John Mayer, and Arrested Development live in the Atlanta area.

Although La Face Records is no longer in Georgia, its presence during the 1990s is, according to the authors of the survey, largely responsible for the development of a number of entertainment-related businesses in the area.

The Atlantis Music Conference is an annual three-day event along the lines of South by Southwest, and Georgia State University has a music business program that has been in existence for a number of years.

Comparing Atlanta to Seattle and Denver, Atlanta's success was essentially initiated by the L.A. and Babyface partnership. Even after that dissolved, the corps of writers, record producers, and talent that evolved from La Face Records has enabled the scene to continue. Although Seattle had powerful acts during the heyday of grunge, there wasn't really a comparable infrastructure.

Conclusion

A single producer, recording artist, or production team can have a major influence on the development of a regional music scene. Jimmy Jam, Terry Lewis and Prince in Minneapolis, LA Reid and Babyface in Atlanta, and Missy Elliott in Philadelphia all function as magnets—drawing artists, writers, producers, and songwriters into their musical orbit. The effect escalates, and soon a new generation develops, placing their own imprint on the scene.

Regional musical scenes can be nurtured and assisted by government grants, managers, agents, music publishers, and recording studios, but it takes something magical and unpredictable to really fan the flames.

Chapter 15 Resources

The most useful book about the Seattle music scene that I have found is Clark Humphreys *Loser: The Seattle Music Story*, published by Ferral Books, in Portland in 1995. Other books are listed in the Appendix.The information about the Denver music scene comes from my thirty years of living there and input from my friends and colleagues Frank Jermance, Jim Mason, and Harry Tuft. The Georgia survey was conducted by Kelly D. Edmiston and Marcus X. Thomas, and published in the 2004 *MEIEA Journal*.

CHAPTER 16

The Music Business in Canada

Canada is the uncharted northern neighbor of the United States. The average statesider probably knows more about his local football team than he knows about Canada. So this chapter is as much for statesiders who are curious about music in Canada as it is for Canadians.

Although Canada is geographically larger than the United States, the population is about 10% that of the U.S. The nation is divided into provinces instead of states; each province has one or two major cities. There are four national political parties plus one that operates only in Quebec. Canada is the leading importer of American goods, and Canadians usually pay a higher price for most of these products than statesiders do. The Canadian dollar is worth less than the U.S. greenback. For the last few years, the American dollar has been worth between $1.10 and $1.35 Canadian.

The Canadian music scene parallels the one found in the States, but is different in some respects. Radio and TV are divided into the government and private sectors. The government portion is operated by CBC, the Canadian Broadcasting Company. Most of the major Canadian cities are fairly close to the United States border, so that many Canadians can readily watch American TV or listen to American radio stations.

Comparing the two music scenes, there is some good news and some bad news for Canadians. The good news is that the Canadian government is friendlier to the arts than the United States government is. The Canada Council offers quite a few grant programs that offer support to the artist. Provincial programs are also available. To some extent, CBC provides an outlet for local musicians that few U.S. stations can match, and which goes beyond what support N.E.T. or N.P.R. offer in the United States.

In the "bad news department," for a number of years Canada has had much higher unemployment than is found stateside. The large distances between cities also make it much more difficult to tour in the United States. There is nothing that resembles the Boston–New York–Philadelphia–Baltimore–Washington, D.C. corridor of cities to support touring musicians.

Since the 9/11 attacks, musicians have found that touring Canada or the United States requires annoying and expensive paperwork for Canadians working in the U.S. and vice versa.

Staying or Going

Canadian musical artists can follow four possible geographical scenarios in pursuing a professional music career. They are:

1. **Stay in Canada, rely on local support, and don't worry about exporting your music.** Try to play performances in the United States only if it makes geographic sense. In other words, it's easy for a Toronto act to play in Buffalo, not so easy for any Canadian act to play in Florida or California.

2. **Move to the United States.** This is also known as "giving it up." In this plan, the musician decides that since the big bucks are not available in Canada, its easier to just pack up and leave. Of course, you can't stay indefinitely in the United States without becoming a legal immigrant.

3. **Go stateside to tour and, perhaps, to record.** Take the money home and live in Canada.

4. **Stay in the U.S. long enough to establish a career.** Find someone to handle your business in the United States, build a reputation in the U.S., and then return home as an established act who expects to tour and record periodically in the United States.

Few Americans are apt to be familiar with artists who have adopted plan one, because these artists are rarely heard in the States. As in the United States, there are many local musicians who play bars, square dances, weddings, etc. The artist who stays home is in friendly territory and is able to build a stable base of support, and to add new territories with a minimum of discomfort. For example, such a musician might add a teaching or freelance playing opportunity to her normal gigs.

A small number of successful artists have re-located to the United States. Neil Young, Joni Mitchell, and Shania Twain are obvious examples. There are also a few musicians who moved from the United States to Canada. Sometimes this was an accident, sometimes a conscious choice. In the late 1960s, quite a few draft-age Americans fled to Canada to avoid military service in Vietnam.

Some of the Canadian musical artists who originally came from the U.S. include longtime rockabilly star Ronnie Hawkins, singer-songwriter Jesse Winchester, and children's artist Eric Nagler.

Some Canadians, like Ian Tyson and Sylvia Fricker, seem to have pursued a sort of dual residency before returning home to Canada. The third group of musicians, the ones who have stayed in Canada but who aggressively pursued bi-national careers, include Anne Murray, Bryan Adams, Bruce Cockburn,

Gordon Lightfoot, Rush, Avril Lavigne, the Barenaked Ladies, and Sarah McLachlan. These artists use Canada as a base of support, but have been able to chalk up extensive record sales and to make considerable income from stateside tours. It is probably also true that their success in the states has validated these artists in Canada, and actually aided their Canadian careers.

There are three drawbacks for Canadian musicians who try to make it by moving to the States. First of all, the U.S. dollar is worth about $1.20 Canadian (it varies from day to day.) In other words, a Canadian musician who comes south with $1,000 Canadian that she has saved would find that she really only had about $800 in U.S. funds.

Both the U.S. and the Canada make it tough to work in each other's country, and the U.S. government has passed some odd and restrictive rulings that insist that a foreign musical artist needs to be "distinguished." What this usually translates to is that the group must have sufficient notoriety that the immigration people have heard of them. Anyone who works in both the United States and Canada on a fairly regular basis is in the unfortunate position of having to pay double income tax. In other words, they must pay taxes in both countries.

What brings Canadian musicians south is the lure of a much larger pot of gold at the end of the rainbow. One hundred thousand albums represent a platinum sale in Canada, whereas one million are required to achieve similar recognition in the States. Another lure is that most major Canadian labels won't sign an act unless their American counterpart expresses interest. It's too difficult to make big money out of strictly Canadian sales, and so much easier to make large sums of money by selling records in both countries. Under these circumstances, it is natural for Canadians to feel that if an American record company is really going to make the decision about their recording career, why not contact the companion at its home office, rather than through its Canadian affiliate?

It is not only artists that face these problems, but songwriters and record producers as well. Canadian writers Eddy Schwartz and Dan Hill live in Canada, but have achieved success through developing American publishing contacts. There are also several well-known Canadian record producers. Bruce Fairborn, who produced Loverboy, and Bon Jovi lives in Canada, but arranger-composer-producer David Foster lives in Los Angeles and Daniel Lanois in New Orleans.

Government Aid

In addition to grant programs, there are several other government programs that are available to help Canadian artists and record companies. It all started with the Canadian Content Law, or CANCON. This rule requires that 35% of radio programming in Canada must go to records that have at least two out of four components that are Canadian. The components are the recording artist, the lyricist, the music composer, and where the record was produced. In Quebec, a similar rule requires that 65% of airplay be devoted to songs sung in French.

There is some controversy as to the real effects of CANCON. There are record companies that believe that any locally produced Canadian record will almost automatically succeed because of CANCON. Since airplay does not guarantee sales, and there are records, after all, that are competing for the 35% quota, this attitude seems to be highly exaggerated. Broadcasters sometimes complain that there aren't enough quality Canadian recordings to enable them to meet the quota, so they periodically request a reduction in a specific area of music, such as country music. In general, the government is reluctant to accept reduced quotas, and does on only on rare occasions.

Some of the Canadian record companies, particularly the smaller ones, openly admit that they would not be in business were it not for the stimulus supplied by CANCON. It has certainly made it easier to compete with product coming out of the United States.

FACTOR Awards

In 1981, the Canadian radio broadcast industry pooled its money in order to set up a fund designed to boost the recording of music in Canada. The funds are administered by the Canadian Independent Record Production Association (CIRPA.) In 1987, the government announced that it would contribute $25,000,000 to the fund over the next five years. These contributions are made in each province, and information about contacting FACTOR is available in the Resources Section at the end of this chapter. The budget varies from year to year.

There are a number of programs available through FACTOR. It funnels various monies through CIRPA, including a loan program for bands that want to make a CD. The band submits a demo and a precise budget that is judged by a group of music industry professionals. The funding may comprise up to 50% of the record's total budget and the loan must be paid back if the record makes money. If the album stiffs, the CIRPA writes off the loan.

Other programs assist artists in making demos. These grants pay for studio time and recording tape. Studio prices are standardized in this program, so that a band may get an unusually large amount of recording time from a high-class studio.

The costs of these FACTOR programs are split between the broadcasters and the government. The government also sponsors music videos, loans, and a foreign tour loan program. The latter is designed for new groups going abroad who actually anticipate losing money on such a tour.

In her useful book, *Marketing Your Songs*, Valerie Mahonin points out that another government regulation in Canada provides that most radio stations are obligated to spend a certain amount of money on promoting Canadian talent. Some stations produce local entertainment or talent shows, and some sponsor compilation albums that feature local performers. If you are a Canadian, it is worth contacting local radio stations to see if they are involved in this program.

There is a regional agency in Vancouver assisting in the process of record distribution. The rationale is that the center of power, population and expertise is in Toronto, which is too far away to be of any help to the west coast province.

The Bad News

At this writing, the future of the FACTOR program is in doubt. Like many of the western democratic countries, Canada has taken some serious economic hits with the aging of the population and the increased costs of medical care, which in Canada is free. According to a Web site posing on ChartAttack, 60% of Canadian musicians have received funding from FACTOR at some point during their careers. In 2003, the program gave $14 million in grants, including $4 million for audio production one million dollars for video, $1.5 million for marketing, and $2.6 million for touring. If the FACTOR program is eliminated or its budget severely cut, it will be a severe blow to Canadian artists and the Canadian music industry.

Telefilm is a federal fund set up to promote film productionin Canada. The funds must be matched by other investors. The program requires a certain amount of Canadian creative involvement in the project, or the government will not offer support.

Currently, there is a large amount of "runaway" American television and film production in Toronto and Vancouver. The main reason for this is the favorable currency exchange. The government also offers rebates to American film producers, based on the amount of money that is spent on the film in Canada. American TV producer-writer Stephen J. Cannell has a large facility in Vancouver, and his company has trained half a dozen crews in Vancouver to do every aspect of television production. *The X-Files* is just one of a number of American television series shot in Vancouver.

The Canadian Record Market and Montreal

Most of the music business mechanism in Canada is in Toronto, with Montreal providing the headquarters for music recorded in French. Since the province of Quebec is mostly French speaking, the country is divided into two separate musical communities despite its legislated bilingualism. The effect of the two cultures is that an already small market is further fragmented through linguistic and cultural differences. Much of the energy seems to have been generated by the success of the band Arcade Fire. Starting out on the internet with MP3s, the band has sold 220,000 copies CDs on the independent Merge record label.

A Februrary 6, 2005, *New York Times* article by David Carr focused on the Montreal music scene. The article listed numerous music venues, and pointed out that currently there is a powerful Anglo rock scene with such bands as the Stars, Wolf Parade, Pony Up, the Unicorns, the Dears, Godspeed You!, Black Emperors to go with a powerful industrial and dance music scene. There are a number of popular French acts, including Eric Lapointe, Boom Desjardins, Mario Pelchat and Daniel Bélanger, and some relative newcomers on the scene, like La Cowboys Fringant and Kodiak. One observer has even compared the music scene in Montreal to the emergence of Seattle and Austin as important regional music markets, with its relatively reasonable standard of living and its musical energy.

The city also boasts Mutek, an annual electronic music festival, and if one can believe Carr and a similar MSNBC story, a healthy live-music-scene label.

The existence of a bilingual market marks the most obvious difference between the U.S. and Canadian music scenes. Rhythm and blues and black dance music represent a smaller market share in Canada, because of the smaller percentage of black population. Nevertheless Toronto *does* have an urban contemporary record scene.

One rather unusual and odd aspect of the record business in Canada is the success of the Canadian children's record market. The United States has a children's record market that falls into four general areas. One is TV programs, like *Sesame Street*, which features combinations of real people or cartoon characters or puppets. Another is the MOR Disneyland sort of recordings that are old-style Hollywood film scores addressed as much to parents as to children. Another genre is a sort of Disney-ish version of rock and roll songs. These songs contain the same sort of musical and lyric hooks found in pop rock songs. The difference is that these tunes represent cartoon characters or television situations. Essentially, they are simplified rock songs for younger audiences. The fourth style of American children's songs are recordings targeted primarily to teachers and music educators. Such artists and writers as Steve and Greg, Hap Palmer, and Ella Jenkins sell mostly in the schools rather than directly to consumers.

The Canadian children's market, on the other hand, is dominated by folksingers. Some of the popular artists include Raffi, a veritable Pied Piper of children's music, Sharon, Lois and Bram, and Fred Penner. Raffi has also achieved extraordinary success in the U.S. Consequently, a number of American major and minor labels have tried their hand, with varying results, at children's music. The success of the Canadian artists has encouraged a sort of folk American children's genre, featuring artists like Cathy Fink and Marcy Marxer, Joe Scruggs, Tom Chapin, and others.

Many of the successful Canadian performers have fueled their record sales by developing their own television shows. The Nickelodeon TV network has picked up some of these shows in the United States.

Festivals

Another part of the Canadian music scene is the incredible summer festival circuit, which includes, Winnipeg, Vancouver, and Edmonton, among many other, smaller venues. These giant folk festivals bring in talent from all over the world, as well as featuring local and Canadian artists. Thousands attend the performances, which include workshops on specific musical instruments and styles, craft displays, and folklife-oriented events. The Vancouver Folk Festival has even spawned its own record label and record distribution outlet, called Festival. The Dukhs and the Be Good Tanyas are among the younger artists that have emerged on the Canadian folk scene.

Performing Rights

Canada's performing rights organization is called SOCAN, the Society of Composers, Authors, and Music Publishers of Canada. It operates similarly to the way ASCAP and BMI work in the United States.

Canada has only about 600 radio stations, so that performance rights in Canada generate only a small percentage of what airplay produces in the United States. Canadian writers receive performance royalties for Canadian movie performances, a right that composers in the United States do not enjoy.

More Aspects of the Music Business in Canada

CARAS (Canadian Academy of Recording Arts and Sciences) is the Canadian equivalent of NARAS, and the Juno Awards correspond to the Grammy Awards in the United States. Canadian Music Week is an annual event held each March in Toronto, where A&R personnel, music publishers, and other industry luminaries hold seminars and go to the local clubs to view perform-ances of hundreds of Canadian artists and bands. Vancouver holds a similar event each year.

There are three cable TV music networks in Canada, and MTV has just announced that it is about to join the pack: Music (Music parallels MTV), Musique Plus (the French music television network in Quebec), and CMT (deals with country music). Quebecois music tends to be more MOR than the music found in the rest of Canada. The language barrier limits sales and prevents most of these records from crossing over to the English-speaking market. Céline Dion, who sings in English, is an international superstar.

We have already mentioned the phenomenal growth in the Canadian film and television business, largely an artifact of the cheaper (than U.S) Canadian dollar. Toronto and Vancouver have a number of trained film and television crews and post-production facilities. Because Vancouver has both mountain and ocean locations, it is particularly attractive to Hollywood producers. Besides the savings in dollars, producer Stephen J. Cannell, in an 1996 interview in the magazine *Variety on Production* has pointed out that the Canadian unions are more willing to be flexible in re-working rules to fit the needs of a particular shoot. The dollar savings include everything from wages to hotel and food expenses. Cannell's facility in Vancouver was partly financed through loans from the Canadian government.

The Canadian music business has several pluses when compared to the scene in the States. First of all, there is government support through the CANCON laws, and government participation with the broadcasters in the FACTOR program. Secondly, there is an awareness of alternative music forms, and the willingness of the Canadian people to buy independently produced albums in such areas as children's music. The big money is not readily available in Canada, and possibly this accounts for a somewhat more open musical attitude in the music business itself.

Major Label Interest

In the last four years, Universal Music Canada has become a major player in the Canadian music scene by picking up distribution of more than half a dozen independent labels based in Montréal and Toronto. They also own a minority interest in Maple Core, an alternative rock label that has such artists as promising singer-songwriter Kathleen Edwards and old favorites the Cowboy Junkies under contract.

Chapter 16 Resources

A number of books, organizations, and trade papers are listed in the Appendix, but the single best resource on the Canadian music business is the *Music Directory Canada*, published by Norris-Whitney Communications in Ontario (last published in 2001). It has extensive lists of Canadian music business organizations, government agencies, radio stations, record companies, and virtually everything else you would want to know in researching the Canadian music business.

CHAPTER 17
Songwriting Income

Every song that is recorded brings in income from a variety of sources. These revenue streams are usually referred to as a "bundle of rights." Prior to 1914, songwriters and composers in the United States did not receive compensation for the performance of their music in public. They received most of their income from the sales of sheet music. At that time, records existed in the form of cylinders and generated relatively little income to writers or performers.

Composers and publishers became increasingly aware that although their music was performed in public, they did not receive any compensation for these performances. A group of composers and publishers established the American Society of Composers, Authors, and Publishers (ASCAP) to collect these monies. This was done by licensing the performance of music in public places. Establishments using music paid flat fees to ASCAP based upon the size of the venue and the annual budget for entertainment. When radio stations began to be licensed for the performance of music, they paid an annual fee based on the gross of their yearly advertising income.

Toward the end of the 1930s, ASCAP tried to raise these fees, and the broadcasters organized their own performing rights society, BMI (Broadcast Music Incorporated), to compete with ASCAP. When BMI was formed, ASCAP was almost totally controlled by Tin Pan Alley songwriters and the people who wrote music for Broadway shows and films, as well as classical composers. BMI deliberately sought out country and blues writers, partly because they were denied entrance to ASCAP. When rock and roll became a significant factor in the mid-1950s, BMI became a viable competitor to ASCAP. By this time, another much smaller performing rights organization called SESAC, the Society for European Stage Authors and Composers, had entered the picture. Unlike the other non-profit organizations, SESAC was a privately-held company.

Over the years, the broadcasters fought with the performing rights organizations over the fees that they had to pay for performing rights. This percentage has varied from approximately 1% to 2% of the station's advertising gross. The broadcasters accused ASCAP and BMI of violating federal antitrust regulations. As a result of many lawsuits, ASCAP and BMI now operate under federal judicial decrees. The rates that they charge are adjusted in lengthy negotiations between the societies and the broadcasters, with the courts mediating or adjudicating the resulting fees. Recently, ASCAP has negotiated agreements with radio stations for specific amounts of money, rather than a percentage of gross income. On ASCAP's side, this offers guaranteed income, and for the stations it limits their costs.

Although the local broadcasters technically own BMI, it is a non-profit organization, which, in reality, operates in a similar manner to ASCAP. Thus, BMI has found itself in court fighting against some of the very broadcasters who nominally own it.

Blanket and Per Program Licenses

Most radio and television stations have blanket licenses, which means that they can play any songs they wish as often as they may choose. Stations that rarely play music buy per program licenses, which are proportionately more expensive, but still economically feasible if the station rarely programs music.

Legal Controversies

For years, the media has been fighting to reduce or eliminate the system of blanket licensing. These fights have taken place in court, and in the U.S Congress. It seems as though there is always legislation in Congress to change the licensing system. These attempts have varied from the broadcasters' seeking to license music directly from the composer to eliminating licensing fees for certain venues, such as small restaurants or beauty parlors. Currently, any establishment that uses two speakers and broadcasts music for the entertainment of its customers, must pay these fees. The single exception is record stores, which clearly aid in the sale of records and therefore bring in income to composers and music publishers. There are also recently legislated exemptions for particularly small venues.

Every time a new medium of transmission arises, such as cable TV or the Internet, new negotiations must take place to establish the rights of composers and publishers to their intellectual property. The broadcasters often use the new technologies to re-open the arguments as to the necessary payments for these rights. It is difficult to understand why anyone can rationally argue that intellectual property differs from any other sort of invention, trademark or copyright. The problem is that the media can enjoy substantial income from reducing or eliminating these fees.

Some Tips to Local Composers

If your music is used on local television or for commercials, you are entitled to synchronization fees. These are not set fees, as is the case for royalties on the sale of records (as of 2006, 9.1 cents per song, or 1.75 cents a minute, whichever is greater.) If you are writing music that is intended for local use only, it is advantageous for you to have your own music publishing company. Generally, publishers and writers split income on a fifty-fifty basis. If you are seeking to get recordings of your songs by major artists, music publishers have the contacts and the ability to access these people. They can also license you songs for movies, TV shows, commercials, and sheet music. *

Common Fallacies

In the twenty some years I have been teaching and writing about the music business, I have constantly encountered several common, incorrect notions. First of all, there is some sort of word-of-mouth fantasy that has convinced musicians that they can copy up to four bars of music without penalty. There is nothing in the copyright law that says that you can copy *anything* without penalty. The law restricts "substantial similarity," and that word is defined in a court proceeding. It is a bad idea to assume that you can borrow *anything*. Another common error is the notion that you can mail a song to yourself and that that constitutes a valid copyright. Courts are unlikely to agree. An envelope could be steamed open, and changed to one with an earlier postmark. The cheapest way to copyright your songs is to make a tape of up to ten songs, and announce each title. Use form SR and send it to the Register of Copyrights at the Library of Congress. The cost is $30, and the address is in the Appendix. You will get a receipt back, and now there is a copy of your tape that you can call on if anyone copies your song. The Copyright Office has a dated receipt that proves when that song was received. Now your songs are indeed safe. The SR form copyrights both the song and your performance of it. If you prefer to copyright songs individually, use form PA and write out a lead sheet that contains the melody line, chords, and all lyrics.

In copyright suits, there are two fundamental elements that must be proved: similarity of the song in question and that author's ability to access your work. In most instances, you must be able to prove that the author of the new work at some point heard your song.

New Income Streams

New income sources for songwriters include the use of songs in video games, royalties from digital sales, the use ofsongs as ring-tones on cellular phones, and the ever-increasing use of songs in movies, TV shows, and in commercials.

---

*For further information, see my book, *The Music Business: Career Opportunities and Self-Defense*, third revised edition, Three Rivers Press, 2003.

Chapter 17 Resources

An invaluable resource for accessing publishers is the annual *Songwriter's Market*, published by Writer's Digest. There are many books about songwriting and music publishing that are listed along with comments about them in the Appendix of this book.

CHAPTER 18
Music and Technology Futures

Note: This chapter, until noted, was written by Ron Sobel, CEO of North Star media, former vice president of ASCAP, Los Angeles, and an adjunct professor at California State at Pomona and the University of Colorado at Denver. From his vantage point in Los Angeles, Ron is in an ideal position to comment on the way that music will be transmitted in the twenty-first century.

The recent advances in computer, multi-media, and Internet technology, although revolutionizing most businesses, may be most profoundly felt in the entertainment industry. The changes that are radically and irrevocably altering the film, television, and publishing industries are having a startling impact on the music business. New technologies are exploding old entertainment models, and transforming all aspects of music—from how works are written, financed, produced, and distributed, to their ultimate enjoyment by the consumer.

We live in a highly evolutionary world—one where digitalization, deregulation, and globalization are profoundly re-shaping the creative landscape. The transition from analog to digital, together with the popularity of the Internet, has created a next-generation multi-media marketplace. Current technology allows for the master quality digital transmission and download of music over the Internet. For composers, musicians, and consumers of all genres of music from classical music to rap, we stand at an unprecedented threshold: the door is open for music to become the first major packaged product to make the legendary transition from atoms to bits. That's a scary concept to those with a heavy investment in atom-based technology. But for those of us who choose to embrace new technology, however, the next millennium can bring limitless opportunity. Whether you are a composer, teacher, player, or listener, the tools and resources available to you today simply did not exist ten years ago. As we peer into the future, however, the next ten years promise to be even more dazzling and inventive. The opportunities available to the music community will stem not only from technology, but from innovation, creativity, and perseverance. In a few years, the Internet may have the same impact for emerging artists that radio and major record companies have today. Beyond the Internet, sheer ingenuity and inventiveness will create new opportunities for writers and artists in fields ranging from film to retail to urban architecture. Making demos at home and transmitting them around the world will be commonplace. Roll over Beethoven and tell Tchaikovsky he's being digitally downloaded, and cybercast to Uzbekistan.

Short-Term Technological Hurdles

Before we take the futurist plunge, there are three short-term technological hurdles that need to be addressed. Although there are significant promises and pitfalls to each of these innovations, the only remaining doubts about these no-brainers revolve around when they will be implemented . . . as opposed to whether they will be implemented.

Copyright Protection

The fundamental concern with the creative community is the protection and safeguarding of intellectual property in the digital world. Significant progress has been made in digital watermark technology—the process of placing an imperceptible, embedded fingerprint containing copyright information within the song or film itself. The watermark ensures royalty and licensing agreements are upheld by allowing decoders to monitor any broadcast of the song, whether on the Internet or the radio. In addition to passive watermark safeguards, the industry has very recently cleared a major obstacle to the delivery of digital movies and music into consumers' homes, by agreeing on technology designed to protect content from illegal copying. The encryption technology will require a "digital handshake," or "key," to be used between one device and another before a protected piece of work can be transferred.

Estimated time of implementation: one to four years

Electronic Commerce/E-Cash

In 1997, electric commerce accounted for $7 billion in business-to-business sales, and that number rose to $12.2 billion in 2003. On the business-to-consumer side, nearly $2.75 billion was transacted in 1997, and it is projected that by the year 2000, the number will be increase to about $10 billion.

To make sure that these numbers rise, companies need to assure their customers that no harm will come to them if they choose to make electronic purchases. Companies and online retailers will soothe jittery consumers by installing some basic security precautions, such as firewalls and secure servers. To convince consumers, companies can use technologies that meet the Secure Electronic Transaction (SET) standard set in May 1997. The SET mark, like a Good Housekeeping Seal of Approval for electronic commerce software, assures users that software on the site meets SET specifications and is therefore safe for online transactions.

Estimated time of implementation and acceptance: one to three years

Bandwidth

Much of the content that can be transmitted over the Internet, or any computer connection, is conditioned by the capacity of the connectors and the delivery systems. The larger the delivery "pipeline," the larger the amount of information that can flow through it per second. Together with the dramatic improvement in computing power of PCs, music and multi-media content is rapidly diffusing across a wide range of products available at affordable prices, and the pace of change is accelerating. Indeed, today's high-end PCs boast gains of nearly 40% in capacity and memory over last year's models. The transition to large capacity T-1 lines, and the eventual wireless transmission of multi-media content, will allow for routine real-time delivery of master quality digital music and video to desktop screens.

Estimated time of implementation: two to four years

Perhaps no greater tool exists to enhance the exposure, promotion, and marketing of music than the Internet. Virtually all of the traditional barriers to new writers and new bands are eliminated through the various opportunities that are available on the Net.

Music on the Internet

Online Retailing

The near-impossible challenge of securing shelf space for an unsigned or indie label band at a traditional "brick and mortar" retail record store takes on wholly manageable proportions when dealing with online retailers. Without the need to physically carry CDs in stock, the inventory is owned and warehoused by third parties. Often the bands themselves hold the CD inventory until a sale is generated through the site. Online sites are able to offer audio samples, simple search mechanisms, bio info on the artists, articles, and a much larger inventory than traditional record stores.

Web Pages

The World Wide Web—that section of the Internet that offers easy access to text, graphics, sound, and other multi-media resources—can also be the source of worldwide exposure for a local or major recording act. Whether on a home-made Web page created for a single band, or as part of a larger Web site featuring many different bands, Web pages have grown to be an affordable means of promoting a music project. Sites such as iuma.com include band photos, bios, and audio samples for hundreds of local bands. Tourdates.com lists upcoming tour schedules for local bands according to geographical loca-

---

* Cowles/Simb

tion, genre of music, biographical information, or the music itself, all with simple searches of any of the several Web sites now available that provide such listings. Other recommended sites include artistdirect.com, the Ultimate Band List (ubl.com), Kaleidospace (space.com), and billboardtalent.com.

Internet Cybercasts

Whether live or pre-recorded, the Net is increasingly being used to broadcast music concerts and interviews of well-known and unknown artists. Many traditional radio stations are now simulcasting their programming on the Net, while many of the 2,800 new Internet "radio stations" (sonicnet.com, jamtv.com, thedj.com) can deliver multiple channel options of various kinds of music. Internet radio can display song and artist information as music is played, provide links enabling online purchases of songs being played, and allow for real-time listener feedback and chats. Another recommended site is audionet.com.

Greenhouse Channels

As the graphics, sound, and video elements of the Net move toward convergence with television, the drive to create a new genre of entertainment programming on the Internet is emerging. The notion that interactive, online variety shows featuring a mix of movie reviews, celebrity interviews, stand-up comedy, and music can evolve into major leisure time attractions is fueling the creation of hundreds of show-business-oriented Web sites. Established entertainment sites such as Mr. Showbiz (mrshowbiz.com) and E! Online (eonline.com) are facing competition from next-generation "greenhouse channels," such as asylum.com and musicosm.com. These channels add enhanced personality, with news from local music scenes, performances of demo tapes by unsigned bands, and opportunities to participate and interact with music industry executives. The increasing emergence of these Internet channels will provide yet another vehicle for regional bands and composers to promote their music.

The Evolution of Traditional Music Distribution

The fact that the Net is rapidly becoming a visible means of ordering CDs and promoting new music is only half of the Internet story.

The potential of the Net to deliver digital copies of musical works, downloadable to your own hard drive or recordable CD, represents the most significant change in the manufacturing and distribution of recorded music. Indeed, once the short-term technological hurdles have been overcome, we are only a few small audio tweaks away from routinely ordering and receiving instantaneous digital copies of music works in our homes. We will be able to download the music to whatever source we choose, and access it on demand. This phenomenon, whereby the physical atom-based packaged product called

"CDs" can be replaced by the bit-based download of "data" harbors enormous implications for those businesses who manufacture traditional CDs and ship them to retail stores. Ultimately, the retail stores themselves will be dramatically affected. The transition means, simply, that we will need fewer manufacturing plants, will use less natural resources, will need fewer trucks and less fuel to ship product, and we will need fewer and smaller "brick and mortar" retail record stores to warehouse and display CDs. The cost savings to consumers can be significant. Fully 65% of the price of today's CDs are attributed to costs that disappear with a digital download. Some folks may prefer, in 2004, to take the time to drive to their local record store and pay $15.99 for a CD. Others, I assume, will prefer to stay at home and download the same music for $5.

Beyond the Internet

Notwithstanding the breadth of opportunity that the Internet presents for the music community, there are equally diverse innovations occurring in music beyond the Net. For both the established and emerging musician, the retail, leisure, and film industries are in a process of revolutionizing their retailing concepts, and are embracing broader and deeper uses of music to attract and retain customers.

The Store Strikes Back: Retail's Revenge

The retail store, facing competitive challenges from catalogs, the Home Shopping Network, and the Internet was expected to roll over and play dead. What happened? Instead of convenience, retail had to give shoppers the one element that technology could not replace—a grander, bigger, more exhilarating experience, beyond mere service. It needed to provide services that the customer could not get at home. Indeed, inventive retailers have come to embrace the very tools of audio-visual, multi-media technology that nearly threatened their existence. From Times Square to Niketown, the music and entertainment have become the touchstone of new retailing. From wide-screen music videos to pre-recorded background music to live bands and performers, the entertainment/experiential component of retailing has never been more important. The opportunities for inventive musicians will grow.

Themed Environments

Themed restaurants—those that mix food with music and entertainment— are attracting more visitors and tend to be more profitable than the non-theme dining establishments. According to a 1998 *Los Angeles Times* article, the average restaurant generates annual revenue of $500,000 to $1 million. Annual sales at theme restaurants range from $4 million to $14 million. Hard Rock Cafe, Marvelmania, and Quark's Bar and Restaurant at "Star Trek: The Experience" in

Las Vegas, are the pioneers of restaurant ventures that have brought music from the background to the foreground. The trend to utilize entertainment and music-driven multi-media in restaurants will continue to provide new outlets for the innovative music maker.

Desktop Filmmaking

In an era of monstrous feature film budgets and costly post-production, today's desktop PC allows for the use of affordable graphics programs—including over-the-counter editing and image processing software—to create finished films for less than $25,000. These more affordable methods of making films will generate not only more films, but the need for more music in films. In much the same way that indie record labels and grassroots distribution allowed more bands to make records, the desktop PC will allow for more films and music to lead a grassroots film distribution market into tours of colleges and small art theaters.

Architectural Entertainment

In the drive to give people more reason to leave their homes, city planners, developers, and architects are embracing a new discipline: experiential design. The Fremont Street Experience, for example, in downtown Las Vegas, attracts twenty-five thousand visitors nightly to a computer-generated animation and music show projected on a screen topping the four-acre complex. Two million lights and 540,000 watts of sound make up the world's largest graphics display system. Coupled with projects that are taking cinema out of the theater and into "entertainment environments" —projecting movies outdoors on the side of ten-story buildings, in theme parks, warehouses, casinos, and 360-degree circular theaters—music will be an integral part of next-millennium urban culture.

New Developments

Outside of the recording studio itself, a musician's greatest tool is now the Internet. Whether used for market research, education, promotion, advertising, or sales, the Internet provides enormous access and opportunity to every musician and band . . . no matter where you live.

The once-daunting barrier of obtaining major label distribution for independent artists is eroding as the mechanics of Internet sales become increasingly easy, affordable, and understandable. Placing your CD or songs for sale on Web sites such as Cdbaby.com, Amazon.com, or iTunes.com establishes global presence for your music. It is not uncommon for unsigned indie bands to sell a few thousand CDs from their own Web site and Internet retailers. And selling even a few thousand CDs when you keep $10 or more per CD can generate significant income.

In addition to providing a worldwide "retail store" for selling CDs, the Internet also allows for a very affordable means of staying in contact with your fan base. Newsletters, schedules of upcoming concert tours, and band merchandise are now all within easy access of every fan . . . and soon-to-become fans. Gone are the days when radio airplay is the only means of getting your music heard or of generating news or excitement about your act. Internet promotion, or "viral" word-of-mouth, is rapidly becoming a mainstream, inexpensive way to advertise and market your band.

Three other technological advances are also changing the way that you can market and promote your music. Advances in *cell phone technology* are only months away from linking a home computer, stereo, and car sound system into a seamless, commercial-free music zone. The service will allow new phones to function as music hubs, enabling the download of songs, television episodes, and radio programming from an Internet-connected computer, and opening the door for ever-widening exposure (and sales) of songs and music videos.

Blogs, the virtually free means to publish and post articles, commentary, music, and videos through online "web-logs," and *podcasting*, the emerging technology that allows individuals to create their own radio broadcasts and deliver them over the Web, are both significant factors in allowing artists to promote their music from their homes at very low cost. As these technological advances gain mainstream acceptance, the savvy musician can take advantage of one or more of these tools in his or her attempt to gain a wider audience. The notion that an artist can make a living in a local hometown music market is rapidly becoming a realistic, practical and preferred path to commercial success.

Final Thoughts by Dick Weissman

In the first portion of this chapter, Ron Sobel has presented a sketch of how the future will look to aspiring musicians, composers, record companies, retail stores, and consumers. A single issue of *Billboard* on February 28, 1998, had stories about an Internet label called J-Bird, and Putamayo, a world music label, adopting innovative marketing techniques by tie-ins with a coffee retailer. A friend of mine had his ATM machine ask if he wanted to order any CDs. These things are happening for quite a while now.

So much has occurred in the world of technology since the last edition of this book. In 1999, N2k started selling digital singles for 99 cents. But it was the Apple iPod that revolutionized the legal sale of digital music. According to BBC News In 2004 there were over one hundred and forty million digital music tracks sold, and the iPod was responsible for 87% of these sales. About 5% of album sales are now taking place over the Net, and although this is way below the wildly inflated estimates that researchers of the 1990s anticipated, it is clearly going to be an increasing share of the pie.

Satellite radio is becoming an increasingly useful source for new music, as a handful of companies own hundreds of radio stations, and are increasingly reluctant to program new or innovative music.

Blue Sky and Free Music

This brings up the subject of the wild-eyed fanatics who predicted in the mid-1990s that the record business would be dead within ten years, and the Internet would totally dominate the music business. The reality of the situation is that the record business is wounded, but far from dead. Television didn't kill the market for books or movies, although had predicted that this would be the case.

Some of the same "futurists" are asserting that the copyright act is too protective, that music should be distributed at a lower cost, and that record companies are dinosaurs, unfit for the twenty-first century.

It is true that business models are changing in the record business. Some of these models are loosening up and giving artists more rights to their own music. On the other hand, there is an impetus for record companies to demand increasing control over various aspects of artists' property. In their stimulating book, *The Future of Music: Manifesto for the Digital Music Revolution*, David Kusek and Gerd Leonhard praise Sanctuary Records, a British-based company that has been successful in selling records in the tens and hundreds of thousands by limiting the costs of recording. The authors point positively to Sanctuary's control of artist management and merchandising rights. It is true that Sanctuary allows the artist to retain control of the masters. Certainly, revenue *usually* peaks during the early years of a record release. EMI has attempted some similar artist-record company partnerships. To paraphrase George Herbert Bush, "Read my lips!" Isn't this expansion of control over the artist's property exactly the sort of thing that artists objected to from the giant, multi-national record companies? Moreover, Sanctuary has just recently suffered some disastrous financial reverses, and is reportedly locking in its horns, limiting or eliminating its book business, and laying off dozens of employees.

I am also skeptical about the so-called slotting fees where an artist can pay to get their product on a file-sharing network. How is this different from payola?

On the other hand, Kusek and Leonhard make some useful suggestions about digital distribution—raising such useful ideas as subscription fees for music, as are used for cable television, or licensing fees paid to an Internet service provider. Renting records is another option for those who don't want to spend $15 to $18 to discover that they don't like most of an album. For years, renting records has been legal in Japan and obviously the video rental business is a major business in this country. It is interesting to me that some of the same consumers who seem willing to pay money for satellite radio, object to paying money for records.

The authors also point to the tie-ins with the fashion industry that have created considerable income for such urban music entrepreneurs as Russell Simmons and P. Diddy. I see nothing wrong with these gentlemen creating more wealth for their empires, I simply doubt that this is going to work for most aspiring young artists.

I have become especially concerned about how file to file sharing effects songwriters. Artists can still tour and sell merchandise, but songwriters derive their income from record sales and the use of their songs on broadcast media. If we take away income from the sales of records, how will songwriters be able to make a living?

Acting as though record companies and music publishers are always the heavies may enable hackers to rationalize their theft of music, but it isn't going to create new revenue streams for artists. New models of revenue sharing and what are essentially record company-artist partnerships are going to emerge from the spread of new media technologies, but the artist (and the reader) should have the same skepticism about giving their rights away to new technologies as the skepticism they have developed toward record companies.

New Revenue Sources

As we put this book to bed, it becomes clear that we are going to see an increasing number of technological advances and changes in the industry. The explosion of the short ringtone has led to ring tones that include an entire song, and even ringback tones, which the caller, not the recipient of the call receives. In Korea digital sales bring in more revenue than the physical ales of CD's in record stores, and in the United States Musicland's Sam Goody's record stores, with other 400 retail outlets, has just declared bankruptcy. Clearly the digital world is going to change the existing record stores into entertainment centers, with frequent live music performances. This is already happening in many cities. Sooner or later digital sales will exceed sales of physical units in all parts of the world.

New Formats

In an attempt to create excitement and to give consumers better value, record companies are starting to create new music formats. New albums are new often packaged with free DVDs that are specifically aimed at expanding the consumer's contact with an act. There are also double sided disks now being sold where one side is a CD, and the other side is a DVD. These are obvious attempts to lure the consumer, and to make it harder for computer hackers to readily rip a product.

Summary

The purpose of this book is to provide a practical guide to working in local and regional music scenes. If you have read through the book then you have developed a reasonably good idea of the differences between working in a major music market, and pursuing a career in a secondary market, or even one that hasn't yet developed. This means that you should learn as much as you can about what goes on in every aspect of the music and music-related community. Investigate freelance work, recording studios, booking agents, songwriters' organizations, music schools and stores, and any available grant programs. Even if the bulk of your musical time and energy is taken up with a specific performing group, it is important for you to do some freelancing.

Look at your musical talent as being in a state of evolution, no matter what your age. Whatever you are doing now, you should be able to look forward to improving and polishing your musical skills, as well as expanding the sort of music that you can perform and understand. This may mean studying with a local teacher, or on your own. If you do take classes or lessons, approach your teachers with enthusiasm, but don't hesitate to question or challenge them.

Try to approach long-range commitments to jobs or performing groups by projecting the situation five years into the future. How will accepting this particular opportunity advance your musical goals? We all go through phases where we take musical jobs that may not fulfill our deepest desires or talents, but if this keeps happening to you, there is either something wrong with the breadth of your music business contacts, or, frankly, you are allowing yourself to settle into a musical rut. If you lock yourself into a very specific musical style or approach, your employment opportunities may evaporate when that music loses favor with the public. You need to do what you want, but you also need to be realistic about your professional opportunities. This sort of approach may make you move to a different town, but it shouldn't necessarily be one of the North American "Big Four" music markets.

Remember, this is the music *business*. Treat it like a business endeavor. Buy the type of musical instrument that will assist in advancing your career and your musical skills. Keep adequate tax records in order to avoid unpleasant surprises from your friends at Internal Revenue. If you make a long-term commitment to a musical group, make sure there's room for musical give-and-take from all the people involved.

By this time, you should have a good understanding of the basics. You need a good demo and a press kit. A Web site can be a valuable tool, especially if you have CDs or merchandise to sell. You need some good pictures of your group, and a demo that looks and sounds good. With these tools at your command, you should be able to find a decent local agent, or, if need be, do the booking yourself.

Unless you know how to get excited about selling your act in the same way that music excites you, you will need to find one or more booking agents. If they can't get you more money than you can get yourself, you should not utilize their services.

Investigate working in more than one group, or both as a soloist and in a group. This will expand your possibilities of employment. It is much easier to get a grant if you work alone, because grant monies are generally limited. Try your hand at songwriting, arranging, composing, and developing a home studio. With today's technology, a home studio has become increasingly affordable. Learn how to play new instruments, or develop new techniques on the instruments that you are already playing.

Consider supplementing your income by teaching. Balance your teaching hours with your writing and playing time, unless you find that teaching is the must fulfilling area of music for you. Contact your local recording studios and try to get work as a studio musician or singer. Developing good studio skills will help you in your own songwriting and arranging, and can provide an excellent source of income, irregular as it may be.

Get involved in any music organizations that you can. Your local union can assist you in getting jobs, and it can help with instrument insurance and can assist you in joining a medical plan. Get involved in your local union, go to meetings, and make your voice heard. Vote in elections and stand up for what you believe in.

The same holds true if there is a songwriters' organization in your community. You can use it to find collaborators, and to get feedback on your work.

If you set up a home studio, try to get some work writing jingles or background scores for local industrial films or slide shows. If the studio develops a reputation, consider renting it out to other musicians or composers. If you start to do much jingle or film work, be sure to be paid creative fees and to file union contracts. Contact local advertising agencies, film producers, and editors to find additional work.

If your band wants to make a CD, develop a mailing list to build a solid base of local support. Consider making and distributing your own record, and use your existing fans as a starting point. Look into developing a Web page and selling your product on the Internet. Remember, just creating a web site is not going to do much for you if you do not continually add to it, giving the consumer of fan some reason to return for additional visits.

If your recording gets some reviews, add them to your press kit. Raise your performance price, as the demand for your group grows. While you're at it, consider making a video, particularly if your local union, local college, or cable TV outlet provides you with the possibility of doing one free of charge.

If your goal is to build a national reputation, pursue the possibility of finding a personal manager in a major music market. You can develop songwriting contacts by making an occasional trip to a major city, and establishing an on-going relationship that builds through mail, faxes, and phone calls. Don't get discouraged by rejection. Stay in there and keep pitching. A career is measured in years, not months. Every record company in England turned down The Beatles, until they met George Martin. Behind most overnight successes are long-term struggles.

If you are truly serious about developing a national career, you will need to spend some time in a major music center in order to find a heavyweight personal manager, a national booking agent, a big-time entertainment lawyer, and a recording deal. You may, at that time, want to consider the possibility of staying there. Be aware of the trade-offs. The competition is much stiffer, and you will probably face several really tough years of establishing yourself in a new and often strange place. Remember, you can always go to a major market and return home at a later time. The important thing is to honestly evaluate your career in terms of the way your musical and business goals are unfolding.

Another alternative may be to move in the opposite direction, and channel your musical activities into part-time work. Many part-time musicians are content with playing occasional jobs, without the full-time commitment or the insecurity that a full-time musical career may bring. You may possess extraordinary musical skills, but they may be unsuited for the sort of music that is lucrative where you happen to live. The issues of staying or going, and working part-time or full-time are all choices that you must make for yourself. It's your life, and you have the ability to change it.

Get involved in developing your regional music scene into a powerful one. Use the examples cited in this book, and apply them to your locale. Try to get your local union, your city government, local songwriting organization, and even business groups to participate in developing a local music scene through their financial support and media coverage. The more musical opportunities that develop in your market, the better chance at getting your piece of the musical and financial pie. Don't bad-mouth other musical groups, but try to support them in their own struggles. If anyone experiences success in your musical community, it can only help the other people in the community.

Above all, avoid whining. Musicians have many opportunities to support themselves through their music. Imagine being a dancer whose low-paying career is about over at the age of thirty five. For every Tom Cruise or Julia Roberts, there are thousands of unemployed actors. Artists pay 40% to 50%* of their gross to galleries, and are responsible for their own framing costs and the cost of materials. I have known many musicians who are unknown to the general public, but are able to generate reasonable incomes and long-term careers. It isn't easy, but there are probably more musicians leading a "middle-class" lifestyle than can be found in any of the other art-related professions.

If you live in Canada, you have many of the same choices. Staying or going may mean staying in Canada or going to the states to access the more lucrative

---

* Some New York galleries are now demanding 60% of the gross!

opportunities. Whatever you do, become aware of the governmental grants available and the FACTOR programs that provide a source of assistance to Canadian musicians.

If you write songs or instrumental music, you will need to join a performing rights organization. Join the one where you feel the most rapport and support in terms of developing contacts with publishers and record companies.

There is much promise in the new musical technologies and delivery systems for music. Keep up with technology, but try to make it work for you, not the other way around. Before you buy equipment, decide what fits your musical style and preference, what is economically feasible for you to purchase, and what will be outmoded in six months.

The Appendix of this book is designed to serve as a tour guide for your trip through the world of the music industry. Consult it from time to time as your goals and needs shift.

Whatever happens, don't lose your enthusiasm or your sense of humor. Retain some objectivity while looking at the business and your own career. You'll need all of these qualities plus some luck to survive and get what you want. Keep your ears open. I wish you the best of luck.

Chapter 18 Resources

The best way to keep up with current and future developments is to read as many music-related periodicals as you can. The Sunday editions of the *New York Times* and the *Los Angeles Times* often have articles about new developments in the entertainment industry. Books necessarily become dated very quickly in a world of rapid change. Remember that it takes six months to a year to produce a book. Often a writer has done the research over a much longer period of time. You may be reading a 1999 book that contains information researched in 1992!

Books about music on the Internet started to appear in the mid-1990s. One reference is Brad Hill's *The Virtual Musician: A Complete Guide to Online Resources and Services*. It was published by Schirmer Books in 1996, and contains a CD-Rom. More recent books are David Kusek and Gerd Leonhard's *The Future of Music: Manifesto for the Digital Music Revolution*, Berklee Press, 2005 and Mark W. Curran's *Sell Your Music: The Musician's Survival Guide to Direct Distribution* on the Internet, NM Books, 2001.

CHAPTER 19

Questions and Answers

I have taught hundreds of students over the last fifteen years. I was a full-time college professor at the University of Colorado at Denver, and have taught classes at the University of Oregon, the University of Denver, the Liverpool Institute for Performing Arts, and I have done music business workshops or lectures in Jamaica, Austin, Santa Cruz, Salt Lake City, and Portland, and I have attended seminars taught by others. Below are some of the most typical questions that students ask me about the music business.

This is not intended as legal advice but to provide you with general guidelines. When in doubt about your legal rights, consult a lawyer

Do I need to copyright my songs?

One of the most compelling reasons to copyright songs is that if you have registered a copyright with the Copyright Office in Washington, D.C. you are entitled to damages of as much as $150,000 a song. You can still recover royalties, if you can provide some form of proof that you wrote a song, and that the person who "borrowed" it had some access to it.

Is there any point to sending out unsolicited tapes to record companies or music publishers?

Most books advise against it. *However*, interviews with record company people in *The Music Connection*, my favorite music business periodical, consistently indicate that about a third of the people interviewed do listen to unsolicited tapes. Another third say ambiguously that "you can figure out some way to get to me," and about a third say they will not accept such tapes. I assume that the middle group mean that they can be contacted through secretaries, at music conferences, or through people that know them. I would caution the reader that unsolicited apes rarely result in record deals. On the other hand, *someone* has to win the lottery.

Do I have to pay BMI or ASCAP to perform songs by written by other people?

It is the venue owner who must pay them. However, if you are promoting a concert, you are the responsible party.

Should I enter songwriting contest? And what do you think about Taxi?

Songwriting contests are a long shot. If you enter one, despite the fact that they all say that the quality of your demo doesn't matter, it does matter. The judges will be listening to dozens and dozens of songs. If you can't sing, get someone else to sing for you.

Taxi is a service that for a fee critiques your music and gets it to A&R people and companies that use songs in films and television. They advertise quite a bit, and their ads include testimonials. So far no one has become a superstar through Taxi, but some people have had their music placed or gotten record deals.

My feeling is that if you live in a remote area, and have no manager or other contacts in the business, then Taxi might be a viable option. If you have a manager they should be helping you with record deals or song placements. I have to admit that have a certain prejudice against paying someone a flat fee to shop my music, especially when I don't know that person.

I'm not a performer. Can I make a living as a songwriter?

Because many people write their own songs, it's harder to make a living as a songwriter than it was years ago. One way to handle the situation is to co-write songs with artists or record producers. Both of them have the ability to get sons recorded. If you are a good songwriter, it is possible to get a staff writing deal with a publisher that pays you a weekly salary. The money is an advance against royalties. There are more artists in country music that don't write their own songs then in rock music.

Consequently, you may want to look at Nashville as a place to find outlet for your songs. For film and television music, New York and Los Angeles are better markets.

Why do we need a band agreement? We're all friends and trust one another.

After two or three years on the road and some hit records, you may find that your friendships have long since ended. Think of it as an insurance policy that protects all of the people involved.

Are independent record labels better for an artist than signing a major label deal?

They both have their pros and cons. Independent labels usually provide a more personal environment, and there is more direct interaction between the artist and the label. They also tend to be better at promoting innovative music. They may give you more creative control, in terms of album covers, notes, etc.

Large labels have bigger promotional and recording budgets, and have better distribution capabilities. If your objective is essentially to be a superstar, larger labels are a better alternative. If you are more concerned with personal relationships and artistic control, independents may be better.

Many artists believe that independents are more honest in their business dealings. It all depends on the company—I have seen some independent record contracts that are worse than typical major label deals.

I want to get a job working in the music business. What do you think about college music business programs?

They can be a good way to break in provided that the college has an active internship program, and that the people teaching there have actually worked in the business, and have contacts that you can use. Some things to look for:

- How large are the classes?
- Where are graduates of the program now working?
- What sorts of jobs have the teachers had in the business, and are they still working in the industry?
- Will the program help you to get an internship, or do you have tomake the contacts on your own?
- Have students from the program interned in Los Angeles, Nashville, or New York?

AFTERWORD
The Global Marketplace

In 1997, I did a one-week teaching residency at the Liverpool Institute for Performing Arts in England. This is a school of performing arts that was literally built in Paul McCartney's primary school, with McCartney himself providing some seed money and enlisting some of his friends and associates to assist in establishing a school for the twenty-first century. The students come from all over the world, but particularly from various countries of Europe. The technical facilities are marvelous, and go far beyond what any college could afford. To me, that isn't what the school is all about. The atmosphere is somewhat chaotic, but dynamic and interesting. Everywhere there are dancers, singers, musicians, actors, and would-be entrepreneurs, learning and practicing their craft in a college setting, but not the sort of college setting that typically governs a college performing arts program. Yet, this *is* a college, with three sets of programs. There is a college degree program (three years in England), a one-year certificate program, and an evening program. The evening program is designed for local residents, most of them in bands. It isn't so hard to imagine a young, possibly wiser, McCartney emerging from this program.

During the last ten to twenty years, we have seen the American share of the world record market go from about 65% to 55%. This has happened because Asia, South America, and other territories are starting to sell CDs in quantity. Imagine what will happen as China and India become important factors in the world record market. It isn't difficult to see the American share of the record business become half of what it is today by the middle of the twenty-first century.

At the same time, world record sales have, for the most part, declined. Major labels have actually closed branches in some countries because of the problem of piracy. In a number of countries, especially China and Indonesia, there is a tremendous problem with illegal duplicators. These are not record consumers sharing files on their computers, but people literally duplicating CDs and cover art, and selling product for bargain basement prices. Periodically, the United States has pressured the Chinese government, and they have cracked down on a handful of illegal CD duplicators. A few months go by, and the factories re-open for business. Their product is sold not only in China, but all over Asia and Africa.

While this process has been going on, the ownership of the major record and film countries has become increasingly international. As we discussed earlier in this book, the Warner Record Group is now the only American-owned record company. How will this shift of ownership and market share transform the world record business?

America is one of the few countries in the world where young people don't quickly learn one, two, or three foreign languages. For years, the entertainment business has been rooted in the English language. In most other parts of the world a large portion of the population is reasonably fluent in two or three languages. As more and more Spanish-speaking people become part of the American demographic tapestry, this picture will inevitably change.

Sooner or later, there will be a supergroup made up of representatives from three or four continents. They will speak and sing in four or more languages, and the demand for them will truly be global. They will be welcomed in all parts of the world because they are representative of people from all over the world. They will from different cultures, and be of different colors, and once a group like this exists, there will be many others that will copy this approach.

Other seemingly inevitable developments in the music industry will involve a much more creative utilization of music video. The music and the video will complement one another, and yet may lead artistically in different directions. This will overcome the typical over-simplification of music videos, which often fall into dull stereotypes.

Just as Ron Sobel explained how music retailing and distribution will change dramatically, so will the art of performance. As the world of technology shrinks the geographic world, the art and style of performance will inevitably change. If it doesn't, people will have no more desire to go to live performances than they will to go to retail record stores. The art of performance must evolve as dramatically as the methods of music merchandising, or there will be no reason for people to buy tickets.

Part of this change will be the integration of regional and territorial music styles into the overall universe of popular music. Another part of it will be the integration of dance, theater, and music into what we have historically called music performance. More than ever, people will be seeking meaningful if broader based experiences when they listen to music. It's a difficult time, an evolutionary time, and an exciting time. With vision and planning it can be your time.

Resources for Afterword

Look for my forthcoming book, *The International Music Business*, co-authored with Arthur Bernstein, of the Liverpool Institute for Performing Arts and Naoki Sakine, who represents Sony Records in seventeen Asian countries, published by Routledge in 2006. For details about the Australian music business, check out Shane Simpson's *Music Business*, published by Omnibus Press in London in 2002.

APPENDIX

State Art Councils

Alabama State Council on the Arts
1 Dexter Ave.
Montgomery, AL 36150-1800
334/242-4076
www.arts.state.al.us

Alaska State Council On The Arts
411 W. 4th Ave., Suite 1E
Anchorage, AK 99501-234
907/269-6610

American Samoa Arts Council
PO Box 1540
Pago, Pago AS 96799
0116846334347

Arizona Commission on the Arts
411 W. Roosevelt Ave.
Phoenix, AZ 85003
602/255-5882
www.ArizonaArts.org

Arkansas Arts Council
1500 Tower Bldg.
323 Center Street
Little Rock, AK 72001
501/324-9766
www.arkansasarts.com

California Arts Council
1300 I St., Suite 930
Sacramento, CA 95814
916/322-655
www.cac.ca.gov

Colorado Council on the Arts
750 Pennsylvania St.
Denver, CO 80203-3699
303/894-2617
www.coloarts.state.co.us

Connecticut Commission on the Arts
755 Main St.
Hartford, CT 06103
860/566-4770
www.ctarts.org

Delaware Division of the Arts
820 N. French St.
Wilmington, DE 19801
302/577-3540
www.artsdel.org

District of Columbia Commission on the Arts and Humanities
410 8th St. NW, 5th Floor,
Washington, DC 20004
202/724-5613
www.dcarts.dc.gov

Florida Division of Cultural
Dept. of State, The Capitol
Tallahasse, FL 32399-0250
904/484-2980
www.flordia-arts.org

Georgia Council on the Arts
503 Means St. NW, Ste. 115
Atlanta, GA 30318
404/685-2787
www/gaarts.org

Hawaii State Foundation
44 Merchant St.
Honolulu, HI 96813
808/586-0306
www.hawaii.gov/sfca

Idaho Commission on the Arts
PO Box 83720
Boise, ID 93720-0008
208/334-2119
www.state,id.us/arts

Illinois Arts Council
State of Illinois Center
100 W. Randolph St., #10-500
Chicago, IL 60601
312/814-6750
www.state.il.us/agency/iac

Indiana Arts Commission
402 W. Washington St., #072
Indianapolis, IN 46204
317/232-1268
www.IN.gov/arts

Iowa Arts Council
State Capitol Complex
600 E. Locust St.
Des Moines, IA 50319
515/281-4451
www.culturalaffairs.org/iac

Kansas Arts Commission
700 SW Jackson, Suite 1004
Topeka, KS 66603
782/296-3335
ww.arts.state.ks.us

Kentucky Arts Council
31 Fountain Place
Frankfort, KY 40601
502/564-3757
www.kyarts.org

Louisiana Division of the Arts
P.O. Box 44247
Baton Rouge, LA 70804
225/342-8180
www.crt.state.la.us

Maine Arts Commission
55 Capitol St.
State House, Station 25
Augusta, ME 04333
207/287-2724
www.mainearts.com

Maryland State Arts Council
601 N. Howard St., 1st Floor
Baltimore, MD 21201
410/767-6555
www.msac.org

Massachusetts Cultural Council
10 St. James Ave., 3rd floor
Boston, MA 02116
617/727-3668
www.massculturalcouncil.org

Michigan Council for the Arts
1200 6th Ave., Executive Plaza
Detroit, MI 48226-2461
517/241-4011
www.michigan.gov/ha

Minnesota State Arts Board
Park Square Court
400 Sibley S., Suite 200
Saint Paul, MN 55101-1949
651/215-1600
www..arts.state.mn.us

Mississippi Arts Commission
239 N. Lamar St., 2nd Floor
Jackson, MS 39201
601/359-6030
www.arts.state.ms.us

Missouri Arts Council
111 N. 7th St., Suite 105,
St. Louis, MO63101
314/340-6845
www.missouriartscounci.org

Montana Arts Council
PO Box 202201
316 North Park Ave., Rm. 252
Helena, MT 59620
406/44-4-6430
www.art.state.mt.us

Nebraska Arts Council
3838 Davenport
Omaha, NE 68131-2329
402/595-2122
www.nebraskaartscouncil.org

Nevada State Council on the Arts
602 N. Curry St.
Carson City, NV 89710
702/687-6680
www.dmla.clan.lib.nv.us/doc/arts

**New Hampshire State Council
on the Arts**
40 N. Main St., Phenix Hall
Concord, NH 03301
603/271-2789
www.state.nh.us/nh/us/nharts

**New Jersey State Council
on the Arts**
20 W. State St., 3rd Floor, CN 306
Trenton, NJ 08625-0306
609/292-6130

New Mexico Arts Division
228 E. Palace Ave.
Santa Fe, NM 87501
505/827-6490
www.nmarts.org

New York State Council on the Arts
915 Broadway
New York, NY 10010
212/627-4455
www.nysca.org

North Carolina Arts Council
Dept. of Cultural Resources
Raleigh, NC 27699-4632
919/733-2111
www.ncarts.org

North Dakota Council on the Arts
Office of Arts, 800 Governor Drive
Bismarck, ND 58501-4086
701/328-3954
www.state.md.us/arts

**Commonwealth Council for Arts
Northern Mariana Islands**
P.O. Box 5553 CHRB
Saipan, MP 96950
670/322-9982
www.nasaa-arts.org/aoa/nmar.shtml

Ohio Arts Council
722 E. Main St
Columbus, OH 43205
614/466-2613
www.oac.state.oh.us

State Arts Council of Oklahoma
PO Box 52001-2002, Jim Thorpe Bldg.
Oklahoma City, OK 73152-2001
405/521-2931

Oregon Arts Commission
775 Summer St. NE
Salem, OR 97310
503/986-0082
www.oregonartscommission.org/
main.php

Pennsylvania Council on the Arts
216 Finance Bldg.
Harrisburg, PA 17120
717/787-6883
www.artsnet.org/pca/pca

Institute of Puerto Rican Culture
P.O. Box 4184
San Juan, PR 00905-4184
787/725-5137
www.icp.gobierno.pr

**Rhode Island State Council
on the Arts**
95 Cedar St., D Suite 103
Providence, RI 02903-1024
401/277-3880
www.risca.state.ri.us

South Carolina Arts Commission
1800 Gervais St.
Columbia, SC 29201
803/734-8696
www.state.sc.us/arts

South Dakota Arts Council
Office of Arts, 800 Governor Drive
Pierre, SD 57101-2294
605/773-3131
www.state.sd.us/deca/sdarts

Tennesse Arts Commission
404 James Robertson Parkway,
Ste. 160
Nashville, TN 37243-0708
615/741-1701
www.arts.state.tn.us

Texas Commission on the Arts
P.O. Box 13406, Capitol Station
Austin, TX 78711
512/463-5535
www.arts.state.tx.us

Utah Arts Council
617 E. South Temple St.
Salt Lake City, UT 84102
801/236-7555
www.arts.utah.gov

Vermont Council on the Arts
136 State St., Drawer 33
Montpelier, VT 05633-6001
802/828-3291
www.vermontartscouncil.org

Virgin Islands Council on the Arts
P.O. Box 103
41-42 Norre Gade
St. Thomas, VI 00804
802/774-5984

Virginia Commission forthe Arts
223 Governor St.
Richmond, VA 23219
804/225-3132
www.arts.state.va.us

Washington State Arts Commission
P.O. Box 42675
234 E. 8th Ave.
Olypmia, WA. 98504-2775
360/753-3860
www.arts.wa.gov

West Virginia Department of Culture & History
1900 Kanawha Blvd. East
Cultural Center
Charleston, WV 23303
304/558-0240
www.wvculture.org

Wisconsin Arts Board
101 E. Wilson St., 1st Floor
Madison, WI 53702
608/266-0190
www.arts.state.wi.us/static

Wyoming Arts Council
320 Capitol Ave.
Cheyenne., WY 82002
307/777-7742
www.wyoarts.state.wy.us

Regional Arts Organizations

Arts Midwest
Hennepin Center for the Arts
2908 Hennepin Ave., Ste. 200
Minneapolis, MN 55408-1954
612/341-0755
www.southernarts.org
www.artsmidwest.org

Arts Northwest
P.O. 1354
Port Angeles, WA 98362
360/417-9290
www.artsnw.org

Consortium for Pacific Arts & Cultures
2141-C Atherton Rd.
Honolulu, HI 96822
808/946-7381

Mid America Arts Alliance
912 Baltimore Ave., Ste. 700
Kansas City, MO 64105
816/421-1388
www.maaa.org

Mid Atlantic Arts Foundation
202 North Charles St., Ste. 401
Baltimore, MD 21202
410/539-6656
www.midatlanticarts.org

New England Foundation for the Arts
266 Summer St., 2nd floor
Boston, MA 02210
617/951-0010
www.nefa.org

Southern Arts Federation
1800 Peachtree St., Ste. 808
Atlanta, GA 30309
404/874-7244

Western States Arts Foundation
1743 Wazee St., Ste. 500
Denver, CO 80202
303/629-1166
www.westaf.org

Canadian Arts Councils

Alberta Arts Development Branch
901 Standard Life Centre
10405 Jasper Ave.
Edmonton, Alberta T5J 4R7
780/427-6315
www.cdgov.ab.ca

B.C. Council for the Performing Arts
P.O. 9817 State Provincial Govt.
Victoria, BC V8W 9W3
250/356-1718
www.bcarts.council.ca

Manitoba Arts Council
525-93 Lombard Ave.
Winnipeg, MN R3B 3B1
204/945-2237
www.artscouncil.mb.ca

New Brunswick Arts Council
39 King St.
Saint John, NB E2L 4W 3
506/635-8019
www.nbac.ca/services

Newfoundland and
Labrador Arts Council
P.O. Box 98
St. John's, NL A1C 5H5
709/726-2212
www.nlac.hf.ca

Nova Scotia Arts &
Culture Partnership
1800 Argyle St., Ste. 402
Halifax, NS B3J 2R5
902/424-4442
www.ns.ca/dtc/culture

Northwest Territories
Division of Culture/Heritage
1320 Yellowknife
NT S1A 2L9
862/873-7551
www.ece.gov/nt.ca/divisions/
culture/heritage

Ontario Arts Council
151 Bloor St., #500
Toronto, ON M55 1T6
416/961-1660
www.arts.on.ca

Prince Edward Island
Council for the Arts
15 Richmond St.
Charlottetown, PEI C1A iH7
902/368-4410
www.peiartsocuncil.com

Quebec Conseil des Arts et des
Lettres du Quebec
79 Boul. René-Lévesque Est, 3e étage
Québec, Québec G1R 5N5
418/643-1707
www.calq.gouv.qc.ca

Saskatchewan Arts Board
2240 Broad St.
Regina, SK S4P 3V7
306/586-1250
www.osac.sk.c2

For sound recording loans, new talent demo awards and international tour support:

Foundation to Assist Canadian Talent On Record (FACTOR)
335 King St. W., 5th floor
Toronto, ON M5V
416/351-1361

Video FACT Video Foundation to Assist Canadian Talent
266 Richmond St. West, Suite 501
Toronto, ON M5V 1W
5416/546-8896
http://www.muchmusic.com/music/videofact/info.asp

State Humanities Councils

Alabama Humanities Foundation
2217 Tenth Court South
Birmingham, AL 35205
205/558-3840
www.ahf/net

Alaska Humanities Forum
421 W. 1st Ave., Ste. 300
Anchorage, AK 99501
www.akhf.org

Arizona Humanities Council
Ellis-Shackelford House
242 N. Central Ave.
Phoenix, AZ 85004
602/257-0335
www.aahumanities.org

California Council for the Humanities
312 Sutter, Ste. 601
San Francisco, CA 94108
415/391-1474
www.calhum.org

Colorado Endowment for the Humanities
1490 Lafayette St., Ste. 101
Denver, CO 80218
303/894-7951
www.ceh.org

Connecticut Humanities Council
955 S. Main St., Ste. E
Middletown, CT 06457
203/685-2260
www.ctculture.org

Delaware Humanities Forum
100 W. 10171 St., Ste. 1009
Wilmington, DE 19801
302/657-0650
www.dhf.org

The Humanities Council of Washington, DC
925 U Street NW
Washington, DC 20001
202/387-8391
wdchumanities.org

Florida Humanities Council
599 Second St. South
St. Petersburg, FL 33701
727/553-3800
www.flahum.org/

Georgia Humanities Council
50 Hurt Plaza, S.E.
Suite 595
Atlanta, Georgia 30303
404/523-6220
www.georgiahumanities.org

Guam Humanities Council
111 Chalan Santo Papa
Hagatna, Guam 96910
671/472-4461
www.guamhumanitiescouncil.org

Hawaii Council for the Humanities
First Hawaiian Bank Bldg.
3599 Waielae Ave., Rm. 23
Honolulu, HI 96816
808/732-5402
www.hihumanities.org

Idaho Humanities Council
217 West State St.
Boise, ID 83702
208/345-5346
www.idahohumanities.org

Illinois Humanities Council
203 N. Wabash Ave., Ste. 2020
Chicago, IL 60601-2417
312/422-5580
www.prairie.org

Indiana Humanities Council
1500 N. Delaware St.
Indianapolis, IN 46202
317/638-1500
www.ihc4u.org

Iowa Humanities Board
100 Oakdale Campus
Iowa City, IA 52242-5000
319/335-4153
http://www.uiowa.edu/~humiowa/

Kansas Humanities Council
112 West Sixth St., Ste. 210
Topeka, KS 66603
913/357-0359
www.kansashumanities.org

Kentucky Humanities Council
206 E. Maxwell St.
Lexington, KY 40508
859/257-5932
www.kyhumanities.org

**Louisiana Endowment
for the Humanities**
938 Lafayette St., Ste. 300
New Orleans, LA 70113
504/529-2357
www.leh.org

Maine Humanities Council
674 Brighton Ave.
Portland, ME 04112-1012
207/773-5051
www.mainehumanities.org

Maryland Humanities Council
108 W. Center St.
Baltimore, MD 21201
410/771-0650
www.mdhc.org

**Massachusetts Foundation
for the Humanities**
66 Bridge St.
Northampton, MA 01060
www.mfh.org

Michigan Humanities Council
119 Pere Marquette Dr., Ste. 3B
Lansing, MI 48912
517/372-7770
michiganhumanities.org

Minnesota Humanities Commission
987 E. Ivy Ave.
St. Paul, MN 55106
612/774-0105
www.thinkmhc.org

Mississippi Humanities Council
3825 Ridgewood Rd., Rm. 311
Jackson, MS 39211-6453
601/432-6752
www.mshumanities.org

Missouri Humanities Council
543 Hanley Industrial Court, Ste. 201
St. Louis, MO 63144
314/781-9660
www.mohumanities.org

**Montana Commission
for the Humanities**
311 Brantly Hall
University of Montana
Missoula, MT 59812-8214
406/243-6022
www.umt.edu/lastbest

Nebraska Humanities Council
Lincoln Center Building, Ste. 225
215 Centennial Mall South
Lincoln, NE 68508
402/474-2131
www.nebraskahumanities.org

Nevada Humanities Committee
1034 N. Sierra Street
Reno, NV 89507
775/784-6587
www.nevadahumanities.org

**New Hampshire
Humanities Council**
19 Pillsbury St.
P.O. Box 2228
Concord, NH 03302-2228
603/224-4071
www.nhhc.org

**New Jersey Council
for the Humanities**
28 West State St., 6th Floor
Trenton, NJ 08608
609/695-4838
www.njch.org

**New Mexico Endowment
for the Humanities**
Onate Hall, Room 209
University of New Mexico
Albuquerque, NM 87131
505/277-3705
www.nmeh.org

**New York Council
for the Humanities**
150 Broadway, Ste. 1700
New York, NY 10038
212/233-1131
www.nyhumanities.org

North Carolina Humanities Council
200 South Elm St., Ste. 403
Greensboro, NC 27401
336/334-5325
www.nchumanities.org

North Dakota Humanities Council
2900 Broadway East, Ste. 3
P.O. Box 2191
Bismarck, ND 58502
701/255-3360
www.nd-humanities.org

**Northern Mariana Islands Council
for the Humanities**
P.O. Box 506437
Saipan, MP 96950
670/235-4785
cnmi.humanities.org.mp

Ohio Humanities Council
695 Bryden Road
P.O. Box 06354
Columbus, OH 43206-0354
614/461-7802
www.ohiohumanities.org

Oklahoma Humanities Council
Festival Plaza
428 West California, Suite 270
Oklahoma City, OK 73102
405/235-0280
www.okhumanitiescouncil.org

Oregon Council for the Humanities
812 SW Washington St., Ste.225
Portland, OR 97205
503/241-0543
www.oregonhum.org/

Pennsylvania Humanities Council
325 Chestnut St., Ste. 715
Philadelphia, PA 19106
215/925-1005
www.pahumanities.org

**Fundación Puertorriqueña
de las Humanidades**
109 San Jose St., 3rd floor
Box 9023920
San Juan, PR 00902-3920
787/721-2087
www.fphpr.org

**Rhode Island Committee
for the Humanities**
385 Westminster St., Ste. 2
Providence, RI 02903
401/273-2250
www.uri.edu/rich

**The Humanities Council of
South Carolina**
1308 Columbia College Dr.
P.O. Box 5287
Columbia, SC 29250
803/691-4100
www.schumanities.org

South Dakota Humanities Council
Box 7050, University Station
Brookings, SD 57007
605/688-6113
web.sdstate.edu/humanities

Tennessee Humanities Council
1003 18th Avenue South
Nashville, TN 37212
615/320-7001
tn-humanities.org

Texas Council for the Humanities
Banister Place A
3809 South Second Street
Austin, TX 78704
512/440-1991
www.humanitiestexas.org

Utah Humanities Council
202 West 300 North
Salt Lake City, UT 84103-1108
801/359-9670
www.utahhumanities.org

Vermont Council on the Humanities
11 Loomis Street
Montpelier, VT 05602
802/262-2626
www.vermonthumanities.org

Virgin Islands Humanities Council
5-6 Kongens Gade, Corbiere Complex
Suites 200B and 201B
St. Thomas, VI 00802
340/776-4044
www.vihumanities.org

**Virginia Foundation for the
Humanities and Public Policy**
145 Ednam Dr.
Charlottesville, VA 22903-4629
804/924-3296
www.virginia.edu/vfh

**Washington Commission
for the Humanities**
615 Second Avenue, Suite 300
Seattle, WA 98104
206/682-1770
www.humanities.org

West Virginia Humanities Council
1310 Kanawha Blvd. East, Suite 800
Charleston, WV 25301
304/346-8500
www.wvhumanities.org

Wisconsin Humanities Council
222 South Bedford Street, Suite F
Madison, WI 53703-3688
608/262-0706
www.wisconsinhumanities.org

**Wyoming Council
for the Humanities**
1315 E. Lewis Street
Laramie, WY 82072-3459
307/721-9244
www.uwyo.edu/humanities

Young Audiences
(Note: Not all branches have web sites.)

**National Office –
Young Audiences Inc.**
115 East 92nd St.
New York, NY 10128-1688
212/831-8110
www.youngaudiences.org

Arizona
Santa Cruz County Young Audiences
P.O. Box 1571
Nogales, AZ 85621
520/287-0800
youngaudiences@nusd.k12.az.us

California
Young Audiences of Northern California
San Francisco
415/974-5554
www.ya-nc.org

Santa Clara Office of Education
San Jose
408/453-6677
www.ya-nc.org

Young Audiences of Kern County
Bakersfield
661/832-0109
www.stroudpuppets.com/YA/

Young Audiences of San Diego
San Diego
619/282-7599
www.yasandiego.org

Colorado
Young Audiences of Colorado
Denver
720/904-8890
www.youngaudiencescolorado.org

Connecticut
Young Audiences of Connecticut
Hamden
203/230-8101
www.yaconn.org

District of Columbia
Young Audiences of Washington, DC
202/944-2790

Georgia
Young Audiences,
Woodruff Arts Center
Atlanta
404/733-5293
www.yawac.org

Indiana
Young Audiences of Indiana
Indianapolis
317/925-4043
www.yaindy.org

Louisiana
Young Audiences of New Orleans
504/523-3525
www.ya4la.org

Maryland
Young Audiences of Maryland
Baltimore
410/837-7577
www.yamd.org

Massachusetts
Young Audiences of Massachusetts
Somerville
617/629-9262
www.yamass.org

Michigan
Young Audiences of Michigan
Detroit
313/417-9850

Minnesota
Young Audiences of Minnesota
St. Paul
www.youngaudiencesofmn.org

Missouri
Kansas City Chapter of Young Audiences
Kansas City
816/531-4022
www.kcya.org

Young Audiences of St. Louis
St. Louis
314/968-5554
www.yastl.org

Montana
Young Audiences of Western Montana
Missoula
406/721-3194

New Jersey
Young Audiences of New Jersey
Princeton
609/243-9000
www.yanj.org

New York
Young Audiences/New York
New York City
212/319-9269
www.yany.org

Rochester Chapter of Young Audiences
Rochester
585/530-2060
www.yarochester.info

Young Audiences of Western New York
Buffalo
716/881-0917
www.yawny.org

Ohio
Young Audiences of Greater Cleveland, Inc.
Cleveland
216/561-5005
www.yagc.org

Oregon
Young Audiences of Oregon and
SW Washington
Portland
503/225-5900
www.ya-or.org

Pennsylvania
Young Audiences of
Eastern Pennsylvania
Philadelphia
215/772-0460
www.yaep.org

Texas
Young Audiences of Abilene
915/677-1161
www.abilenecac.org/ya.html

Young Audiences of North Texas
Dallas
214/520-9988
www.yanorthtexas.org

Young Audiences of Houston
713/520-9264
www.yahouston.org

Young Audiences of Northeast Texas
Tyler
903/561-2787
ya@tyler.net

Young Audiences of Southeast Texas
Beaumont
409/835-3884
www.geocities.com/~yasetx

Virginia
Young Audiences of Virginia
Norfolk
757/466-7555
www.yav.org

National Arts & Humanities Councils
Don't overlook the more generous grant programs offered by the following:

National Endowment for the Arts
100 Pennsylvania Ave., NW
Washington, DC 20506
202/682.5400
www.nea.gov

**National Endowment
for the Humanities**
1100 Pennsylvania Avenue, NW
Washington, DC 20506
1-800-NEH-1121
www.neh.gov

Canada Council
350 Albert St.
P.O. Box 1047
Ottawa, ON K1P 5V8
1-800-263-5588
www.canadacouncil.ca

In addition to government grants, there are numerous private foundations and organizations that have grant programs. For information in your state, check with the local arts and humanities councils, or the reference librarian at your local library. There are numerous books about grants that describe available grants, and offer tips about how to write successful proposals. Check into the latest publications of the *Washington International Arts Letter,* 1321 4th St., SW, Washington, DC, 20204, and the materials available from the Foundation Center, 79 Fifth Ave., New York, NY 10003-3076 (www.fdncenter.org). The Foundation Center also sells computer printouts that list specific grant areas, such as grants for composers. There are branch offices in Atlanta, Cleveland, San Francisco, and Washington, DC.

University libraries are a good place to look for information about grants. Many universities have extensive grant programs that support as substantial amount of their research. The librarians in these facilities are quite familiar with grant programs.

Arts Organizations Dealing with Special Populations
(Alphabetically by state.)

Performing Tree
Los Angeles Unified School District
1320 W. Third St.
Los Angeles, CA 90017
213/482-8831

Artreach
3400 W. 38th Ave.
Denver, CO 80212
303/433-2882
www.artreach.denver.org

Access
Durham Arts Council
120 Morris St.
Durham, NC 27701
919/682-5519

Artreach-Dallas, Inc.
626 N. Hill St.
Dallas, TX 75219
214/219-2006

Cultural Experiences Unlimited
P.O. Box 808
Norfolk, VA 23501
804/625-7857

Artreach
152 W. Wisconsin Ave., #434
Milwaukee, WI 53203
414/271-4704

Volunteer Lawyers for the Arts Groups

In deference to the fact that many artists and musicians cannot afford adequate representation, a number of lawyers contribute their time at little or no costs to aid artists in obtaining this help. Volunteer Lawyers for the Arts is a national organization that compiles an annual directory that lists each of the organizations that offer such help, along with their criteria for eligibility, and what costs they may require for this service. You can purchase this directory by writing to the Volunteer Lawyers for the Arts, 1 East 53rd St., Sixth Floor, New York, NY 10022-4201, 212/319-ARTS, www.vlany.org. The list printed below is printed with the kind permission of the Volunteer Lawyers for the Arts, without the detailed information about costs and service that appears in their directory.

California
Beverly Hills Bar Association
Barristers Committee for the Arts
300 S. Beverly Dr., #201
Beverly Hills, CA 90212
310/553-6644

California Lawyers for the Arts
(Sacramento)
926 J St., Ste. 811
Sacramento, CA 95814
916/442-6210

California Lawyers for the Arts
(San Francisco)
Fort Mason Center, Building C,
Rm. 255
San Francisco, CA 94123
415/775-7200

California Lawyers for the Arts (Santa Monica)
1641 18th St.
Santa Monica, CA 90404
310/998-5590

Colorado
Colorado Lawyers for the Arts
P.O. Box 48148
Denver, CO 80204
303/722 7994

Connecticut
Connecticut Volunteer Lawyers
for the Arts
Connecticut Commission on
Culture and Tourism
755 Main St.
Hartford, CT 06103
203/566-4770

District of Columbia
Washington Area Lawyers for the Arts
810 15th St., Ste. 900
617/550-7600
Washington, DC 20005
202/393-2826

Florida
Volunteer Lawyers for the
Arts of Western Florida
14700 Terminal Blvd., Ste. 229
Clearwater, FL 33762
727/453-7860

Georgia
Southeast Volunteer Lawyers for the Arts
c/o Bureau of Cultural Affairs
675 Ponce De Leon Ave., 5th Fl.
Atlanta, GA 30308
404/873-3911

Illinois
Lawyers for the Creative Arts
213 W. Institute Pl., Suite 403
Chicago, IL 60610
312/649-4111

Kansas
Mid-America Arts Resources
c/o Susan J. Whitfield-Lofgren, Esq.
P.O. Box 363
Lindsborg, KS 67456
913/227-2321

Louisiana
Louisiana Volunteer Lawyers for the Arts
225 Baronet Street, Suite 1712
New Orleans, LA 70112
504/523 1465

Maine
Maine Lawyers and Accountants
for the Arts
43 Pleasant St.
South Portland, ME 04106
207/799-9646

or 4 Dane St.
Kenneybunk ME 04043
207/985-1199

Massachusetts
Volunteer Lawyers for the Arts of
Massachusetts, Inc.
249 A Street, Studio 14
Boston, MA 02210
617/350-7600

Minnesota
Minnesota Resources and
Counseling for the Arts
308 Prince St., Ste. 270
St. Paul, MN 55101
612/292-4381

Missouri
St. Louis Volunteer Lawyers and
Accountants for the Arts
3540 Washington
St. Louis, MO 63103
314/652-2410

Montana

Montana Volunteer Lawyers for the Arts
P.O. Box 8687
Missoula, MT 59807
406/721-1835

New Hampshire

Lawyers for the Arts
New Hampshire Business
Committee for the Art
One Granite Pl.
Concord, NH 03301
603/224-8300

New York

Albany/Schenectady League of Arts Inc.
19 Clinton Ave.
Albany NY 12207
518/449-5380

Volunteer Lawyers for the Arts
1 E. 53rd St., 6th Floor
New York, NY 10022
212/319-2787;

North Carolina

*North Carolina Volunteer
Lawyers for the Arts*
P.O. Box 26513
Raleigh, NC 27611
919/990-2575

Ohio

*Volunteer Lawyers and Accountants
for the Arts-Cleveland*
113 St. Clair Ave.
Cleveland, OH 44114
216/696-3525

*Toledo Volunteer Lawyers and
Accountants for the Arts*
608 Madison, Ste. 1523
Toledo, OH 43604
419/255-3344

Oregon

Northwest Lawyers and Artists, Inc.
621 SW Morrison St., Ste. 1417
Portland, OR 97205
503-/95-2787

Pennsylvania

*Philadelphia Volunteer Lawyers
for the Arts*
251 South 18th St.
Philadelphia, PA 19103
215/545-3385

Western Pennsylvania Professionals
P.O. Box 19388
Pittsburgh, PA 15213
412/268-8437

Rhode Island

Ocean State Lawyers for the Arts
P.O. Box 19
Saunderstown, RI 02874
401/789-5686

South Dakota

South Dakota Arts Council (SDAC)
800 Governors Drive
Pierre, SD 57501
605/773-3131

Texas

Artists' Legal and Accounting Assistance
P.O. Box 2577
Austin, TX 78751
512/476-4458

*Lawyers and Accountants of
North Texas for the Arts*
P.O. Box 2019
Cedar Hill, TX 75106
972/291-9010

Texas Accountants & Lawyers for the Arts
1540 Sul Ross
Houston, TX 77006
713/526-4876

Utah
Utah Lawyers for the Arts
P.O. Box 652
Salt Lake City, UT 84110
801/482-5373

Washington
Washington Lawyers for the Arts
1634 11th Ave.
Seattle, WA 98122
206/328-7053

Canada
Canadian Artists' Representation
Ontario (CARO)
183 Bathurst St., 1st floor
Toronto, ON M5T 2R7
416/340-7791

U.S. Locals of the
American Federation of Musicians (AFM)

The union is making a real effort to service today's traveling musicians, and has introduced a 24-hour 800 hotline, which offers immediate legal help to musicians who are having contractual problems with clubs or promoters. The number is 800/ROAD-GIG.

The AFM is currently consolidating some of the smaller locals of the union. Because this process is rapidly changing the jurisdiction of various locals, to find out which local services your territory look in the Yellow Pages under unions. Many of the locals have names likes the Denver Musicians Association, or they can be found under the heading American Federation of Musicians. You can contact the American Federation of Musicians at 1501 Broadway, Suite 600, New York, NY, 20036, 212-869-1330. www.af,.org The Canadian office is at 75 The Donway West, Mills, ON M3C 2E9 416/391-5161; www.afm.org/public/departments/canada.

Songwriters' Associations (U.S.)

(Note: these addresses often shift as officers of the organizations change. To make sure your information is current check the annual Songwriter's Market, or consult ASCAP, BMI, or SESAC. Note many of these organizations don't have web sites, and operate out of the homes of the organization's officers. These contacts will change from time to time.)

Alabama
Alabama Songwriters Guild
P.O. Box 272
Garden City, AL 35070
256/352-4873

Alaska
Alaska Songwriters Association
P.O. Box 33552
Juneau, AK 99803
907/789-0613

Arkansas
Arkansas Songwriters Association
6817 Gingerbread Ln.
Little Rock, AR, 72204
501/565-8889

California
*Northern California
Songwriters Association*
855 Oak Grove
Menlo Park, 94025
415/327-8296

San Diego Songwriters Guild
3368 Governor Dr., Ste. F-326
San Diego, CA 96122
619/225-2131

Colorado
Colorado Music Association (COMA)
8 East 1st Avenue, #107
Denver, CO 80203
213/462-1108
www.coloradomusic.org

Connecticut
Connecticut Songwriters Association
40 Bruggeman Pl.
Mystic, CT 06355
860/572-9285

District of Columbia
Songwriters Association of Washington
4200 Wisconsin Ave. N.W.,
PMB 106-137
Washington, DC, 20016.
301/654-8434

Florida
*North Florida Christian
Music Writers Association*
P.O. Box 6113
Jacksonville, FL 33236

Songwriters Association of Jacksonville
P.O. 10394
Jacksonville Beach, FL 32207

Hawaii
Hawaii Songwriters Association
P.O. Box 655
Pahoa, HI 9677
808/965-8901

Illinois
Chicago Songwriters Collective
www.chicagosongwriters.com

Indianapolis
Indianapolis Songwriters Association, Inc.
P.O. Box 44724
Indianapolis, IN 46244-0724

Kansas
United Songwriters Association
6429 Leavenworth Rd.
Dept. 2130, 1715 Marty
Kansas City, KS 66104
913/788-7716

Great Plains Songwriters Association
708 Massachusetts, Ste. 208
Lawrence, KS 66044

Kentucky
Louisville Songwriters Cooperative
P.O. Box 16, Peewee Valley, KY 40056
503/241-1645

Louisiana
Louisiana Songwriters Association
P.O. Box 80425
Baton Rouge, LA 70898-0425

Massachusetts
Boston Songwriters Workshop
14 Skelton RD.
Burlington, MA 01803

Michigan
Michigan Songwriters Association
P.O. Box 26044
Fraser, MI 48026

Minnesota
Minnesota Association of Songwriters
Minneapolis, MN 55458

Missouri
Missouri Association of Songwriters
HCR1 Box 157E
Eminence, MO 66466

Missouri Songwriters Association
693 Green Forest Dr.
Fenton, MO 63026
314/343-6662

Nevada
Las Vegas Songwriters Association
P.O. 42683, Las Vegas, NV 89116-0683
702/223-7255

New York
The Songwriter Advocate
47 Maplehurst Rd.
Rochester, NY 14617
716/266-0679

North Carolina
Central Carolina
Songwriters Association
1144 Amber Acres Ln.
Knightdale, NC 27545
919/266-5791

Ohio
Songwriters & Poets Critique
11599 Coontz Rd., Orient, OH 43146
614/877-1727

Oklahoma
Tulsa Songwriters Association
P.O. Box 254, Tulsa, 74101-0254
918/665-3334

Oregon
Portland Songwriters Association
1920 N. Vancouver
Portland, OR 97227
503/727-9072

Pennsylvania
Philadelphia Songwriters Forum
332 Eastwood Ave.
Feasterville, PA 19053

Pittsburgh Songwriters Association
124 W. Edgewood Dr.
McMurray, PA 15317-3364

Tennessee
The Tennessee Songwriters Association
P.O. Box 2664
Hendersonville, TN 38077-2664
615/824-4555

Knoxville Songwriters Association
P.O. Box 603
Knoxville, TN 37901
423/933-4488

Memphis Songwriters Association
1494 Prescott St., 38111
Memphis, TN 38122
901/677-0906

Nashville Songwriters Association
1701 West End Ave., 3rd Floor
Nashville, TN 37203
www.nashvillesongwriters.com

Texas
Austin Songwriters Group
P.O. Box 2578
Austin, TX 78768
512/338-1200

Dallas Songwriters Association
3630 Harry Hines Blvd. Box 20
Dallas, TX 75219
214/750-0916

Fort Worth Songwriters Association
8301 Boat Club Rd., #312
Fort Worth, TX 76179
817/236-3855

Vermont
New England Songwriters Association
P.O. Box 207
Jamaica, VT 05343
802/874-4360

Virginia
*Charlottesville Area
Songwriters Association*
P.O. Box 4825
Charlottesville, VA 22905
804/975-2272

*Southwest Virginia
Songwriters Association*
P.O. Box 698
Salem, VA 24153-0698
540/387-7541

Washington
*Pacific Northwest
Songwriters Association*
P.O. Box 98564
Seattle, WA 98198
206/824-1568

Wisconsin
Songwriters of Wisconsin International
P.O. Box 1027
Neenah, WI 54957-1027
920/725-1609

Canada
Pacific Songwriters' Association
Box 15453, 349 W. Georgia St.,
Vancouver, British Columbia, V6B-5B2
604/876-SONG

Songwriters Association of Canada
3600 Billings Ct., #204
Burlington, ON L7N 3N6905
681-6320

Performing Rights Organizations

The American Society of Composers, Authors and Publishers, ASCAP
www.ascap.com

1 Lincoln Plaza
New York, NY 10023
212/595-3050

3500 W. Hubbard St., 2nd Floor,
Chicago, IL 60610
312 481-1194

2 Music Sq. W.
Nashville, TN 37203
 615/742-5000

541 Tenth St. NW
Atlanta, GA 30318
404/351-1224

420 Lincoln Rd., Ste. 385
Miami Beach, FL 33139
305/673-3446

Broadcast Music, Inc. (BMI)
www.bmi.com
20 W. 57th St.
New York, NY 10019
212/586-2000

8730 Sunset Blvd.
Los Angeles, CA 90069
310/659-9109

10 Music Sq. E.
Nashville, TN 37203
615/291-6700

5201 Blue Lagoon Dr., Ste. 310
Miami, FL 33126
305/266-3636

SESAC INC
www.sesac.com
20 W. 57th St.
New York, NY 10019
212/586-5430 or 800/826-9996

55 Music Sq. E
Nashville, TN 37203
615/320-0055

CANADA
Society of Composers, Authors & Music Publishers of Canada (SOCAN)
5201 Blue Lagoon Dr., Ste. 310
41 Valleybrook Dr.
Don Mills, ON M3B 2S6
416/445-8700
www.cosa.ca

Other Music Business Organizations

American Association for Music Therapy
9455 Colesville Rd., Ste. 1000
Silver Spring, MD 20910
589/517-5209
www.musictherapy.org
Publishes a journal and newsletter, approves college music therapy programs, offers job referrals and a list of colleges, offering music therapy programs.

American Federation of Radio & Television Artists (AFTRA)
260 Madison Ave.
New York, NY 10016
212/532-0800
A union for radio and television performers; particularly important for singers who do radio or television commercials. Regional offices in Atlanta, Boston, Buffalo, Chicago, Cleveland, Dallas-Fort Worth, Denver, Detroit, Fresno, Honolulu, Houston, Kansas City, Los Angeles, Miami, Milwaukee, Nashville, New Orleans, Omaha, Peoria, Philadelphia, Phoenix, Pittsburgh, Rochester, Sacramento, San Diego, San Francisco, Schenectady-Albany, Seattle, St. Louis, Stamford, Tri-State-Indiana, Ohio, Kentucky, Minneapolis-St. Paul, and Washington-Baltimore.

American Guild of Musical Artists (AGMA)
7 Pine Ct.
Westfield, NJ 07090
908/BEETHOVEN

American Symphony Orchestra League (ASOL)
33 W. 60th St.
New York, NY 10023-703
212/262-5162

Americans for the Arts
1 E. 53rd St.
New York, NY 10222
212/223-2787

Associated Council of the Arts
570 5th Ave.
New York, NY 10018
212/345-6655

Association of Independent Music Publishers
P.O. Box 69473
Los Angeles, CA 90069
818/771-7301

156 W 56th St., Ste. 1803
New York, NY 10022
212/758-6157
www.aimp.org

California Copyright Conference
P.O. Box 57962
Sherman Oaks, CA 91413
818/379-3312
www.theccc.org

Canadian Academy of Recording Art (CARAS)
335 King St. NW, Ste. 501
Toronto, ON M5V 1J6
416/4853235
www.carasonline.com

**Canadian Association
for Music Therapy**
Wilfrid Laurier University
Waterloo, ON N1L 3C5
519/834-1970
www.musictherapy.ca

Country Music Association (CMA)
One Music Circle S
Nashville, 37203
615/244-2840
www.cmaworld.com

Gospel Music Association
7 Music Circle N.
Nashville, 37203
615/242-0303

**Music Educators
National Conference**
1902 Association Dr.
Reston, VA 22091
703/860-4000
www.menc.org

**National Academy of Recording
Arts & Sciences (NARAS)**
3402 Pico Blvd.
Santa Monica, CA 90405
310/392-3777
www.grammy.com
*There are local chapters of NARAS in
Atlanta, Austin, Chicago, Los Angeles,
Memphis, Miami, Nashville, New York,
Philadelphia, San Francisco, Seattle, and
Washington, D.C.*

**National Association for Cam
Activities (NACA)**
P.O. Box 6828
Columbia, SC 29260
800/732-6222
www.naca.org

**National Association of Music
Industry Professionals (NARIP)**
P.O. Box 102446
Tolucca Lake, CA 91610
818/769-7207
www.narip.org

**National Association of
Music Merchants (NAMM)**
5140 Avenida Encinas
Carlsbad, CA 92008
619/438-8001
www.namm.org

**National Association of
Record Merchandisers (NARM)**
9 Eves Dr., Ste. 120
Marlton , NJ 080
856/596-2221
www.narm.com

**National Music
Publishers Association**
711 Third Ave.
New York, NY 10017
212/834-0100
www.nmpa.org

**Recording Industry Association
(RIAA)**
1020 Nineteenth St. NW,
Washington, DC 20036
202/775-0101
www.riaa.com

**Society of Audio Professionals
(SPARS)**
9 Music Sq. S., Ste. 222
Nashville, TN 37203
800/777-77217
www.spars.com
*SPARS sets up criteria for the profession
of audio engineering, and is active in
college engineering programs.*

Songwriters Guild of America (SGA)
1510 Harbor Blvd.
Weehawken, NJ 07087-6732
201/867-7603
www.songwritersresiuces.network.com

Women in Music National Network
31121 Mission Blvd., Ste. 123
Hayward, CA 94544
510/471-1752
www.womeninmusic.com
Consult this group for similar organizations in other cities. Members include all music retail chains and most record labels.

Colleges Offereing Two and Four Year Degree Progams in Music Industry, Music Merchandising & Audio Engineering in the United States and Canada

For this information we suggest that you consult the following:

MUSIC BUSINESS PROGRAMS
Visit the web site for the Music & Entertainment Industry Educators Association (MEIEA): meiea.org.

MUSIC ENGINEERING PROGRAMS
Consult the annual Mix Directory, published by MIX, 6400 Hollis St., #12, Emoryville, CA 94608, 510/653-3307.

MUSIC MERCHANDISING PROGRAMS
A free listing is available from the National Association of Music Merchants (NAMM), 5140 Avenida Encinas, Carlsbad, CA 92008, 619/438-8001.

SCHOOLS OFFERING MUSICAL INSTRUMENT REPAIR COURSES
Five Towns College
2165 Seaford Ave., Seaford, NY 11783
516/424-7000

Red Wing Vocational & Technical Institute
Red Wing, MN 55066
612/388-8271

Renton Vocational & Technical Institute
3000 NE 4th St.
Renton, WA 98056
425/235-2352

Spokane Falls Community College
3140 Fort George Wright Dr.
Spokane, WA 99204
509/459-3500

State University of New York, Agricultural & Technical College at Morrisville
Morrisville, NY 13048
315/684-6046

Trinidad State Junior College
Trinidad, CO 71082
306/846-5011

Western Iowa Technical
Community College
4647 Stone Avenue
Sioux City, IA 51106
712/274-6400

Music Trade Papers

Billboard
1515 Broadway
New York, NY 10036
www.billboard.com
A must for people in the business.

National Weekly Variety
310 Park Ave. South
New York, NY 10036

Daily Variety
5700 Wilshire Blvd., Ste. 120
Los Angeles, CA 90036
Mostly film and television, but occasional music coverage and want ads.

Hits
14958 Ventura Blvd.
Sherman Oaks, CA 91403

Hollywood Reporter
5055 Wilshire Blvd., 6th Fl.
Los Angeles, CA 94105

Music Row
1231 17th Ave. S.
Nashville, TN 37212

Pollstar
4333 N. West Ave.
Fresno, CA 93705
Focuses on live performances.

Radio and Records
2044 Century Park
W. 41st Floor
Los Angeles, CA 90067

Songwriters' Tip Sheets

Music Supervisor 411
SES Publishing
8441 Sunset Blvd., #1771
Los Angeles, CA 90069-1911
Many databases for TV and film.

Song Placement Guide
889 Vale View Dr.
Vista, CA 92083-91403

Songcasting
15445 Vista Rd.
Sherman Oaks, CA 91403

Magazines for Songwriters

American Songwriter
121 17th Ave.
Nashville, TN 37203

Performing Songwriter
P.O. Box 158519
Nashville, TN 37215-9998

Words And Music
41 Valleybrook Dr.
Don Mills, ONT
M3B 2S6
Canada

Radio Tip Sheets

The Album Network
120 N. Victory Blvd.
Burbank, CA 91502

Free Local and Regional Publications

Practically every major city has a local entertainment guide. Most of these publications are available free at music stores or entertainment-related venues. My favorite of all of these is the Music Connection, 6640 Sunset Blvd., #201, Hollywood, CA 90026, or musiconnection.com.

The Music Connection publishes frequent lists of A&R people, Music Supervisors for film and TV, managers, music publishers, etc. Out-of-towners can subscribe to the magazine.

Magazines: The Best and Most Interesting

Acoustic Guitar
P.O. 469120
Escondido, CA 92046

American Harp Journal
3006 Woodlawn Ave.
Falls Church, VA. 22042

American Recorder (the instrument)
P.O. Box 1067
Jackson, NJ 08527

American Record Guide
4412 Braddock St.
Cincinnati, OH 45204

Audio
P.O. Box 52548,
Boulder, Co. 80322

Banjo Newsletter
P.O. Box 3418,
Annapolis, MD 21403

Broadcasting
1735 De Salle St.
Washington, DC 20018

Bass Player
2600 Campus Dr.
San Mateo, CA 94403   .

Black Music Research Newsletter
c/o Columbia College
600 S. Michigan Ave.
Chicago, IL 60605

Bluegrass Unlimited
9514 James Madison Highway
Warrenton, VA 20186

Cadence
Cadence Bldg
Redwood, NY 13769

Canadian Composer   .
41 Valleybrook Dr.
Don Mills, ON M3B 2S6
Canada

Chamber Music America
305 7th Ave., 5th floor
New York, NY 10001

Chart Magazine
P.O. Box 332, Willowdale Station A
York, Ont., M2N 5S9, Canada

CMJ New Music Report
151 W. 20th St., 12th Floor
New York, NY 10001

Coda (modern jazz)
Box 1002, Station 0
Toronto, ON Canada M4A 2N4

Dirty Linen (folk music)
P.O. 66600
Baltimore, MD 21239

Down Beat
190 W. Park Ave.
Elmhurst, IL 60126

Electronic Musician
6400 Hollis St., #12
Emeryville, CA 94608

Ethnomusicology
Morrison Hall, Rm 005
Blomington, IN 47905-2501

Flute Talk
200 Northfield Rd.
Northfield, IL 60093

Goldmine (for record collectors)
Krause Publications
600 E. State St.
Iola, WI 54990

Grammy
c/o NARAS
3402 Pico Blvd., Ste. 963
Santa Monica, CA 90405

Guitar Player
411 Borel Ave., Ste. 100
San Mateo, CA 94402

Guitar World
1115 Broadway, 8th Floor
New York, BNY 10010

The Instrumentalist
200 Northfield Rd.
Northfield, IL 60093

The International Musician
1501 Broadway
New York, NY 10036
Journal of the Musicians Union,
includes want ads for symphony jobs.

Jazz Educators Journal
Box 724
Manhattan, KS 66502

Jazz Iz
2650 N. Military Trail
Fountain Sq. II Bldg, Ste. 140
Boca Raton, FL 33431

Jazz Times
8737 Colesville Dr., 9th flr.
Silver Spring, MD 20910-3921

Journal of Country Music
4 Music Sq. E.
Nashville, TN 37203

Keyboard
2600 Campus Dr.
San Mateo, CA 94403

Living Blues
Center for the Study of Southern
Culture
University of Mississippi
University, MI 38677

**Maximum Rock'N'Roll
(punk and alternative music)**
P.O. Box 460760
San Francisco, CA 94146-0760

**Millimeter (motion picture
and TV production)**
Primemedia Business
2104 Harvell Circle
Bellevue, NE 68005

**Mix (recording studios
and recording)**
6400 Hollis St., #12,
Emeryville, CA 94608

Musical America
424 W. 33rd St.
New York, NY 10001

Modern Drummer
12 Old Birdge Rd.
Cedar Grove, NJ 07009-1288

Musical Merchandise Review
21 Highland Circle, Suite 1
Needham, MA 02494

Music Educators Journal
1904 Association Dr.,
Reston, VA 22091

**Music Trades (music stores and
musical instrument manufacturers)**
P.O. Box 432,
Englewood, NJ 07631

**New York Times
(Sunday Arts section)**
220 W. 43rd St.,
New York, NY 10036

**No Depression
(alternative country music)**
P.O. Box 31332,
Seattle, WA 98103

Opera News
Dept. 70, Lincoln Center Plaza
New York, NY 10023-6593

Popular Music & Society
Routledge Publications
315 Chestnut St.
Philadelphia, PA 19106

Pro Sound News
(recording studios and equipment)
460 Park Ave.,
New York, NY 10016

Punk Planet
(essential reading for punk fans)
4229 N. Honore
Chicago, IL 60613

Recording Magazine
5412 Idylwild Trail, Suite 10
Boulder, CO 80301-3523

Rolling Stone
1290 Ave. of the Americas
New York, NY 10014-0298

Sheet Music
P.O. Box 5253,
Boulder, CO 80323

Sing Out! The Folk Song Magazine
PO. Box 5253
Bethlehem, PA 18015-0253

Stereo Review
P.O. Box 55627,
Boulder, CO 80322-5627

Up Beat (for music retailers)
190 W. Park Ave.
Elmhurst, IL 60126

Vibe (hip-hop)
PO Box 57540
Boulder, CO. 80323-7540

Washington International Arts
Letter
325 Pennsylvania Ave. SW
Washington, DC 20003

Bibliographies

The "Top Ten" books will give you a good general picture of the music business. The bibliography that follows them consists of other books with useful information.

Braheny, John. *The Craft and Business of Songwriting.* Cincinnati: Writer's Digest Books, Revised Ed., 2003. John Braheny probably knows as much as anyone about how songs are created and merchandised.

Flanagan, Bill. *Written in My Soul: Conversations with Rock's Greatest Songwriters.* Chicago: Contemporary Books, 1987. Flanagan interviewed a number of important songwriters and examines their creative processes.

Rapaport, Diane Sward: *How to Make and Sell Your Own Record.* New York: Prentice Hall, 1999, 5th Edition. An important resource for anyone who contemplates producing and/or marketing their own record or tape.

Shemel, Sidney, Wm. Krasilovsky, and John Gross. *This Business of Music, and More About This Business of Music.* New York: Billboard Publications, 9th Edition, 2003, and 5th Edition, 1994.

Small, Christopher. *Music. Society. Education.* New York: Schirmer Books, 1977. A wonderful book about music, education and society.

Songwriter's Market. Annual. Cincinnati Writer's Digest, annually.

Wallis, Roger, and Krister Malm. *Big Sounds From Small Peoples: The Music Industry in Small Countries.* New York: Pendragon Press, 1984. A superb and thought-provoking book.

Weissman, Dick. *The Music Business: Career Opportunities and Self-Defense.* Crown Publishers, New York. 3rd Revised Edition, 2003. A clear and informative book, even if I did write it.

Audio Engineering

Mix Bookshelf. 6400 Hollis St., #12, Emoryville, CA 94608, 800-223-9604 or in California 800-641-3349. Has a detailed catalog of books on this subject. It also includes audio and video tapes, music software, and books on the music business.

Crane, Larry, ed. Tape Op: *The Book About Creative Music Recording.* Venice, Ca: Ferra House, 2000. A good collection of articles.

Computers

Books about computers become out-dated so rapidly, that we suggest you look for the most recent issues at your music or book stores.

Cultural Study of Music

Bennett, H. Stith. *On Becoming a Rock Musician.* Amherst: U. of Mass, Press, 1980. Difficult reading, but worth it.

Cashmore, Ells. *The Black Culture Industry.* New York: Routledge, 1997. A study of black culture and white corporate control.

Chapple, Steve and Garafalo, Reebee. *Rock N'Roll Is Here to Pay.* Chicago: Nelson-Hall, 1977. Dated but useful.

Ewbank, Alison J. and Papageorgiou, Fouli T. *Whose Master's Voice: The Development of Popular Music in Thirteen Cultures.* Westport, CT: Greenwood Press, 1997. It's a global music business, remember?

Frith, Simon. *Sound Effects: Youth, Leisure and the Politics of Rock 'N' Roll.* New York: Pantheon Books, 1981.

Garfield, Simon. *Money For Nothing: Greed and Exploitation in the Music Industry.* Boston: Faber & Faber, 1986.

Hebdige, Dick. *Cut 'N' Mix: Culture, Identity and Caribbean Music.* New York, Methuen & Co., 1986.

Kelley, Norman, Ed. R &B: *Rhythm & Business.* New York: Akashic Books, 2002. A collection of of articles covering various aspects of black music and its place in the commercial marketplace. A useful book.

Neal, Mark Anthony. *What the Music Said: Black Popular Music and Black Public Culture.* New York: Routledge, 1999. Covers the relationship of black popular music to the life of the black community.

Rahn, Jay. *A Theory for All Music: Problems and Solutions in the Analysis of Non-Western Forms.* Toronto: University of Toronto Press, 1983.

Taylor, Timothy D. *Global Pop: World Music World Markets.* New York: Routledge, 1997. This book studies specific pop artists from around the world.

Note: Routledge Press publishes many books on cultural studies that touch on music and the media.

Film

There are many useful books on the technique of writing film scores. Business aspects are detailed in:

Faulkner, Robert A. *Music on Demand: Composers and Careers in the Hollywood Film Industry.* New Brunswick, NJ: Transaction Books, 1982. The way film composers get work and how their careers operate.

Rona, Jeff. *Synchonization from Reel to Reel.* Milwaukee, WI: Hal Leonard, 1995.

Legal and Economic Matters

Biederman, Donald, and Berry, Pierson, Silfer and Glasser. *Law and Business in the Entertainment Industries.* Dover, MA: Auburn House Publishing Co., 1987. Informative and very "lawyerish."

Muller, Peter. *Music Business: A Legal Perspective.* New York: Greenwood Press, 1993.

Thal, Peter M. *What They'll Never Tell You About the Music Business.* New York: Billboard Books, 2002. A useful guide to industry contracts and practice.

Vogel, Harold L. *Entertainment Industry Economics.* Cambridge, England: Cambridge University Press, Revised Edition, 1995.

Commercials

Karmen, Steve. *Who Killed The Jingle How A Unique American Art Form Disappeared.* Milwaukee: Hal Leonard, 2005. The past and present-day economics of the jingle.

Also see Resources, Chapter 7.

Copyright

Chickering, Robert B, and Susan Hartman. *How to Register a Copyright and Protect Your Creative Work.* New York: Charles Scribner's Sons, 1987.

Frith, Simon and Lee Marshall, editors. *Music and Copyright: Second Edition.* New York: Routledge, 2004. A series of artiles about international copyright.

Nimmer, Melville B., et. al. *Entertainment Litigation Including Unfair Competition, Defamation, Privacy.* St. Paul, West, 4th Ed., 1991.

Samuel, Edward. *The Illustrated Story of Copyright.* New York: Thomas Dunne Books, 2000. A well-written book that covers music, books and the internet.

Weinstein, David A. *How to Protect Your Creative Work.* New York: John Wiley & Sons, 1987.

Wilson, Lee. *The Copyright Guide.* New York: Allworth Press, 1996.

Gigs

Casola, Mary. *The Independent Working Musician.* Vallejo, Ca. Mix Books, 1998. A reasonable approach.

Heflick, David. *How to Make Money Performing in Schools.* Oreint, WA: Silcox Productions, 1996.

Hooper, David and Lee Kennedy. *How I Make $100,0000/Year in the Music Business.* Nashville: Kathode Tay Music, 2003. A prety slim book for such a strong promise.

Jackson, Randy. *"What's Up Dawg?" How to Become a Superstar in the Music Business.* New York: Hyperion, 2004. Jackson is one of the judges on American Idol. The book offers some good inspiration, but not too a whole lot of specific information.

McLeod, Douglas, and Kimberli Ranson. *House Concerts: A Guide for Musicians and Hosts.* Austin: Wordworks Publications, 1999.

Mitchell, Billy. *The Gigging Musician: How to Get, Play and Keep the Gig.* San Francisco: Backbeat Books, 2001. Mitchell is a working musician, and this short book offers some good practical information for the freelance musician.

Popyk, Bob. *The Business of Getting More Gigs as a Professional Musician.* Milwaukee: Hal Leonard, 2003. Some good tips of self-promotion, The book is intended for freelance casual musicians, and isn't terribly useful for the touring musician.

Shih, Patricia. *Gigging: A Practical Guide for Musicians.* New York: Allworth Press, 2003. Probably the most useful of this group.

Taylor, Livingston. *Stage Performance.* New York; Pocket Books, 2000. This is a book about performing on the job. Taylor is stimulating and opinionated.

The Internet and Current Issues Involving New Media
Curran, Mark W. *Sell Your Music: the Musician's Survival Guide to Direct Distribution on the Internet.* Simi Valley, CA: NMD Books, 2001. Includes information about marketing and interviews with web site artists.

Kusek, Dave, and Gerd Leonhard. *The Future of Music: Manifesto for the Digital Music Revolution.* Boston: Berklee Music Press, 2005. The authors are impassioned fans of the net and file sharing, and they make a good, if overdrawn case for the latter.

Souvignier, Todd, and Gary Hustwit. *The Musicians' Guide to the Internet,* 2nd edition. Milwaukee: Hal Leonard, 2002. Good nuts-and-bolt information.

On copyright issues and file sharing, also see the books of law professor Lawrence Lessig.

Local and Regional Music Scenes
Azerad, Michael. *Screaming Life: A Chronicle of the Seattle Music Scene.* San Francisco: Harper Collins West, 1995. Contains a CD and many photographs by Charles Peterson.

Berry, Jason, Jonathan Foose, and Tad Jones. *Up from the Cradle of Jazz: New Orleans Music Since World War II.* Athens, GA: University of Georgia Press, 1986. A superb book.

Bowman, Rob. *Soulsville U.S.A.: The Story of Stax Records.* New York: Schirmer Books, 1997. A detailed study of Stax and the Memphis music scene.

Endres, Clifford. *Austin City Limits.* Austin: University of Texas Press, 1987. The story of the television show, plus information on the local music scene.

McDonough, Jack. *San Francisco Rock: The Illustrated History of San Francisco Rock.* San Francisco: Chronicle Books, 1985.

Morrell, Brad. *Nirvana and the Sound of Seattle.* New York: Omnibus Press, 1996.

Reid, Jan. *The Improbable Rise of Redneck Rock.* New Edition,. Austin: University of Texas Press, 20004. A useful if subjective exploration of the roots of the Austin scene.

Willoughby, Larry, *Texas Rhyme.* Austin: Texas Monthly Press, 1984.

Also see Resources, Chapter 15. Note' There are also quite a few locally published books about specific music scenes that are available mostly in the towns that the author is writing about.

Music Business in Canada

Coxson, Mona. *Some Straight Talk About the Music Business.* Toronto: CM Books, 2nd Edition, 1989. Strong opinions, generally worthy of your consideration. One of the few available books about the Canadian music business.

Jennings, Nicholas. *Before the Gold Rush: Flashbacks to the Dawn of the Canadian Sound.* Toronto: Viking Press, 1997.

Also see Resources, Chapter 16 for the invaluable Music Directory, Canada.

Music Business in General

Barrow, Tony, and Newby, Julius. *Inside the Music Business.* London: Routledge, 1995. The best book I have found about the music business in England.

Baskerville, David. *Music Business Handbook & Career Guide. 7th edition.* Thousand Oaks, CA: Sage Publications, 2005. Dr. Baskerville was a pioneer in the field of music business education.

Borg, Bobby. *The Musician's Handbook: A Practical Guide to Understanding the Music Business.* New York: Billboard Books, 2003. The first section of the book, on getting gigs and organizing a career is the best. The rest of the music duplicates materials that are readily available elsewhere.

Burlingame, Jon. *For the Record.* Hollywood: Recording Musicians Association, 1997. A history of the RMA, an organization of recording musicians within the Musicians' Union.

Davison, Marc. *All Area Access: Personal Management for Unsigned Musicians.* Milwaukee, Hal Leonard, 1997. This is really a book on self management for musicians. It is extremely detailed, and should convince 98% of musicians why they need a personal manager and an agent if they plan to pursue a national career.

Eskelin, Gerald. *Lies My Music Teacher Told Me.* Woodland Hills, CA: Stage 3 Publishing, 1994. Deals with the disparity between the way music is usually taught and how it is actually performed.

Goldberg, Justin. *The Ultimate Survival Guide to the New Music Industry: Handbook for Hell.* Hollywood: Lone Eagle, 2004. A useful book that comes with a floppy disk that includes numerous resources.

Hall, Charles W. and Taylor, Frederick J. *Marketing in the Music Industry.* Needham Heights, MA: Simon & Schuster Custom Publishing, 1996.

Hull, Geoffrey P. *The Recording Industry.* Second Edition, New York: Routledge, 2004. Some useful charts and numbers, but quite dry.

Kashif. *Everything You'd Better Know About the Music Industry.* Venice, CA: Brooklyn Boy, 1995. Very oriented towards commercial music.

Moore, Steve. *The Truth About the Music Business: A Grassroots Business and Legal Guide.* Boston: Thomson Course Technology, 2005. A useful guide that goes a bit overboard; it covers everything from dental insurance to wills.

Nagger, David, and Jeffrey D Brandstetter. *The Music Business Explained in Plain English.* Revised ed. San Francisco: Daje Publishing, 2003 If you've never read anything about the music business, this book packs a surprising amount of information in one skinny volume.

Passman, Donald S. *All You Need to Know About the Music Business.* New York: Simon & Schuster, 5th Edition, 2003. Passman is a top entertainment attorney in Hollywood, and his book, though written in a somewhat irritating wise-guy style contains a lot of useful information, mostly about major label deals.

Music Industry Careers

Beeching, Angel Myles. *Beyond Talent: Creating a Successful Career in Music.* New York: Oxford University Press, 2005. A reasonable guide, especially of classical musicians.

Field, Shelly. *Career Opportunities in the Music Industry Revised Edition.* New York: Facts on File Publications, 2000; 5th edition, 2004.

Highstein, Ellen. *Making a Living in Looking Glass Land: A Guide to Survival and Business Skills for the Classical Performer.* 4th edition. New York: CAG, 2003. A must for classical musicians.

Personal Management

Dumler, Egon & Cushman, Robert F. *Entertainers & Their Professional Advisers.* Hollywood, IL: Dow Jones-Irwin, 1987. Covers many topics dealing with other areas of entertainment, such as the movie business. There is an excellent fifteen-page chapter on personal management by long-time manager Dee Anthony.

Eliot, Marc. *Down Thunder Road: The Making of Bruce Springsteen.* New York: Simon & Schuster, 1992. This book was written with the participation of Mike Appel, Springsteen's former manager. Its primary value is to see the perspective of a hard-working and frankly, greedy, starmaker.

Frascogna, Xavier M. Jr., and Hetherington, H. Lee. *Successful Artist Management.* New York: Billboard Publications, 4th Revised Ed., 2004.

Kragen, Ken with Graham Jefferson. *Life Is a Contact Sport: Ten Great Career Strategies That Work.* New York: William Morrow & Co., 1994. Kragen is an incurable optimist, and these are his shrewd guidelines for success.

Marcone, Steven. Managing *Your Band: Artists Management, The Ultimate Responsibility.* Wayne, N.J.: High Marks Publishing 2003. Practical advice.

Promotion-Concerts & Records

Lathrop, Tad. *This Business of Music: Music Marketing & Promotion.* Revised ed. New York: Billboard Books, 2003. Fills a real void in books about the industry.

Stein, Howard, and Ron Zallkind,. *Promoting Rock Concerts.* New York: Schirmer Books, 1979. A systemactic and sensible presentation.

O'Shea, Shad. *Just for the Record.* Cincinnati: Positive Feedback Press, 1986. Amusing and rather longwinded on many aspects of the music business. The section on promoting records in local and regional markets is useful and coherent.

Publicity

Gibson, James. *Getting Noticed: A Musician's Guide to Publicity & Self-Promotion.* Cincinnati: Writer's Digest Books, 1987. There are many useful ideas in this book, sometimes overwhelmed by its sheer mass of detailed suggestions.

Pinsky, Raleigh. *101 Ways to Promote Yourself.* New York: Avon Books, 1997.

See Resources, Chapter 3.

Radio

Hall, Claude & Barbara. *This Business of Radio Programming.* New York: Billboard Publications, 1977. An excellent book—needs updating to follow the changes in radio formats and programming.

Halper, Donna L. *Radio Music Directing*. Boston: Focal Press, 1991.

Note: There are many books by former disc jockeys about their lives in the business. Although most of these books are amusing, they rarely offer much in the way of hard facts. There are also some recent books about various aspects of FM radio. Most of the current books about the music business have a section on radio.

Recording (History and Discussion, not Technical Audio)
Eisenberg, Even. *Explorations in Phonography*. New HYork: McGraw-Hill Books, 1987. Thoughtful and opinionated esssays about various aspects of recording.

Gelatt, Roland. *The Fabulous Phonograph*. New York: Collier Books, 1977.

Gronow, Pekka and Ilpo Saunio. *An International History Of The Recording Industry.*, London; Cassell, 1998. A fascinating book.

Read, Oliver & Welch, Walter C. *From Tin Foil to Stereo*. Indianapolis: Howard W. Sams, 2nd Edition, 1976.

Zak, Albin J. III. *The Poetics of Rock: Cutting Tracks, Making Records*. Berkeley: University of California Press, 2001. How the recording process has developed.

Record Production
Burgess, Richard James. *The Art of Record Production*. London: Omnibus Press, 1997. A good guide to current techniques and producers.

Cunningham, Mark. *Good Vibrations: A History of Record Production*. Surrey, UK: Castle Communications, 1996. This book is very focused on English Music.

Howard, David N. *Sonic Alchemy: Visionary Music Producers And Their Maverick Recordings.* Milwaukee; Hal Leonard, 2004. From george Martin to dr. Dre.

Kalmar, Veronika. *Label Launch: a Guide to Independent Record Recording, Promotion and Distribution*. New York; St. Martin's Griffin, 2002. Includes information about selling on the internet.

Schwartz, Dayelle Deanna. *Start & Run Your Own Record Label*. Revised 7 expanded Edition. New York: Billboard Books, 2003. For those who want to actually start their own label.

Stokes, Geoffrey. *Star Making Machinery*. Indianapolis: Bobbs-Merrill, 1976. A detailed description of how Commander Cody recorded an album, plus a lot of informative details on how a record deal is negotiated with a major company.

Tobler, John and Grundy, Stuart. *The Record Producers*. New York: St. Martin's Press. Another book of interviews.

White, Paul. *Recording and Production Techniques For the Recording Musician.* London: Sanctuary Publishing Corp., undated.

See Resources, Chapter 9.

Songwriting and Music Publishing

Citron, Stephen. *Songwriting.* New York: William Morrow & Co., 1985. A good general guide.

Davis, Sheila. *The Craft of Lyric Writing.* Cincinnati: Writer's Digest Books, 1985.

Davis, Sheila. *Successful Lyric Writing: A Step by Step Course & Workbook.* Cincinnati: Writer's Digest Books, 1988. Davis' books are excellent resources for serious students of the song lyric. They include many detailed examples, and thoughts about how the revision process works.

Hall, Tom T. *The Songwriter's Handbook.* Nashville: Rutledge Hill Press, 1987. Hall is one of the masters of story songs; he explains how he writes songs, and why you can too.

Kasha, Al, and Joel Hirschorn. *If They Ask You, You Can Write a Song.* New York: Simon & Schuster, 1979. A good general guide to the craft of songwriting.

Kosser, Michael. *How to Become a Successful Nashville Songwriter.* Nashville: Porch Swing Press, 1981. Contains good, practical information, especially about the process of collaboration.

Lydon, Micahel. *Songwriting Success; How To Write Songs For Fun And (Maybe) Profit.* New York: Routledge, 2004. Comes with a CD that expands on matters covered in the text.

Mahonin, Valerie. *Market Your Songs.* Calgary: Songsmith Publications, 1986. A guide to marketing songs in Canada.

Pattison, Pat. *Writing Better Lyrics.* Cincinnati: Writer's Digest, 1995. You may not agree with everything here, but it should give you plenty of ideas to think about.

Pickow, Peter & Appleby, Amy. *The Billboard Book of Songwriting.* New York: Billboard Publications, 1988. Excellent, with many references to current songs.

Poe, randy. *Music Publishing.* Revised edition. Cincinnati: Writer's Digest, 2005.

Webb, Jimmy. *Tunesmith; Inside The art Of Songwriting.* New York; Hyperion, 1998. A very useful book for advanced songwriters who can read music.

Weissman, Dick. *Songwriting; The Words, the Music & the Money.* Milwaukee: Hal Leonard, 2001. Comes with a CD of the songs and examples.

Whitsett, Tim. *Music Publishing: The Real Road to Music Business Success.* Revised ed. Emeryville, CA: Mix Books, 2005. See Resources, Chapter 11.

Studio Work
Faulkner, Robert A. *Hollywood Studio Musicians: Their Work and Careers in the Recording Industry.* Chicago: Aldine-Atherton, 1971. A superb study of the nature and evolution of careers in the world of the recording studio.

Women in Music
Carson, Mina, Lisa Lewis, and Susan M. Shaw. *Girls Rock! Fifty Years of Women Making Music.* Lexington: University of Kentucky Press, 2004. An excellent study.

Drinker, Sophie. *Music and Women.* New York: Coward McCann, 1948. The essential book on the role of women in music and music making.

O'Brien, Lucy. *She Bop: The Definitive History of Women in Rock, Pop and Soul.* London: Continuum, 2002. A valuable history.

Placksin, Sally. *Women in Jazz: 1900 to the Present.* Distributed by Putnum, Wideview Books, 1982.

Whitly, Sheila, Ed. *Sexing the Groove: Popular Music and Gender.* London: Routledge, 1997. 16 articles by various writers.

Zaimont, Judith Lang, ed. *Women in Music: An International Perspective.* Vols. I and II. New York: Greenwood Press, 1983 and 1986.

Musical Styles:
Classical Music
Bernstein, Seymour. *Monsters and Angels: Surviving a Career in Music.* Milwaukee: Hal Leonard, 2002. A personal odyssey.

Epstein, Helen. *Music Talks: Conversations With Working Musicians.* New York: McGraw Hill, 1987. A revealing book about famous and lesser known classical musicians and teachers.

Furlong, William Barry. *Season with Solti.* New York: Macmillan, 1974. A fascinating study of the interactions of players in the Chicago Symphony.

Hart, Philip. *Orpheus in the New World.* New York: Norton, 1973. A detailed and informative study of the symphony orchestra in the United States.

Country Music
Goldsmith, Thomas, ed. *The Bluegrass Reader.* Urbana: University of Illinois Press, 2004. A wide-ranging collection of articles.

Hemphill, Paul. *The Nashville Sound: Bright Lights & Country Music.* New York: Pocket Books, 1971. Contains many valuable insights.

Malone, Bill. *Don't Get Above Your Raisin: Country Music and the Southern Working Class.* Urbana, IL; University of Illinois Press, 2002. Malone is one of the best informed writers in this field of music.

Willis, Barry R. *America's Music: Bluegrass.* Franktown, Colorado: Pine Valley Music, distributed by Mel Bay, 1997. An encyclopedic work.

Jazz
Spellman, A.B. *Four Lives in the Bebop Business.* New York: Schoken Books, 1970. Some editions of this book are called Black Music, Four Lives. A sobering book on the difficulties of making a living as a jazz artist.

Note: There are dozens of biographies and autobiographies of jazz figures, and numerous histories about jazz styles.

Rock 'n' Roll
Friedlander, Paul. *Rock and Roll: A Social History.* Boulder, Colorado: Westview Press, 1996. Particularly good for 1950s and '60s rock.

Garofalo, Reebee. *Rockin' Out: Popular Music in the USA.* Boston: Allyn and Bacon, 1997. Garofalo is an excellent commentator on the relationship between music and culture.

Gillette, Charlie. *The Sound of the City.* New York: Dutton, 1970. Still the best overall history of rock.

Rap
Rose, Tricia. *Black Noise: Rap Music and Black Culture in Contemporary America.* Hannover, NH: Wesleyan University Press, 1994. The best book to date.

There are many interesting autobiographical works by rappers, including Ice T, Chuck D, and L.L. Cool J. Also see the list under Cultural Study of Music.

Blues & Soul
Peter Guralnick is a superb, sympathetic writer with fine musical sensibilities. The first two books also include some material on country music.

Guralnick Peter. *Feel Like Goin' Home: Portraits in Blues & Rock 'N' Roll.* New York: Random House, 1981.

Guralnick Peter. *Lost Highway: Journeys & Arrivals of American Musicians.* Boston: David Godine, 1979.

Guralnick Peter. *Sweet Soul Music: Rhythm & Blues and the Southern Dream of Freedom.* New York: Harper & Row, 1986.

The Chicago Public Library has an excellent bibliography of books, periodicals and directories on the business of music, which they actually stock. Write to Music Information Center, Visual & Performing Arts, Chicago Public Library, 78 E. Washington, Chicago, IL 60602, 312/269-2886. There has been a recent spate of biogrpahies of blues musicians- some of the best are Elijah Wald's books on Robert Johnson and Josh White an Robert Gordon's book about Muddy Waters.

MIDI, Sampling, Drum Machines, etc.
These books become dated so quickly, I suggest that you look for the latest books available.

Etc...
Alfonso, Barry. *The Billboard Guide of Contemporary Christian Music.* New York; Billboard Books, 2002. Includes a number of interviews with important figures.

Goldstein, Jeri. *How to be Your Own Booking Agent.* Revised Ed. Charlottesville, VA: The New Music Times, 2004. Recommended under Resources.

Kaye, Deena, and James Le Brecht. *Sound and Music for the Theatre.* New York: Back Stage Books, 1992.

Korpe, Marie, ed. *Shoot the Singer: Music Censorship Today.* London; Zed Books, 2004. Comes with a CD of censored songs.

Mandell, Jim. *The Studio Business Book.* 2nd ed. Emeryville, CA: Mix Books, 1995.

Schuyler, Nina. *The Business of Multimedia.* New York: Allworth Press, 1995.

Shagen, Rena. *Booking and Tour Management for the Performing Arts.* New York: Allworth Press, 1996. A practical guide to touring.

Sievert, Jon. *Concert Photography.* San Francisco: Humble Press, 1997. A unique guide.

Wimble, David. *The Indie Bible.* 6th edition. New York; Music Sales Corp., 2004. Contains a valuable list of contacts for getting CD's reviewed, radio play resources, etc.

Directories (and other publications)
Billboard, Musical America, Performance and Pollstar all publish annual guides that variously list venues, agents, managers and all sorts of information about recording. Two other useful guides are the Recording Industry Sourcebook, available from Sourcebook, 3301 Barham Blvd., Suite 300, Los Angeles, CA 90068, and The Yellow Pages of Rock, available from The Album Network, 120 N. Victory Blvd., Burbank, CA 91502. Also check out the Musician's Atlas, published annual by the Music Resource Group, 38 Porter Place, Montclair, NJ 07042.

Miscellaneous Books for Musicians

Buttwinick, Marty. *How to Make a Living as a Musician.* Glendale, CA: Sonata Publishing, 1993. Career Strategies for the Working Musician.

Halloran, Mark, Ed. *The Musician's Business & Legal Guide.* Englewood Cliffs, NJ: Prentice Hall, 1991. A collection of articles of varying value.

Hustwit, Gary. *Releasing an Independent Record.* San Diego, CA: Rock Press, 1995, Fifth Edition. Strategies, directories, etc.

Kohn, Al and Bob. *The Art of Music Licensing.* Englewood Cliffs, NJ: Prentice Hall, 2nd ed. 1997. Describes every conceivable music license. Not for the novice.

Stanfield, Jana. *A Musician's Guide to Outrageous Successs: Making and Selling CD's and Cassettes.* Nashville: Jana Stans Tunes Music, 1996. Includes a section on cyberspace marketing.

Instructional Tapes and Videotapes

Jamey Abersold
P.O. Box 1244, New Albany, IN 47150
Many jazz instructional tapes and CDs.

Homespun Tapes
Box 694 F, Woodstock, NY 12498
Audio and video instructional tapes for folk,bluegrass, country music and jazz.

Music Minus One Records
50 Executive Blvd., Elmsford, NY 10523
A pioneering company in this fieldAlfred Music, Mel Bay Publications, Hal Leonard, Music Sales Corp. and Warner Bros. Publications all produce taped instructional materials. For addresses see the list of music print publishers below.

Promotional Tools

ABRACADABRA, c/o Rick Abramson 1010 Palm Avenue, West Hollywood, CA 90069 supplies a catalog of T-shirts, mugs and other such giveaways that a band can use to promote itself or to sell to fans. Look for similar companies in your city or region.

Alternative Radio Lists

Lists are available in various styles of music from Icebird Record Company, P.O. Box 216, Lakebay, WA 98349, 206/884-9705. The lists are available on disk or in printed form.

Music Print Publishers

Most music publishers no longer print music. They exist for the purpose of getting artists to record songs that the publishers own. These publishers then receive revenue from record sales, performances on radio and television, and other uses of their songs.

The publishers listed below print sheet music collections and instructional folios.

Alexander Publishing
3537 Old Conejo Rd., Ste. 101,
Newbury Park, CA 91320
Specializes in high-tech oriented music.

Alfred Music Publishing, Inc.
16380 Roscoe Blvd., P.O. Box 10003,
Van Nuys, CA 91406
School band, choral and instructional books.

Mel Bay Publications
4 Industrial Dr., Pacific, MO 63069
Guitar, instrumental methods and collections.

Cherry Lane Music Co.
10 Midland Ave.
Port Chester, NY 10573
Heavy metal and rock and pop material.

International Music Publishing Co.
5 W. 37th St.
New York, NY 10018
Specializes in classical music.

Neil Kjos
P.O. Box 178270
San Diego, CA 92177-8270

Hal Leonard Publishing Corp.
7777 W. Bluemound Rd.
Milwaukee, WI 53213
Pops, standards, rock, band and choral music. Distributes other publishers.

Music Sales Corp.
225 Park Ave. S.
New York, NY 10003
A strong catalog in folk-related instructional materials. Also includes jazz and rock publications.

A great resource for books about the music business is the Music Books Plus catalog. Call 1-800-265-8481 to get one.

INDEX

A-DATs, 10, 30, 79, 105, 180
accordion, 142
Ackerman, Will, 109
Acoustic Junction, 181
ADA, 98
Adams, Bryan, 186
advances, 101–2, 130, 132
advertising, 110
advertising agencies, 80–81, 83, 84, 166, 168, 207
AFTRA. *See* American Federation of Radio and Television Artists
agents, booking, 39–42, 93
  dealing with, 42–44, 63, 77, 123–24
  finding, 39–42
  for jingle writing, 85
  local, 4, 6, 14, 29, 206
  meal breaks viewed by, 42, 90
  national, 138–39
  in Seattle, 177
  union, 43
Albini, Steve, 167
Albuquerque music market, 3, 169
Aldridge, Ron, 146
Alexakis, Art, 168
Alfred Music, 133
Alger, Pat, 126–27
Alice in Chains, 176, 177
Allen, David, 168
Allen, Paul, 177
Allen, Woody, 146
Alligator label, 167
Allman Brothers, 159
Alternative Distribution Alliance, 167
alternative rock, 155, 161, 167, 192
A&M Records, 181
amateur musicians, 150
Amazon.com, 202
American Federation of Musicians, 63–75
  advantages and disadvantages of, 66
  benefit concert rule, 38
  Canadian work and, 187
  contracts, 43, 70, 71–72, 81, 83–84, 90, 92, 97, 207
  importance of joining, 43, 63–64, 208
  as information source, 3, 19, 33, 40, 115
  job listings, 148
  list of locals, 236
  part-time musicians in, 145
  protections offered by, 92
  as source of contacts, 68–70
  as source of work, 7, 65, 67–68
  video demos and, 31–32

wage scales, 47, 69–70, 77, 81, 89, 91, 93
  work dues, 93
American Federation of Radio and Television Artists (AFTRA), 64, 65, 82
American Society of Composers, Authors and Publishers (ASCAP), 111, 119, 130–31, 193–94, 211
Amoeba Music, 161
analog tape, 105–7
Ann Arbor, Michigan, 162
Anthony, Dee, 136–37
Antone, Clifford, 163
Antone's, 163
Antony & The Johnsons, 167
Appell, Dave, 154
Apple iPod, 100, 203
Arcade Fire, 189
architectural entertainment, 202
Ardent Recording Studios, 157
Arista Records, 159, 164, 181
Armadillo World Headquarters, 163
arranging, 116, 133
Arrested Development, 183
artist-in-residence programs (AIR), 6, 7, 48–51, 75
artistdirect.com, 200
Artists in the Schools, 48
ArtReach, 48
Arts Councils, 75–77
  Canadian, 224–25
  listed by state, 219–23
  national, 232
  regional, 223
Arts Northwest, 44
arts organizations dealing with special populations, 233
ASCAP. *See* American Society of Composers, Authors and Publishers
Aspen, Colorado, 9, 14, 180
Aspen Festival, 133
asylum.com, 200
Athens music market, 3, 159, 162
Atkins, Chet, 163
Atlanta music market, 3, 159, 183–84
Atlanta Rhythm Section, 159
Atlantic Records, 156, 179
Atlantis Music Conference, 184
attitude, 7, 23–24, 68–69, 101, 115, 151
attorneys. See lawyers, music business
audionet.com, 200
auditions, 23, 32, 40, 44, 50, 148
Austin, Dallas, 159
Austin City Limits, 163, 164

Austin Community College, 164
Austin music market, 3, 144, 162–64
Avenue Q (musical), 131
Azoff, Irving, 181

B-52's, 159
Babyface, 184
Bad Animals Recording Studio, 176
Baez, Joan, 161
Ball, Marcia, 163
ballet companies, 148
BAM, 135
band agreements, 24, 212
bandwidth, 199
Banff Festival, 133
bar codes, 111
bar scene, 21, 40, 41
Bare Naked Ladies, 187
Barnes and Noble, 97
Bartholomew, Dave, 155
bass, acoustic, 53–54
bass, electric, 53–54
Bay Area music market, 159–61
Be Good Tanyas, 191
Beach Boys, the, 179
Bear Creek Studio, 177
Beatles, the, 15, 100, 154, 207
Beckett, Barry, 158
Bee, Tom, 169
Bélanger, Daniel, 190
Bell, Thom, 155
Bellingham, Washington, 177, 178
benefit concerts, 38, 43–44
Benjamin, Bennie, 154
Bennett, Tony, 136
Bergan, Ron, 135
Berklee College of Music, 85
Best Buy, 99
Better Than Ezra, 156
big bands, 92
Big Head Todd & the Monsters, 111, 180, 181
Bill Black Combo, 157
Bill Graham Presents, 161
Billboard, 138, 169, 203
billboardtalent.com, 200
bios, 32–33
Black, Jack, 154
Black Emperors, 190
Blackwell, Chris, 158
blanket licenses, 194
Bliesener, Mark, 182
blogs, 203
Bloomington music market, 162, 167, 169
bluegrass, 169
Bluegrass Unlimited, 133
blues, 142, 155, 157, 158, 163, 165, 168, 169
BMG, 95, 97, 156, 161

BMI. See Broadcast Music, Incorporated
Boeing Corporation, 177
Bon Jovi, 187
Booker T. and the MG's, 156, 169
booking agents. See agents, booking
booking yourself, 37–39
Bossin, Bob, 10
Boston music market, 3, 142, 149, 161
Boulder, Colorado. See Denver-Boulder music market
Bowman, Rob, *Soulsville, U.S.A.: The Story of Stax Records*, 157
Braheny, John, *The Craft and Business of Songwriting*, 128
brass, 54
Bread and Roses (San Francisco), 48
Bright Eyes, 11, 96, 169
Broadcast Music, Incorporated (BMI), 111, 119, 130–31, 193–94, 211
Broadcasting Yearbook, 110
Brooks, Garth, 127
Brooks, Meredith, 168
Brown, Sawyer, 158
Bryson, Peabo, 183
Buck, Peter, 178
Buffalo, New York, 11, 173
Buffett, Jimmy, 163
Built to Spill, 179
Bumbershoot Festival, 178
"bundle of (performance) rights," 193
Burnside, 168
Burrell, Kenny, 154
business managers, 46, 105
Butler, Jerry, 167

cable television, 8, 32, 47, 180, 191, 194
Cajun music, 142, 155
Calgary music market, 3
Cameo Parkway Records, 154
Canada, music business in, 44, 48, 169, 185–92, 208
Canada Council, 185
Canadian Academy of Recording Arts & Sciences (CARAS), 191
Canadian Broadcasting Company (CBC), 185
Canadian Content Law (CANCON), 187–88, 192
Canadian Federation of Musicians, 187
Canadian Independent Record Production Association (CIRPA), 188
Canadian Music Week, 191
Cannell, Stephen J., 189, 191–92
Canyon Records, 169
Capricorn Records, 159
Caribou Studios, 181
Carl Fischer, 133

Caroline, 98
Carr, David, 190
Cash, Johnny, 156
cassettes, 12, 102, 109
casual work, 77, 92
caterers, 6
Catero, Fred, 160
Catero Records, 160
CD players, tempo-adjustable, 18
Cdbaby.com, 202
CDR format, 12, 102–3
cell phones, 203
Chadbourne, Eugene, *I Hate the Man Who Runs This Bar*, 12
chamber music groups, 148
chambers of commerce, 46
Chapel Hill music market, 3, 162, 173
Chapin, Tom, 190
Checker, Chubby, 154
Cherry Lane Music, 133
Cherry Poppin' Daddies, 168
Chess Records, 167
Chicago (group), 179
Chicago music market, 1, 3, 142, 167
Chicano music, 180
children's music, 190, 192
chord charts, 117
Christian music, 179
church music, 8
Cincinnati, Ohio, 172
CIRPA. See Canadian Independent Record Production Association
Clark, Bud, 168
classical music, 63–64, 133, 147–49, 161, 166, 181–82
classified ads, 20, 148
Clear Channel Communications, 161
Cleveland music market, 3, 172–73
CMT Canada Network, 191
Cockburn, Bruce, 186
collaborations, 117–18
collecting bad checks, 91–92
college circuit, 14, 44
college degree programs, 213, 243–44
college teaching, 56
Collins, Phil, 103
Colorado Arts Council, 7
Colorado Springs, Colorado, 182
Colorado Symphony, 181–82
Columbia Artists Management, 148
Columbia Records, 160
Colvin, Shawn, 142
commercials, 47, 65, 74, 85, 148, 194–95
commitments, 123–24, 143, 206
Commodores, the, 154
Community Concerts, 148
compact discs (CDs), 102
    financing and marketing, 9–13, 105
composing and composers. *See also* songwriting

college courses, 116
    for film, television, and commercials, 85–87, 148
    grants for, 75–77, 206
    income, 193–95
    opportunities for, 8, 79
    teaching positions for, 148
    technology and, 150–51
computer-driven hard-disc systems, 10, 30
computers, 103, 150–51, 197–201
Concord Records, 160
conferences, 44
Conley, Earl Thomas, 158
consignment, 108–9
constructive criticism, 22
contacts, making, 124–34, 140–41
"continuing education," 116
contractors, 67–68, 147
contracts. *See also under* American Federation of Musicians
    with agencies, 124
    with clubs, 42–43, 92
    with managers, 44–46, 137–38
    publishing, 127
    record, 95
    union, 43, 70, 71–72, 81, 83–84, 90, 92, 97, 207
convention work, 4, 6, 40, 42, 90, 110, 181
copyright, 8, 118, 127, 195, 198, 204, 211
Cornelius Brothers, the, 158
costumes, 26, 33
country music, 142, 158, 162–64, 169, 172
cover art, 12, 107, 112
cover bands, 21
cover charges, 39
Cowboy Junkies, the, 192
Cowboy Mouth, 156
Cowboys Fringant, La, 190
Cray, Robert, 168
creative fees, 82, 86, 207
credits, 34, 129
Creed, Linda, 155
Creedence Clearwater Revival, 160
Criteria, 158
Crosby, Stills, Nash and Young, 158
cue sheet, 86
Cushman, Robert F., *Entertainers and Their Professional Advisers*, 136–37
cybercasts, 200

Dallas-Fort Worth music market, 3
dance bands, 146
Dandy Warhols, the, 168
Danoff, Bill, 125, 126
Davis, Carl, 167
Davis, Chip, 169
Dears, the, 190
Def Jam South, 183
Delmark label, 167
demos, audio, 29–31, 40, 81, 128,

129–30, 139, 206, 212
demos, video, 31–33, 40, 207
Denver, John, 126, 179, 180
Denver-Boulder music market, 2, 3,
   9, 131, 179–83
Denver Center for the Performing
   Arts, 179
Denver Symphony, 181
depreciation schedules, 26
Desjardins, Boom, 190
desktop filmmaking, 202
Detroit music market, 153–54, 169,
   172
Dickinson, Jim, 157
DiFranco, Ani, 11, 96, 173
digital downloads, 100, 195,
   197–98, 200–201, 203, 204
Dion, Céline, 18, 191
Dirty Linen, 133
discos, 99
DJ Screw, 165
Doe, Ernie K., 155
Domino, Fats, 155
door charges, 91–92
Dorsey, T. J., 167
Dotsero, 182
double-sided disks, 205
doubling fees, 68
Dovells, the, 154
Downbeat, 133
Dressy Bessy, 181
drinking, 42, 90, 145
drug use, 145, 147, 160
drum machine, 53–54, 79
drums, 53–54, 103
Duke Records, 165
Dukhs, the, 191
Dumler, Egon, *Entertainers and
   Their Professional Advisers*,
   136–37
Dupri, Jermaine, 159, 183
Durham, North Carolina, 162
DVD formats, 205
Dylan, Bob, 100, 103, 155, 165

e-mail, 129
Eagles, the, 180
Eaglin, Snooks, 156
early music ensembles, 149
Eddy, Duane, 154
Edmonds, Babyface, 159
Edmonton Folk Festival, 191
education, music, 14, 17–19, 85,
   115–16, 171, 212. *See also*
   teaching music
Edwards, David, 181
Edwards, Kathleen, 192
electronic commerce, 198
Elliott, Missy, 155, 184
Emerson, Lake and Palmer, 136
EMI, 204
Eminem, 154
Endino, Jack, 175
engineers, recording, 101–2
enthusiasm, maintaining, 14
eonline.com, 200

equipment, 23, 25–27. *See also*
   recording equipment; sound
   systems
Estefan, Gloria, 14, 158
Everclear, 168
expenses. *See also* taxes
   attorneys' fees, 139
   booking agents' commis-
      sions, 39
   business managers, 46
   equipment purchases, 25–26
   logs, 26, 27
   personal managers, 44–45
   producers, 101–2
   recordings, 9–13, 82–83,
      103–5, 172, 188
   tip sheets, 130
   work dues, 93
Experience Music Project, 177–78

Fabulous Thunderbirds, the, 163
FACTOR Awards, 188–89, 192, 208
Fahrenheit, 182
Fairborn, Bruce, 187
"fake books," 117
Fame Studios, 157–58
Fantasy Records, 159, 160
fashion industry tie-ins, 205
festivals, summer music, 133–34,
   191
Fey, Barry, 179, 180, 181
file sharing, 95, 100, 205, 215
film editors, 47
film music, 8, 47, 64, 85–87, 148,
   202, 207
film work, 148, 166, 169, 189,
   191–92, 212
financing. *see* expenses
Fink, Cathy, 190
Firefall, 179, 180
First Edition, 9
Fischbach, John, 156
Flanagan, Bill, *Written in My Soul*,
   119–20
Fleetwoods, 175
Fogelberg, Dan, 125, 179, 180
Fogerty, John, 160
folk music, 142, 159, 161, 165
folk-rock, 181
Foo Fighters, the, 179
Forster, Nick, 182–83
Foster, David, 187
foundations, 6, 50, 77
Franklin, Aretha, 19, 157
Fray, the, 181
Freakwater, 167
Fremont Street Experience, 202
Frey, Glenn, 180–81
Fricker, Sylvia, 186
Friedman, Kinky, 162
Frissell, Bill, 178
Fromholz, Steve, 162
Fugazi, 11, 96

Gamble and Huff, 155
Garcia, Jerry, 160

Gateway Studio, 103
Gaye, Marvin, 154, 172
Geffin Records, 168
General Motors, 96
Georgia State University, 184
Geto Boys, 165
Giant Records, 181
Gillette, Charlie, *Making Tracks*,
   157–58
Gilmer, Jerome, 3
globalization, 197–98, 215–16
goals, setting, 23–24, 123–24, 135,
   151–52, 205–6
Godspeed You!, 190
Gonzales, Corky, 180
Good Music Agency, the, 166
Goodman, Benny, 92
Goodman, Steve, 167
Gordy, Berry, 153–54
gospel music, 157, 158
Graham, Bill, 160, 161
Grammy Awards, 77
grants, 6, 48–51, 75–77, 148, 206
   in Canada, 185, 208
Grateful Dead, the, 159, 160
Green, Al, 157
greenhouse channels, 200
Griffith, Nanci, 163
Grisman, David, 142
Grohl, Dave, 179
Grokster, 100
group lessons, 57
groups, forming, 20–24, 103–4,
   123–24, 143, 212
GRP Records, 182
Grundman, Bernie, 103
"grunge," 175–76
Guercio, Jim, 179
Guggenheim, Ted, 182
guitar, acoustic, 53–54, 105
guitar, electric, 53–54, 105, 142
Gurlanick, Peter, *Sweet Soul Music*,
   157
Guthrie, Arlo, 11, 96

Haggard, Merle, 163
Hal Leonard Corporation, 116, 133
Hall, Rick, 157–58
Hall, Tom T., *The Songwriter's
   Handbook*, 125
Handy, W. C., 157
"happy hour" gigs, 41
hard disc recording, 106–7
Hard Rock Cafe, 201
Harold Melvin and the Blue Notes,
   155
harpsichord, 54
Harry Fox Agency, 111
Hawkins, Ronnie, 186
Hayes, Isaac, 156
Hayes, Louis, 154
Heart, 176
heavy metal, 175
Hendrix, Jimi, 177
Hill, Dan, 187
hip-hop, 183

Holland, Dozier and Holland, 154
Hollywood Bowl Symphony, 133
home studios. *See* recording
  studios
Hooters, the, 155
Hootie & The Blowfish, 96, 111
Hopkins, Lightnin', 163
Hot Rize, 9
house concerts, 6–7, 91
House of Blues, 181
housing developments, age-based,
  48
Houston music market, 3, 165, 172,
  173
Huey Lewis & The News, 160
Humanities Councils
listed by state, 225–29
national, 232
Humphrey, Clark, *Loser: The Seattle
  Music Story*, 176, 177, 178
Hunter, Charley, 160

Images, 182
Impressions, the, 167
improvisation, 117
income
advances, 101–2, 132
apportioning in groups, 21, 89–90,
  92–93
arrangers, 133
attorneys', 139
creative fees, 82
door charges, 91–92
doubling fees, 68
file sharing and, 205
guarantees, 41–42
home studio rental, 87
from Musicians' Union, 64
part-time, 145–52
private lessons, 57–58
residuals, 65, 81, 84
of road manager, 26
royalties, 86, 95, 101–2, 127, 132,
  138, 191, 193–95
session fees, 81–82
setting prices, 38–39, 40, 42, 77
songwriting, 193–95
staff writers, 125
success and, 141–42
synchronization fees, 194–95
versatility and, 208
Indigo Girls, the, 96, 183
industrial films, 47
instructional materials, 14, 132–33
instructional videos, 18–19
International Music Publishers, 133
International Musician, 148
Internet, 95, 100, 111, 194, 197,
  199–200, 202–3, 207
Interscope, 97
investors, raising money from,
  10–11, 105, 172
"invisible work," 4–5
Island Records, 158
iTunes.com, 202
iuma.com, 199

J-Bird label, 203
Jackson, Mahalia, 167
Jackson, Michael, 95, 154
Jackson, Mississippi, 172
Jackson, Wayne, 157
Jackson Five, the, 154
Jagged Edge, 183
Jam, Jimmy, 143, 166, 184
jam sessions, 78
Jamerson, James, 154
Jamey Abersold, 116
Jamie/Guyden Records, 154
jamtv.com, 200
jazz, 142, 156, 160, 161
jazz bands, 116
Jazz Times, 133
Jefferson Airplane, 159
Jenkins, Ella, 190
Jennings, Waylon, 126, 163
jingles, 8, 80–84, 87, 159, 161, 165,
  167, 181, 207
job referrals, 7, 19, 69, 70–71, 73, 77
Jobete Music, 154
John, Elton, 179
Johnson, Michael, 166
Jones, Mike, 165
Joplin, Janis, 160, 163
Jug Band, the, 161
Juilliard String Quartet, 148
jukeboxes, 99
Juno Awards, 191

K-Tel, 165
Kaleidospace, 200
Kazaa, 100
K.C. and the Sunshine Band, 158
Keillor, Garrison, 166
Kenny G., 176, 178
keyboards, 53–54
"keyman" clause, 45, 124, 138
Keys, Alicia, 183
Kill Rock Stars label, 168
King, Jay, 169
King Records, 97, 172
Kingston Trio, the, 159
Kiss, 9
Koch Records, 98, 182
Kodiak, 190
Koerner, Ray and Glover, 165
Kottke, Leo, 166, 180
Kramer, Stanley, 176
KSAN-FM, 160
Kusek, David, *The Future of Music*,
  204
Kweskin, Jim, 161

La Face Records, 159, 184
LA Weekly, 135
Lanois, Daniel, 155, 187
Lapointe, Eric, 190
Lathrop, Todd, *This Business of
  Music, Marketing, and Promotion*,
  99
Latin American music market,
  158–59
Lavigne, Avril, 187

Lawson, Steve, 176
lawyers, music business, 14, 24,
  137, 138, 139–40, 177, 211
Le Doux, Chris, 110
lead sheets, 59–61
leader (of a group), 8–9, 20–21, 24,
  89–90, 92–93
Lear, Norman, 125
Led Zeppelin, 53, 100
Leftover Salmon, 181
legal matters, 193–95. *See also*
  copyright
Leigh, Mitch, 87
Leo Burnett Advertising Agency, 167
Leonard, Pat, 181
Leonhard, Gerd, *The Future of
  Music*, 204
Lewis, Jerry Lee, 156
Lewis, Terry, 143, 166, 184
licenses, 194
Lightfoot, Gordon, 187
L'il Bow Wow, 183
L'il Flip, 165
Lipscomb, Mance, 163
Liss, Scott, 177
literacy, musical, 151
Liverpool Institute for Performing
  Arts, 215
Lomax, Alan, 169
Lone Star Studio, 163
Lorber, Alan, 161
Lorber, Jeff, 168
Los Angeles music market, 1, 2–3,
  14, 129, 212. *See also* music
  markets, major
Los Lobos, 142
Loverboy, 187
Lovett, Lyle, 163
Lowry, Bill, 159
Lucas, George, 161
Luke Skywalker Ranch, 161
Lynn, Loretta, 110
lyric writing, techniques of, 120

Macon, Georgia, 159
Madison, Wisconsin, 162
Madonna, 95, 96, 181
magazines, music, 133, 245–48
magazines, songwriters', 244
Mahonin, Valerie, *Marketing Your
  Songs*, 188–89
mailing lists, developing, 12
Mainstream Records, 160
make-up lessons, 58
Malaco, 158
Mamas & the Papas, the, 9
Mammoth Records, 173
managers. *See* business managers;
  personal managers
Manchester, Melissa, 126
mandolin, 142
Mann, Kal, 154
Mannheim Steamroller, 169
Maple Core, 192
marketing recordings, 107–10,
  189–90

Markeys, the, 156
Marsalis family, 156
Martha and the Vandellas, 154
Martin, George, 207
Marvelmania, 201
Marxer, Marcy, 190
Master P., 156
mastering recordings, 102–3
mastering studios, 12
Matassa, Cossimo, 155
Mattea, Kathy, 126
Mattis, Marv, 131
Maverick, 96
Mayer, John, 183
Mayfield, Curtis, 167
Mays, Douglas, 176
MCA Records, 179, 180, 181
McCartney, Paul, 155, 215
McLachlan, Sarah, 187
meal breaks, 42, 43, 90
Mel Bay, 133
Mellencamp, John, 14, 125, 169
Melody Maker, 175
melody writing, techniques of, 120
Memphis music market, 3, 156–57, 169, 172
Memphis State University, 157
merchandising, 108, 110
Mercury Records, 167
Merge Records, 173, 189
Metallica, 160
MGM Records, 161
Miami music market, 3, 158–59
Miami Sound Machine, 158
microphones, 30, 101
Microsoft Corporation, 177
middle-of-the-road (MOR) styles, 18, 154, 190, 191
MIDI, 53, 54, 79, 107
mileage deductions, 26
Milwaukee, Wisconsin, 142
Minneapolis music market, 3, 144, 165–66, 184
Miracles, the, 154
Mitchell, Joni, 186
Mitchell, Willie, 157
Mix Magazine directory, 3
mixing, 101, 106
Moby Grape, 159, 160
Molina, Jason, 167
Moman, Chips, 157
Monica, 183
Montreal music market, 3, 189–90
Morris, Chuck, 181
Morris/Bliesener Associates, 181, 182
Morrison, Van, 120
Morrissette, Alanis, 96
Mother Love Bone, 175
Motown Records, 153–54, 169, 172
MP3, 100
mrshowbiz.com, 200
MTV, 99, 191
multimedia technologies, 197–201, 208
Murphy, Michael Martin, 162

Murray, Anne, 186
Muscle Shoals, Alabama, 157–58, 169, 172
Muscle Shoals Sound, 157–58
music business organizations, 241–43
Music City News, 135
Music Connection, 135, 211
music distribution, 200–201. *See also* record distribution
music markets, major, 1–3, 118, 124–25, 135–43. *See also* Los Angeles; Nashville; New York
music markets, regional and local. *See also specific cities*
    ebb and flow of, 170–73
    goals and, 123–24, 135–36
    history and development of, 153–73
    opportunities, 14–15
    overview, 1–3
    relocating to, 143–44, 207–8
    researching, 3–4
Music Millennium, 168
Music Minus One, 116
Music Network, 191
Music Performance Trust Fund (MPTF), 7, 43–44, 48, 69, 70–71
Music Row, 135
Music Sales, 133
music stores, teaching at, 56, 58
music therapy, 50–51
music trade papers, 135, 169, 244
music videos, 99, 216
Musician's Atlas, 3
musicosm.com, 200
Musique Plus Network, 191
Mutek Festival, 190
Muzak Corporation, 178
Myrtle Beach, South Carolina, 173

N2k, 203
Nagler, Eric, 186
naming a group, 4, 21, 24
Napster, 100
Nashville music market, 1, 2–3, 125, 126–27, 129, 172, 212. *See also* music markets, major
Nashville Songwriters Association International (NSAI), 119, 132
National Academy of Recording Arts and Sciences (NARAS), 76–77, 155, 180
National Association for Campus Activities (NACA), 44
National Endowment for the Arts (NEA), 76
National Endowment for the Humanities (NEH), 76
National Repertory Orchestra, 133
Native American music, 169
Navarre, 98
Neil Kjos, 133
Nelson, Willie, 162–63, 164
Neptunes, the, 169
Neville, Aaron, 155

New Age music, 110, 142, 161, 181
New Jack City, 169
New Kids on the Block, 161
New Orleans music market, 3, 142, 155–56, 170
New York music market, 1, 2–3, 129, 212. *See also* music markets, major
New York Times, The, 165, 190
newspapers, 135, 168, 176
Nickel Creek, 142
Nickelodeon Network, 190
Nirvana, 175, 176, 179
Nitty Gritty Dirt Band, the, 180
Nivert, Taffy, 126
No Limits, 156
North by Northwest Music Festival, 168
North Star Studio, 179
Novaselic, Krist, 179
nursing homes, 6, 14

Oberst, Conor, 11, 169
O'Brien, Tim, 126
O'Jays, the, 155
Old Town School of Folk Music, 57
Olympia, Washington, 177, 178
Omaha music market, 3, 11, 167, 169
O'Malley, Scott, 182
one-sheets, 108
one-stops, 98
online retailing, 199
open mike sessions, 78
opera companies, 148
organ, 54
Organized Noize, 159
O'Shea, Shad, *Just for the Record*, 110
Outkast, 183
Outside/In (Santa Fe), 48

P. Diddy, 96, 205
packaging the product, 4–6, 29–36
Page, Jimmy, 53
Paisley Park label, 165–66
Palmer, Hap, 190
part-time opportunities, 145–52, 207–8
Paul, Billy, 155
Paul Revere and the Raiders, 175
Pavitt, Bruce, 175, 178
"pay to play" clubs, 91
Peacock Records, 165, 172
Pearl Jam, 14, 155, 175, 176, 179
Pelchat, Mario, 190
Penn, Dan, 157
Penner, Fred, 190
Pension Fund, 64, 75
per program licenses, 194
percussion, 53–54, 105, 116
performing rights organizations, 86, 111, 130–31, 191, 193–95, 208, 240
Perkins, Carl, 156
personal managers, 14, 44–45, 105, 125, 136–37, 177, 207
Peterson, Charles, 175

Phair, Liz, 167
Philadelphia music market, 3, 154–55, 169, 170, 172, 184
Phillips, Sam, 156
Phoenix music market, 3, 169
phone calls, 128–29
photographers, 206
photographs, 32–33, 40
piano, 54
Pickwick International, 165
Pierson, Ed, 179, 182
Pink Martini, 168
piracy, 215
podcasting, 203
Pollstar, 138
Poneman, Jonathan, 175, 178
Pony Up, 190
Portland music market, 3, 103, 131, 144, 162, 168, 178
practicing, 146
Prairie Home Companion, 166
Presley, Elvis, 156
press kits. *See* promotional kits
press releases, 107–8
Price, Lloyd, 155
prices, setting, 38–39, 40, 42, 77
Prince, 165–66, 184
Prine, John, 11, 96, 167
private teaching, 56–59
Pro Tools, 10
producers, record, 100–102, 139, 170, 187
profit-sharing arrangements, 96
promotional kits, 4, 29, 32–36, 37, 40, 69, 109, 113, 206, 207
Provenza, Charley, 149
publicists, 34
publishers, music print, 132–33, 262
publishing, music, 8, 86, 111, 127–30, 139
Putamayo label, 96–97, 203

Quark's Bar & Restaurant, 201–2
Quarterflash, 168
Queensrÿche, 175
Quicksilver Messenger Service, 159

rack jobbers, 98, 165
radio, 99, 109–10, 160, 182–83, 187–88, 189, 191, 193–94, 198
Radio and Records, 169
radio promotion, 45
radio tip sheets, 245
Raffi, 190
Ramsey, Willis Alan, 163
Rangell, Nelson, 182
rap music, 155, 156, 165, 173, 176
Ray, Amy, 96
RCA Corporation, 97, 156
reading music, 18–19, 151
"reasonable limits," 90–91
record card, instrument, 27
record companies, 11, 12–14, 95–97, 99–100, 142–43, 165, 178, 187, 204, 205, 211, 212, 215–16. See *also specific companies*

record deals, 100, 139, 187, 211
record distribution, 13–14, 97–99, 108–9, 165, 168, 189, 202–3, 207
record production, 87, 100–113, 200–201
record promotion and marketing, 45, 107–10, 189–90
record stores, 168, 178, 194, 199, 201
recording budgets, 82–83, 103–5
recording equipment, 30–31, 79–80, 101, 105–7
recording formats, 102
Recording Musicians' Association (RMA), 69–70
recording studios, 105–7, 176–77. *See also specific names*
    home, 10, 30, 31, 79, 84, 87, 101, 130, 150, 154, 206, 207
    rental costs, 10, 31, 79, 84, 106, 130, 188
recording work, 79–84
recordings, self-produced, 11, 12–14, 96, 100–103, 202–3, 207
RED, 98
Red House, 166
Red Knuckles and the Trailblazers, 9
Redding, Otis, 156, 159
regional geography, 124
regional music publications, 245
rehearsals, 20–24, 29
Reid, L. A., 159, 184
rejection, dealing with, 15
R.E.M., 155, 159
Remington, Alan, 38–39
rental instruments, 58
rentals, record, 204
residuals, 65, 81, 84
resort work, 9, 40, 145, 149, 181
returns, 97
reuse payments. *see* residuals
"reversion clause," 127
reviewers, record, 109
reviews, 32–33, 40
Revolution Records, 181
rhythm and blues, 157–58, 167, 172, 190
right-to-work states, 67
Righteous Babe label, 173
Riley, Teddy, 125, 169
ring-tones, 195
Ritchie, Lionel, 154
road manager, 26, 91, 108
Robinson, Smoky, 154
Rocket, The, 176
Rocky Mountain Music Association, 179
Roe, Tommy, 159
Rogers, Kenny, 9
Ronkin, Bruce, 151
Rounder Records, 155
Rowdy Records, 159
royalties, 86, 95, 101–2, 127, 132, 138, 191, 193–95
Rubinson, David, 160
Rush, 187

Rydell, Bobby, 154
Ryko, 98

Sacks, Kevin, 159
Sacramento, California, 169, 173
Saddle Creek Records, 11, 167, 169
St. Paul Chamber Orchestra, 166
sales representative, 85
Sam and Dave, 156
samplers, 54, 86, 87, 150
Samples, the, 181
San Antonio music market, 3, 164, 169
San Francisco Music Fair, 161
San Francisco music market, 3, 142, 149, 159–61
Sanctuary Records, 96, 204
Sanneh, Kelefa, 165
satellite radio, 204
school concerts, 6, 14, 47–48
Schwartz, Eddy, 187
Screen Actors Guild (SAG), 65
Scruggs, Joe, 190
Sea Saint Studios, 155
Seattle music market, 3, 4, 131, 175–79
Seattle Sun, 176
Secure Electronic Transaction (SET) standard, 198
semi-professionals, 150
seminars, songwriting, 118–19, 131
senior centers, 6, 14, 48, 50
sequencers, 86, 87, 107, 150
SESAC. *See* Society for European Stage Authors and Composers
Sesame Street, 190
Seskin, Steve, 125
Sharon, Lois and Bram, 190
showcases, 44
side musicians, 8–9, 92–93
sight-reading, 116–17
Silver Wave Records, 181
Simmons, Russell, 96, 205
Simon, Paul, 157
Sing Out, 133
singles, 99–100, 110
Sir Mix-A-Lot, 176
Sister Rose, 158
16 Horsepower, 181
skill levels, 59–61
slide shows, 47, 207
Slim Thug, 165
slotting fees, 204
Sly and the Family Stone, 160
Smashing Pumpkins, the, 167
Smith, Huey, 155
Smith-Kaye Studio, 176
Smothers Brothers, the, 159
So So Def Recordings, 159, 183
Sobel, Ron, 131, 216
Sobule, Jill, 179
Social Services, Department of, 48, 50
Society for European Stage Authors and Composers (SESAC), 111, 130–31, 193

Society of Composers, Authors and Music Publishers of Canada (SOCAN), 191
software programs, 150
solo acts, 89
solo recitalists, 148
songwriter tip sheets, 245
Songwriters Guild of America (SGA), 119, 132
Songwriter's Market, 127, 128
songwriters' organizations, 3, 21, 117–19, 132, 207
 list of, 237–39
songwriting
 books about, 119–20
 Canadian, 187
 contests, 212
 copyright and royalties, 111
 grants for, 75–77, 206
 improving skills, 119–20
 income from, 193–95
 jingle writing and, 80, 87
 making contacts, 124–29
 opportunities for, 8, 14, 46–47, 149
 performing your own songs, 21, 22, 24
 publishing and, 127–30
 technology and, 207, 208
Sonic Solutions, 103
sonicnet.com, 200
Sony, 95, 176, 183
sound systems, 25–27
Soundgarden, 175, 176, 177, 179
Soundscan, 111
South, Joe, 159
South By Southwest conference, 131, 162, 164
space.com, 200
Special Payments Fund, 64, 70
special populations, 6, 14, 48, 50–51
Spector, Phil, 97
Spinners, the, 155
Springsteen, Bruce, 95
staff writers, 125
Standing in the Shadows (film), 154
Staples Singers, the, 147
Starbucks Coffee, 96
Starland Vocal Band, 126, 157
Starr, Maurice, 161
Stars, the, 190
Stax Records, 156–57, 163
staying or going, 135–44, 186–87, 207–8
Stephenson, B. W., 162
Stephenson, Mickey, 154
Steve and Greg, 190
Stevens, Sufjan, 167
Sting, 103
Stone, Henry, 158
street musicians, 108
Strehli, Angela, 163
Streisand, Barbra, 18
Strictly Canadian, 167
String Cheese Incident, 181
strings, 54

studio musicians and work, 24, 87, 103–4, 117–19, 148, 166, 206
stylists, 33–34
Sub Pop label, 175–76, 178, 179
Subdudes, the, 179
subscription fees, 204
substitute musicians, 93
substitute teaching, 55
success, definitions of, 141–43
summer jobs, 149
Sun Records, 97, 156
sunset clauses, 46
Supremes, the, 154
Susan Silver Management, 177
Sussman, Neil, 177
Swallow Hill Music Association, 182
Swan Records, 154
Swisha House label, 165
Sykes, Keith, 157
symphony orchestras, 63–64, 133, 147–48, 166, 181–82
synchronization fees, 194–95
synthesizers, 8, 53–54, 79, 86, 87, 150
Szymczyk, Bill, 158, 179

Tacoma, Washington, 177, 178
talent, developing, 17–28
Tanglewood Festival, 133
Taos, New Mexico, 162
Target Stores, 165
taxes, 26, 90, 187, 206
Taxi, 212
TCI Corporation, 180
teaching music, 7, 17–19, 54–59, 146, 148, 150–51, 206
Tedesco, Tommy, 117
Tejano music, 164
Telefilm, 191
television, 8, 47, 85–87, 99, 169, 189, 191–92, 194–95, 212. See also cable television
Telluride Festival, 182
Temptations, the, 154
Texas Jewboys, the, 162
thedj.com, 200
themed restaurants, 201–2
Theodore Presser, 133
Thiele, Chris, 142
Thomas, Rufus and Irma, 156
Threadgill, Kenneth, 163
Thrill Jockey Records, 167
tip sheets, 130, 244, 245
Tooth and Nail, 179
Toronto music market, 1, 2–3, 162, 169, 189, 190, 191
tourdates.com, 199–200
tourist bureaus, 46
Toussaint, Allen, 155
Toyota, 96
track sheet, 104
travel, 40, 42–43, 123, 124, 145
traveling shows, 65, 67
True, Everett, 175
Tuatara, 179

Tumbleweed Records, 179
Turner, Ted, 159
Twain, Shania, 186
Two Louies, 168
Tyrone Guthrie Theater, 166
Tyson, Ian, 186

ubl.com, 200
UGK, 165
Ultimate Band List, 200
Unicorns, the, 190
Universal, 95, 97, 167
Universal Music Canada, 192
University of Colorado, 183
University of Georgia, 159
University of Southern California in Los Angeles, 85
University of Texas, 162, 164
University of Washington, 177, 178
Usher, 183

Van Zandt, Townes, 163
Vancouver Folk Festival, 133, 191
Vancouver music market, 3, 169, 178, 189, 191–92
Variety on Production, 192
Vaughan, Jimmy, 163
Vaughan, Stevie Ray, 163
Vee Jay Records, 167
Ventures, the, 175
versatility, developing, 6–7, 53–61, 89–93, 105, 115, 206
video games, 195
videos, music instruction, 18–19
Village Voice, The, 135
vinyl (LPs), 12, 102, 110
Virginia Beach, Virginia, 169, 173
"visible work," 4–5
voice, studying, 19
Volt Records, 156
Volunteer Lawyers for the Arts, 140
 list of, 233–36

Wade, Rico, 159
Walden, Narada Michael, 160
Walker, Jerry Jeff, 162
Wall, Paul, 165
W.A.R. Records, 181
Warner Music Group, 133, 165, 166, 167, 176, 179, 216
Washington, D.C., 126
watermark technology, 198
Watermelon Records, 164
Web sites, 111, 199–200, 202–3, 206, 207
wedding gigs, 92
wedding planners, 6
Weiden and Kennedy advertising agency, 168
Weir, Rusty, 162
Westword, 181
Wexler, Jerry, 156, 158
White Stripes, 154
Willamette Week, 168
Wilson Sisters, 176
Winchester, Jesse, 186

Windham Hill Records, 97, 109,
    111, 160–61
Winnipeg Folk Festival, 133, 191
Winston, George, 111
Winwood, Stevie, 18
wireless transmission, 199
Wishbone Sound, 157
Wolf Parade, 190
Wonder, Stevie, 154, 156, 172
woodwinds, 54
world music, 116, 161, 169, 178, 181
Woven Hand, 181
writers, 33

X-Files, The, 189

Yellow Pages directory, 3, 37, 40, 81
Yonder Mountain String Band, 181
Young, Neil, 186
Young Audiences, 47–48, 49
list of chapters, 229–31

Z., Bobby (Rivkin), 165–66
Z., David (Rivkin), 165–66
Zeitlin, Denny, 146
Zomba, 95, 97
zydeco, 142
Z.Z. Top, 157